PRIVILEGING PLACE

T0355358

Privileging Place

How Second Homeowners Transform Communities and Themselves

Meaghan Stiman

PRINCETON UNIVERSITY PRESS

PRINCETON AND OXFORD

Published by Princeton University Press
41 William Street, Princeton, New Jersey 08540
99 Banbury Road, Oxford OX2 6JX

press.princeton.edu

All Rights Reserved

Library of Congress Cataloging-in-Publication Data

Names: Stiman, Meaghan, 1988–author.
Title: Privileging place : how second homeowners transform
   communities and themselves / Meaghan Stiman.
Description: Princeton : Princeton University Press, [2024] |
   Includes bibliographical references and index.
Identifiers: LCCN 2023040206 (print) | LCCN 2023040207 (ebook) | ISBN 9780691239965
   (paperback) | ISBN 9780691240787 (hardback) | ISBN 9780691239972 (ebook)
Subjects: LCSH: Place attachment—United States. | Second homes—United States. |
   Middle class white people—Housing—United States. | Upper class—Housing—
   United States. | COVID-19 Pandemic, 2020—United States—Influence.
Classification: LCC BF353.5.P56 S75 2024 (print) | LCC BF353.5.P56
   (ebook) | DDC 155.9—dc23/eng/20230922
LC record available at https://lccn.loc.gov/2023040206
LC ebook record available at https://lccn.loc.gov/2023040207

British Library Cataloging-in-Publication Data is available

Editorial: Meagan Levinson and Erik Beranek
Production Editorial: Kathleen Cioffi
Cover Design: Heather Hansen
Production: Lauren Reese
Publicity: William Pagdatoon

Jacket images: Tartila / Adobe Stock

This book has been composed in Adobe Text and Gotham

Printed and bound by CPI Group (UK) Ltd, Croydon, CR0 4YY

For Elyas

For Flight

CONTENTS

TABLES

ACKNOWLEDGMENTS

There are many individuals, groups, and organizations that have made the publication of this book possible. I first thank my interview participants for inviting me into their homes and sharing their stories and experiences with me. This project would not have been possible without their generosity of time and insight.

A huge thanks to Meagan Levinson and the entire editorial team at Princeton University Press. Meagan saw the potential of this project well before I saw it myself and provided the necessary support and encouragement to turn a proposal into a final manuscript. I also thank the two anonymous reviewers who provided highly productive feedback.

Important financial assistance made this research viable. The Initiative on Cities at Boston University provided essential grant funding for the Boston portion of this project, and the Department of Sociology at Boston University provided a Writing Grant and Morris Funding, which allowed me the necessary time and resources to write the early stages of this project in the form of a dissertation. I thank William & Mary for providing a summer research grant, which allowed me to develop these ideas into a book prospectus and manuscript.

There were people during my time in graduate school at Boston University who helped me formulate the very early ideas that make up the pages of this book. Emily Barman, Cati Connell, and Jessica Simes provided valuable insights, pushing me to think about how to bring these two cases together to tell a larger story. The entire Urban Workshop at Boston University's Initiative on Cities and its participants—Ladin Bayurgil, Taylor Cain, Pam Devan, Connor Fitzmaurice, Whitney Gecker, and Sarah Hosman—gave me the space and encouragement to make sense of my early findings.

Since the beginning of graduate school, Japonica Brown-Saracino has served as my dissertation advisor, mentor, and friend. I have never met someone so generous with their time and insights as Japonica, who is always willing to read drafts, provide thoughtful feedback, and think through ideas, however big or small. Few are so fortunate to have such sustained support over the course of their academic careers. I thank her for her commitment to my development as a scholar and writer since this project's inception.

All my colleagues in the sociology department at William & Mary have been vital as I turned this early work into a full manuscript. Brent Kaup deserves a special thanks. Brent read the very first—and very rough—draft of this manuscript and offered some of the most detailed and insightful feedback I have ever received, helping me develop the arguments I make in this book. He has also provided essential mentorship at virtually every step of the book process from beginning to end. Diya Bose, Reya Farber, and Fernando Galeana-Rodriguez have created a wonderful intellectual environment to workshop drafts and brainstorm ideas. They are also brilliant and inspirational people and scholars whose enthusiasm has kept me moving forward even during the very hard times. Finally, I extend a thanks to Tom Linneman, whose everyday guidance and humor have provided the necessary levity to make academic life fun.

Some of the chapters in this book have appeared elsewhere in different versions:

Chapter 1 was adapted from "Second Homes in the City and the Country: A Reappraisal of Vacation Homes in the Twenty-First Century," *International Journal of Housing Policy* 20 (1). © 2020 Meaghan Stiman. Reprinted with permission from Taylor & Francis Ltd.

Chapter 5 was adapted from "Discourses of Resource Dependency: Second Homeowners as 'Lifeblood' in Vacationland," *Rural Sociology* 85 (2). © 2019 Meaghan Stiman. Reproduced with permission of John Wiley and Sons, Inc.

Chapters 6 and 7 were adapted from "Speculators and Specters: Diverse Modes of Second Homeownership in Boston, Massachusetts," *Journal of Urban Affairs* 41 (5). © 2019 Meaghan Stiman. Reprinted with permission from Taylor & Francis, Ltd.

Family and friends have kept me grounded during much of this arduous work. I thank Liz Raposa and Chris Conway for the big and small ways they have supported me over the years—listening to me talk about the book, helping me brainstorm a title, and organizing our family trips together for a much-needed respite from work. In my family, I thank Matthew Stiman, Andrew Stiman, Cassie Stiman, Carolyn Stiman, Shah Bakhtiari, Mariam Bakhtiari, Vicki Sells, and Joseph Kinard for their love, enthusiasm, and childcare help over the past few years. I extend a heartfelt thanks to my parents, Ann and Ralph Stiman, who have been selflessly supportive of my academic aspirations since I was a small child. None of this would have been possible without their constant and absolute support and belief in me. My two children, Kamran and Kian, have borne the brunt of this book project in ways they may not entirely understand. I thank them both for bringing inexplicable joy to my every day and for tolerating the times I was off in my own head or talking to their dad about my ideas—when I should have been building Legos or train tracks with them instead.

Finally, there is no one more deserving of my thanks than my spouse, friend, co-parent, and colleague Elyas Bakhtiari, to whom this book is dedicated. He has helped at virtually every stage of this project from its origins as a research proposal, to the methodological challenges I experienced doing research in Rangeley and Boston, and through the final submission of the manuscript. Thanks for enduring the long distance during fieldwork. Thanks for talking with me about my ideas for hours that somehow turned into years. Thanks for reading and rereading countless drafts with the utmost care and attention. Thanks for being the best parent to our kids and picking up the childcare slack when I needed time and space to write. And most of all, thank you for the patience and optimism you bring to our family every day. I could not have done any of this without you.

PRIVILEGING PLACE

Introduction

THE BAKERS

It's an early Saturday morning at the beginning of June in Rangeley, a small town tucked away in the western mountains of northern Maine. After weeks of anticipation and a long night of traveling, Paul and Carol Baker have just awoken to enjoy the first day of the summer season.[1] They make their way from their lofted bedroom into the kitchen downstairs, opening the dark oak cabinets to find their favorite mugs as they wait for the kettle to whistle. Once their tea has finished steeping, they open the sliding glass door to the back porch where they sit on Adirondack chairs that face the lake, a pristine body of water that rests beneath a vast mountain range. They sit there quietly drinking their tea and listening to loons as the sun slowly rises, making its way through the white pines hovering above.

They spend the rest of their morning chipping away at their "opening chores." After having been away since October, the shrubs need to be pruned, the grass needs to be cut, and this year's garden needs to be planted. But they don't really mind. Carol is an amateur botanist who enjoys spending her days outside among the flowers and trees. Since there are no other obligations—Paul doesn't have to work, Carol doesn't have to attend board meetings—the rest of their afternoon is free. They decide to hike Bald Mountain. At the observation tower at the top, they see Saddleback Mountain, where locals and visitors alike spend their winters skiing and snowboarding. They see Rangeley and Mooselookmeguntic Lakes, where families go boating and fishing all summer long. And they take in the magnificent view that

1

transforms this small town in the summer months from about a thousand permanent residents to nearly five thousand, as second homeowners like them populate its shores and slopes.

After the hike, Paul and Carol decide they don't want to drive to Rangeley's Main Street to eat at the Red Onion or Parkside & Main, where many people flock to at this time of year. They would rather have dinner alone. After grabbing provisions for dinner at the Farmer's Daughter, a small grocer, they find themselves where their day began, on the back porch listening to the birds and the waves that gently crash against the rocky shoreline of the lake. They stay there until the sun has gone down and the stars have come out in the sky.

Rangeley is exactly the type of place Paul and Carol were looking for when they were on a hunt for a second home in the early 2000s. Paul had recently retired from his law practice and Carol had stepped back from her teaching career. After spending over three decades in their hometown, they were ready to be somewhere entirely different. Paul and Carol enjoyed many aspects of their primary home, but to them it felt too urban. They live in a densely populated neighborhood where they often run into neighbors on their way to the local co-op or independent bookstore. Over the years, they longed for houses more spread apart. They longed for green space and seclusion. They longed for rural life. They looked around at places in Massachusetts within easy driving distance from their permanent residence. But the lakes were too small. The houses were too close together. It didn't feel rural enough. Although neither Paul nor Carol had ever lived in Maine before buying a second home in Rangeley, Paul had remembered a hiking trip he took up north to Rangeley as a child with his father. It was a time in his life he remembered fondly. Once he brought Carol to see it for herself, they knew it was the place for them. Carol grew up in rural Pennsylvania, and driving down the dirt roads in Rangeley that wind deep through the woods reminded her of home. She felt comfort in the familiarity. Work and education pulled them away from these types of places, and they moved frequently from city to city up and down the East Coast following the next opportunity. A second home in Rangeley would make it all worth it.

In Rangeley, they purchased a house worth nearly $1 million that, in Carol's words, was "the ugliest place I've ever seen in my life." They did not buy it for the house but for the thirty-two acres of abutting land and nearly 400 feet of waterfront property upon which it sat. They had no interest in renovating this "ugly" home, and they even kept items like couches and dishware left from the previous owners that to Carol were still "serviceable."

They leave this house untouched because most days are spent outside of it. Every morning, they sit on their porch that overlooks the water, drinking tea, reading the paper, and listening to the birds. When they feel so inclined, they hike Bald Mountain, kayak on the lake to find a loon family, or walk the dirt road in search of a bald eagle. Their nights are spent under the stars. This is the Rangeley they wait for all winter long. It is their quiet, unpopulated refuge set in nature. And being here makes them feel like they are the rural people they had left behind long ago.

Paul and Carol are not that involved in most aspects of local life in Rangeley, preferring to keep to themselves. But they do spend much of their down time patrolling the lake for invasive species on behalf of the Rangeley Lakes Heritage Trust, a land trust organization dedicated to conservation across the region. They have begun taking classes on invasive species to educate second homeowners and locals alike on how to preserve and protect the waterways. They also donate to this organization's vast conservation efforts. This includes annual donations of time and money. It also includes a lump-sum donation of the thirty-two acres of land that abuts their property. This protects their vision of Rangeley as an isolated refuge set in nature. And it secures their place within it.

THE FLYNNS

Two hundred miles south, in Boston, Richard and Doris Flynn are ready for their Saturday in the city. They have just arrived at their harborside condo after a two-hour drive from their hometown the night before. They start the morning as they do on most weekends throughout the year; once their coffee has brewed, they move from their kitchen with stainless-steel appliances to their harbor-facing living room that is lined with floor-to-ceiling windows. They spend the next hour watching the sun rise over Boston Harbor, reflecting off the downtown skyline.

Doris doesn't have much time to lounge around. In a few hours she needs to make her way from their condo to Fenway for a weekly class she has been taking on abstract expressionism at the Museum of Fine Arts (MFA). It'll take her about an hour to get from one neighborhood to the other, but she relishes parking her car in the building's garage for the weekend and traversing Boston by foot and public transit. Along the route she takes, she can envelop herself in the city's unique revolutionary history, passing Faneuil Hall Marketplace and the Old State House, preserved historic buildings nestled within the city's modernist skyscrapers. At Park Street Station, she can take the E Line to the museum's front steps. For the next hour she sits next to other erudite strangers listening to a lecture on the latest Hokusai exhibit, an artist whose work depicted the "floating world" of urban opulence during the Edo period in Japan.

Come evening, she meets Richard at the Huntington Theatre, where they spend their evening absorbed in this season's latest play. When the show is over, they can enjoy the longer walk to Copley Station where they will pick up the T to make their way back to their condo, contemplating the architecture as they walk toward Boylston Street—the McKim building of the Boston Public Library, the bell in the campanile of the Old South Church, and the reflection of Henry Richardson's Romanesque Trinity Church in the minimalist Hancock Tower.

This is what Doris and Richard Flynn missed most about Boston, the place where they formed their nascent identities as "city people." They had lived there together for nearly a decade while they were both attending college and in the early stages of their careers, loving the city and the life they fashioned there. According to Doris, it's where they "began." They made the decision to leave when Doris was accepted into a graduate program hundreds of miles away, a move that ended up being a permanent relocation for professional opportunities that materialized for them both. They said goodbye to their Boston life. They bought a house, raised their three children, and put down roots. Their home sits on two and a half acres. They have a barn with a loft, a paddock for horses, and access to riding trails nearby. Doris and Richard enjoyed their hometown but have grown tired of the lack of anonymity in small-town life. After having not lived in Boston for decades, there was always a part of them left unfinished. "We have the country," Doris remarked, "but we long for the city."

In Boston, they hadn't wanted to buy a second home in a so-called up-and-coming or trendy neighborhood. They wanted a neighborhood with access to the part of the city they knew and loved, areas close to downtown where affluent, transient people like them were increasing in numbers year after year. Their condo on the waterfront, worth nearly $1 million, provides quick access to the Freedom Trail, a pedestrian path connecting places like Paul Revere's house, Faneuil Hall, Boston Common, museums, churches, buildings, burial grounds, and parks celebrating Boston's revolutionary history.[2] At any point they can hop on the T and be at the MFA or Symphony Hall in Boston's newly designated Avenue of the Arts. This part of the city contains the memory of Boston they hold close, a city rife with art, music, theater, and rich history.

Richard and Doris don't feel they have the time or occasion to attend neighborhood civic events or block parties. When not traversing the Freedom Trail or Avenue of the Arts, Doris spends her sporadic days in Boston volunteering for a nonprofit organization dedicated to promoting public art in her neighborhood. Annually, they support the institutions they value; they write checks to the Museum of Fine Arts, the Huntington Theatre, and the Freedom Trail Foundation. Funneling resources into these institutions and organizations secures their vision of Boston as a world-class arts and culture destination. These practices also help Richard and Doris tell a story about who they are as *urban people*.

THE FLYNNS AND THE BAKERS

The Flynns and the Bakers are longtime friends who understand each other's motivations for second homeownership as entirely incongruent. The Flynns, city people whose hometown feels too insular and small, can't imagine choosing a more formulaic and typical rural vacation destination like the Bakers. The Bakers, who identify deeply with rural life and have grown tired of the density and pace of their hometown, quip about how a loon's call on a dark summer night might frighten the Flynns. Yet the two couples are not as different as they seem.

The Bakers are not from the city, and the Flynns are not from the country. The couples live no more than two miles apart from each other in the suburbs of a major metropolitan region in New England. It is a place that offers a blend of everything. Paul and Carol can kayak in the river that borders downtown, walk an extensive hiking and biking trail nearby, and frequent a number of state parks within a short driving distance. Richard and Doris can attend museums, watch art-house films at a local independent cinema, and even drive to watch the symphony play outside during the summer months. This region seems to have it all. Despite this abundance of amenities, the Bakers and the Flynns each expressed a personal dissonance with this place. To the Bakers, this community is not rural enough; they spend their days longing for the secluded, slower pace of life they experienced as children deep in the woods. To the Flynns, it is not urban enough; they have spent decades wanting to re-create the days they first met, walking around the bustling streets of Boston. They both longed for the places in which they used to live.

Although this community feels too diluted to give them the sense of place they longed for, it's where they decided to remain, forgoing attachment to urban and rural places for access to a range of work and educational opportunities for themselves and their children that they could not find in places like Rangeley or Boston. This small city, in Doris's words, is "nice." And it is resource rich. It is where Paul and Richard set up their successful law practice, where Carol and Doris obtained their master's degrees, and where their children attended a highly ranked school system. Deciding to stay there opened a world of opportunity for their families. But neither the Flynns nor the Bakers had to make the choice between access to resources in their hometowns and lifestyles they longed for in the city or country. They had enough time and money to have *both*.

Second Homeownership as a Social Problem

The Bakers and the Flynns are among the growing number of second home-owners shaping real estate markets, community, and inequality in the United States.[3] This phenomenon is typically associated with rural destinations, as people seek out natural amenities and lifestyles along the shores of lakes and oceans and in the woods and mountains.[4] However, highly affluent neighborhoods in global cities are beginning to witness a rise in this form of homeownership as urban real estate has transformed into a new asset class for elites and as people now seek out cities as places for leisure, travel, and consumption.[5]

The rise and geographic spread of second-home purchases have come at a cost for the communities that host them, placing immense pressure on housing markets. This is particularly true in more recent years against the backdrop of a nationwide housing shortage.[6] In 2021, the demand for vacation homes began to skyrocket, far outpacing existing-home sales for the first time in recent history.[7] Lured by low interest rates and mortgage fees, viable remote work options, and an escape from disease risk and pandemic life, people began buying vacation homes at unprecedented rates.[8] This devoured the nation's already tenuous housing supply. Some estimates suggest that during this period, the United States had a deficit of nearly four million housing units.[9] Under these tight market conditions, every purchase made by a second homeowner was consequential, both limiting the supply of homes that could be used as primary residences and failing to put another home up for sale to equalize supply and demand—it was a one-two punch.[10]

But second homeowners' influence on housing markets predates the pandemic housing-boom years. They have been altering real estate markets for decades. They are more likely to make highly competitive, all-cash

offers, straining markets in both urban and rural areas.[11] These types of purchases are known to monopolize scarce housing supply and to drive up
real estate prices, shutting out new primary homebuyers and pushing out
permanent residents who cannot keep up with increased property taxes or
rents. Second-home destinations across the city and the country are among
the most highly racially and economically segregated parts of America.[12]

Second homeowners who do take out mortgages often over-leverage
themselves to do so. This contributed significantly to the housing foreclo-
sure crisis of 2008, in which millions of Americans defaulted on their loans.
During this period, second-home buyers contributed to more mortgage debt
than primary-home buyers, making them more likely to default on loans.[13]
Places with more second-home buying saw bigger booms and busts. Analysts
even suggest that the housing crisis in the early 2000s would have been less
severe had it not been for the precipitous rise in second-home buying.[14]

Yet housing markets are not the only place where second homeowners
have left their mark. They also strain community dynamics.[15] Rural communities have been grappling with the presence of second homeowners for over
a century, as productive economies like farming and logging have steadily
declined. Many rural towns are dependent on people like second homeowners to populate their Main Streets throughout the year, relying on them to
build homes, buy groceries, dine out at restaurants, and buy souvenirs as
they consume the bucolic mountains, waterfront, forest, and countryside.
More recent accounts highlight how this in-migration has fueled complex
tensions with permanent residents.

During the early months of the Covid-19 pandemic, reports quickly mul-
tiplied about wealthy New Yorkers fleeing their neighborhoods and taking up
residence in their second homes on the shores of Long Island, New Jersey,
and the Hamptons. They did so to avoid disease risk and to live more comfortably under conditions of lockdown, and many did so without regard for
the communities that hosted them. As more cities began shutting schools
and offices down, remote rural vacation communities beyond the New York
metropolitan region began facing the unwelcome influx of out-of-towners
looking to escape. Some municipalities banned out-of-towners altogether,[16]
some required a two-week quarantine upon arrival,[17] and some locals took
it upon themselves to ensure the safety of their communities.

In one instance in Vinalhaven, a remote island town in Maine, "vigilantes" made sure out-of-staters could not leave the premises of their second
home. With guns in tow, a group of locals cut down a tree to block the
unwelcome visitor to ensure they could not spread Covid-19 to the town.[18]

People feared the spread of disease, max-capacity ICUs, and strain on everyday resources. Despite warnings, many still flocked to their second homes. Such disregard put permanent residents in harm's way, some of whom lived in places that didn't even have so much as a pharmacy, let alone medical facilities, staff, or supplies. But there was nothing these towns could do. Second homeowners still came. And business and political leaders did not want to jeopardize their economic base.

Whereas rural towns feel the presence of second homeowners year in and year out, cities have begun to feel their absence. Entire buildings and blocks of affluent city neighborhoods now appear dark and lifeless, nearly void of people, as transient, non-permanent residents continue buying urban real estate.[19] Some buy as a safe-deposit box, some buy to hide dubiously acquired cash, some buy as a place to crash after the symphony or before jet-setting around the world, and some buy to rent out to other transient people on third-party platforms. Regardless of the intent, the lights are turned off most of the year.[20]

Analysts contemplate what will become of neighborhoods if this trend continues. Some worry that the lack of permanent residents will undermine collective community life. "My block is like a ghost town," confessed Gay Talese to the *New York Times* about his Upper East Side neighborhood. "It's dark on this street at night, and I'm not talking about the summer people in the Hamptons."[21] Others fear that cities will become nothing but places for the super-rich to park their money as real estate rapidly grows as a new asset class. This has led politicians across the globe to vow to ban foreign home-buyers: "No more foreign wealth being parked in homes that people should be living in," Canada's Justin Trudeau declared to his constituents.[22] And many point to how these collective purchases fuel neighborhood change, in which the middle class is being priced out by the upper class, sending a ripple effect of unaffordability and churn throughout a given city.[23]

In no uncertain terms, second homeownership is a social problem. It is a public issue in which these collective practices, and the structures that enable them, accumulate to produce material consequences for others. These more high-profile accounts present a full picture of the costs of second homeownership for host communities. Through their high-end purchases they strain local housing markets and through their presence and absence they alter community life for permanent residents.

But what is missing from these accounts is a fuller picture of how and why specific people deepen these dynamics that disadvantage host communities. Who are some of these second homeowners? What motivates their second-home purchases? How and why do they decide to allocate time, money, and resources within their host communities beyond their transactions in real estate? How do they justify their in-migration? And how does this differ, if at all, across the city and the country?

What is also missing is a more critical look at how second homeowners *and* the places left behind stand to benefit from these processes. How do some people benefit from second homeownership aside from growing an investment portfolio? How and why do they decide to allocate time, money, and resources *between* their primary homes and host communities? How does this not only disadvantage host communities but *advantage* primary-home communities? These gaps motivate the inquiry in this book. A story about second homeownership is not just a story about host communities. It is a larger story about what motivates people to wield their privileges within and between geographies in the twenty-first century.

———

Privileging Place picks up where headlines and housing reports leave off, following the accounts of upper-middle-class people who buy second homes in the city and the country and live permanently in affluent, mostly suburban communities. I spent more than two years talking to second homeowners in Rangeley, Maine, and Boston, Massachusetts, about how they made housing decisions and interacted with the communities around them. What I learned sheds light on part of what is driving second homeownership as a social phenomenon and some of its complex local influence.

The conversations I had about second homes with the people I met turned into conversations about the identities they tied to place—who they felt they were and where they felt they really belonged. They talked at length about what they felt urban and rural places should look and feel like and why they felt so aligned with these types of places. The ideas they had about Rangeley and Boston, and how they saw themselves within them, explained their actions in these communities, including where they decided to buy, how much they were willing to spend, how they developed and maintained social ties, which nonprofit and civic organizations they donated to or volunteered for, which commercial establishments they patronized, and which community meetings they decided to attend, if at all. Understanding the meaning they gave to their actions provided a piece to the larger puzzle of what motivated them to participate in sustaining the larger social problems across the city and the country detailed above. Theoretically, this book makes a case for understanding how such cultural orientations to place help explain some people's second-home purchases and local community influence.[24]

However, as my conversations unfolded, I learned that to really understand what motivated the people I met, their actions in second-home communities, and their broader influence on the social world, I had to understand their relationships to the places where many of their stories began—the suburbs. They talked in detail about why they did not feel like they could tie their identities to their hometowns but why they remained there, even when they would rather have been somewhere else. While I initially set out to study the relationship between second homeownership in urban and rural areas, I realized I had a bigger story to tell, one distinct from popular and academic accounts that typically explore what second homeowners do and why within the delimited sphere of their second-home host communities.[25] Through my conversations, I came to understand that the actions of the second homeowners I met in Rangeley and Boston were always relational with actions in their hometowns—and in ways that advantaged these communities. This book not only offers unique analytical insight into what explained some second homeowners' everyday practices across both urban and rural host communities. It also provides insight into how and why affluent people leverage their privileges across multiple places *at once*.[26]

The Argument: The Pursuit of Place Identity

For the people I met, buying a second home was a way to balance the desire for a meaningful connection to place in the city or the country, while also holding onto material interests in the suburbs. My argument is that second homeownership was a *place-identity project*, in which they used place-specific meanings, attributes, and practices to both attach their sense of self to certain places and engage in everyday actions to accomplish this aspect of their identity.[27] These tensions between viewing the second home as a source of place identity and their hometowns as sites of opportunity shaped why they bought a second home, how they interacted with the communities they traversed, and why they decided to remain in their hometowns when they would rather have been in the city or the country.

The place-identity projects of the people I talked with were motivated by *felt place identities*, in which they more strongly attached their sense of self to the places where they used to live—the city or the country—rather than the places where they permanently resided. Although most of my sample resided permanently in suburbs, they often thought of themselves as fundamentally city or country people. They echoed more critical academic and popular discourse about the suburbs as alienating, places devoid of a coherent character.[28] While once framed as the American dream, offering its residents the best of all worlds with ample greenspace and access to commercial and institutional amenities, the people I met found this liminal and diluted space as the worst of all worlds and the best of none—it was neither urban nor rural enough.[29]

Although their hometowns did not provide them with a sense of place, they made locational choices to move and stay there for access to material resources, including schools, jobs, housing, and what they thought was a nice quality of life. Viewing their hometowns as sites of opportunity, the people I met engaged in everyday practices that reified the notions they held that these communities were resource rich. Using time and money, they supported a wealth of local institutions like schools, health-care infrastructure, and an array of nonprofit and civic organizations. And yet they strategically chose not to invest in these institutions in their second-home host communities because supporting these institutions did not align with—and might have undermined—their sense of place. *Opportunity hoarding* was therefore a key piece of their place-identity projects. The decision to remain in affluent communities and uplift them, at the expense of other places, maps onto enduring methods of social closure, in which affluent people concentrate material resources in already affluent communities, systematically denying other people and places access to the very locational advantages they create.[30]

The people I met leveraged their social position to purchase second homes in the city and the country to recover the sense of place they did not find in their hometowns, giving them the feeling of being in a distinctly *urban* or distinctly *rural* place they desired, transforming their place identities from *felt* into *projects*. Privilege was thus central to their relationship with place identity. Because they only lived there part-time, their projects were developed around narrow and archetypal notions of what best characterized these places, viewing Rangeley as an isolated refuge set in nature and Boston as a site of elite high-cultural consumption. These meanings, however, were not neutral or benign. They built their sense of place from processes that have historically disadvantaged urban and rural people and places. In Rangeley, the people I met maintained notions of *rural* that depended on this community being less resource rich than their own. For the people I met in Boston, their ideas of *urban* depended on the city's historic and contemporary concentrated affluence and enduring racial segregation.

The people I met did not simply emplace themselves where they could feel more like a city or country person. A central feature of their place-identity projects was to engage in everyday practices to make these places look more like how they imagined them. Using an array of philanthropic, consumptive, and voluntaristic practices, they supported local nonprofit institutions that have become stewards of the city and the country, aligning their second-home communities with their envisioned sense of place. In Rangeley, the people I talked with supported a land trust organization to ensure the country remained an isolated refuge set in nature. These practices supplanted supporting other public goods like health care, housing, or internet service that would have benefited permanent residents. In Boston, the people I met supported select cultural institutions to ensure the city remained a site of elite, high-cultural consumption. This contributed to larger processes of neighborhood change and unequal resource distribution in the city. Taken together, the practices associated with their projects helped reproduce the very conditions of spatial inequalities upon which they built their sense of place.

The people I interviewed strategically segmented the various facets of associational life typically related to community—primary and secondary ties, institutional and philanthropic engagement, and place identity—between the multiple places where they lived and owned second homes. This segmentation was patterned by their deeply held notions of what urban, rural, and suburban places were and should have been. Their selective investments in these communities helped align the places where they lived and owned second homes with their imagined ideals, emboldened by broader structural conditions that make places dependent on private practices and philanthropic support of people like them for local growth. Such everyday actions guaranteed parts of the city remained sites of high culture, parts of the country remained places of unadulterated nature, and their hometowns remained a repository of institutional privileges. In the end, their practices ensured that every place was made for people like them.

How Cultural Processes Can Explain Spatial Inequality

To understand how and why some second homeowners' cultural orientations to place can matter for explaining patterns in the social world, I want to take a step back to draw the connections between everyday people, their motivations for social action in local places, and broader patterns of spatial inequality in society.

It is impossible to understand social inequality without understanding its relationship to place. Seemingly national-level structures are built on social dynamics that play out in local places.[31] Residential segregation, or the spatial division by race and class, has served as the building block for virtually every major national-level problem, from the racial wealth gap to racial and economic health disparities.[32] Gentrification enhances wealth accumulation and resource access for gentrifiers in non-white working-class communities while systematically denying longtime residents the very locational advantages gentrifiers create.[33] What is colloquially understood as NIMBYism (not in my backyard) patterns national-level housing affordability and resource access. It is sometimes framed as a process in which powerful local stakeholders fight against policies that affect the use and exchange value of their neighborhoods that might make them more inclusive.[34] These examples illuminate how local problems serve as the foundation for macro-level systems of stratification that pattern everything from housing precarity to wealth inequality to health disparities.

Sociologists study a range of social actors who have a hand in shaping these local-level processes. They study political and business elites who have top-down influence, defining, for instance, national policies that influence the unequal distribution of mortgage acquisitions.[35] They study middlemen like real estate agents, appraisers, building inspectors, landlords, and civic leaders who are involved in defining land use and value and sorting people, goods, and resources across communities in unequal ways.[36] Sociologists also study everyday social actors like longtime residents, doormen, and squatters whose practices define the contours of local life as they resist or navigate neighborhood change.[37] They even study relatively advantaged and affluent residents like gentrifiers, NIMBYs, or even billionaires who use a range of economic, social, and cultural capital to shape communities for everyone.[38] Local-level processes of spatial inequalities like segregation, gentrification, and resource hoarding come to life and pattern macro-level systems of stratification through the aggregate practices of this wide range of people.

In this book, I explore second homeowners as one such group who are involved in shaping many of these processes. Second homeowners are found in some of the most highly segregated parts of America, from cities of extremes to racially and economically bifurcated destinations rich in natural amenities.[39] Second homeowners are gentrifiers, buying property in rural amenity-rich communities and in highly affluent urban neighborhoods, fueling increased property values, and participating in creating a new neighborhood milieu.[40] Second homeowners are also linked to NIMBYism across a range of geographies, guiding land-use policies and practices to serve their interests.[41] They are part of many of the major social problems that a range of environmental, stratification, urban, and rural scholars are motivated to understand. An analysis of second homeowners provides insight into the multiple social actors who shape place-based inequality in ways that coalesce to shape macro-level stratification.

There are a variety of factors that could explain why and how second homeowners shape spatial inequality in communities. These include political-economic conditions, technological advances, racial inequality, and historic and contemporary housing market practices. I focus specifically on the place-based cultural motivations of some second homeowners themselves as one factor that explains how and why they pattern their community engagements in ways that connect to larger patterns of social inequality.[42]

People's cultural orientations to place are valuable to understand as social scientists endeavor to make sense of local-level community processes. Scholars who study community life across urban and rural places like Japonica Brown-Saracino and David Hummon argue that the meanings people give to places have the power to motivate action and inform people's everyday practices in ways that can structure the form and function of communities.[43] Thomas Gieryn developed this argument in his formative essay on place:

> Places are endlessly made, not just when the powerful pursue their ambition through brick and mortar . . . but also when ordinary people extract from continuous and abstract space a bounded, identified, meaningful, named, and significant place.[44]

How people think and feel about urban, rural, and suburban communities in part explains where people move and why they move there. Gentrifiers are not always motivated to move to new neighborhoods to make a quick return on their investment. Scholars have found that many move for a variety of place-specific cultural reasons, including the desire to live alongside people or in neighborhoods they feel are gritty or authentic.[45] Amenity and lifestyle migrants have also been found to forgo more lucrative career opportunities in cities to emplace themselves in natural-amenity-rich rural areas, places where they perceive the good life and real community to be located.[46] The cultural environment people believe a place offers can explain why they uproot their lives to move somewhere new, altering the demographic and topographic features of a given community.[47]

How people think and feel about places also has the power to incite civic and political action in local communities after people have moved. People will pack the halls of neighborhood or city council meetings to fight against zoning changes that might increase the density of their neighborhood to protect its perceived character.[48] People will take to the streets holding signs and yelling chants to decry a Whole Foods that might replace a local grocer to save commercial establishments they associate with a neighborhood's old-timers.[49] People will rally together to protest permits for wind turbines to preserve their notions of what rural landscapes should look like.[50] These actions are not always motivated by a desire to protect property values. People maintain ideas about the character of their neighborhoods and communities and these ideas guide their actions.

Contemporary economic ideologies and structures make the individual-level practices of everyday actors ascendant in communities across the United States. As government funding receded during the 1970s, *neoliberalism* created the conditions in which cities, suburbs, and small towns became increasingly dependent on market-based, private solutions to social problems and community development.[51] Community growth and place-based resources are now largely dependent on political, institutional, and private actors who are motivated to invest in spaces, leading to uneven development within and across these place categories.[52] The political and economic capital from private interests explains, for instance, why some neighborhoods in cities have updated and well-connected transportation routes and why some do not, or why some rural communities have new medical facilities and others are medical deserts.[53] Understanding people's conceptions of places thus provides a piece to the larger puzzle of how and why everyday actors are motivated to participate in local-level community processes that have the power to influence macro-level patterns of social inequality.

However, this book is distinct in its analysis of how second homeowners' and other affluent groups' motivations and actions are typically studied in the context of local places. They are primarily understood only within a singular geography. Gentrifiers are often studied within the neighborhoods they gentrify.[54] Amenity migrants' influence on local life is mainly contained to the rural localities where they make real estate purchases.[55] Even second homeowners are typically understood only within the confines of their host communities.[56] This emphasis on studying a contained geography to understand the influence of affluent people comes from a long line of place-based community scholarship that focuses on geographic propinquity to capture processes of community life—how social ties are formed, how power operates between different social groups, how resources are distributed, how people find a sense of belonging, and how all of this influences people's everyday institutional and commercial practices.[57] Researchers have pointed to the more complex ways people divide their associations across city blocks, streets, neighborhoods, and entire metropolitan areas.[58] However, much research still relies on municipal boundaries to understand how people engage with community life in the twenty-first century.

Such reliance on studying affluent people within municipal boundaries obscures the complexities of the people I talked to. It is not simply that they divided their leisure time and equity between two distinct municipal entities. The people I met also selectively divided their social ties, philanthropy, organizational and institutional involvements, and resources—an entire array of community attachments—between their first- and second-home municipalities in ways that were *patterned* and *relational*. An analysis of their cultural orientations to the places where they lived and owned second homes explained these selective community commitments, providing unique insight into how and why affluent people are implicated in many processes of spatial inequalities at once.

How Place Identity Can Incite Action

There are many different cultural processes that sociologists study to understand how people engage in everyday actions to shape the communities around them. In this book, I explore the pursuit of *place identity*, a specific cultural process of narrative construction that emerged inductively after talking with second homeowners in Rangeley and Boston.[59] This process explained how the people I talked with understood their place in the world, and how and why they divided their community attachments in ways that contributed to reproducing spatial inequalities across the places where they lived and owned second homes.

Lee Cuba and David Hummon have called the relationship between our personal identity narratives and our geographic location *place identity*, the idea that where we live influences who we are and how we think of ourselves.[60] Places, or physical locations that we "invest with meaning and value," are a central feature of identity narrative construction.[61] The "raw materials" we gather over the course of our lives to tell a story about who we are—memories, experiences, understandings, interpretations—are always situated somewhere.[62] Therefore, physical locations help us situate ourselves as we build the story we tell.[63]

I build on this concept, *place identity*, in two ways. First, I suggest that place identities can be *felt*. Typically, place identity is conceptualized as a situated social identity, dependent on one's current geographic location.[64] This can include identification with a range of geographic types including one's home, neighborhood, community, or even region.[65] It can also include one's identification with urban, suburban, and rural places.[66] People call upon their immediate physical environments to tell a story about who they are to others—a city person, a country person, an East Coaster, a West Coaster, a midwesterner, a southerner, and so on and so forth. Yet what is distinct about the people I interviewed is that they use places other than where they live full-time to define themselves, expressing a dissonance between their *felt* place identity and where they permanently reside.

Social theorist Erving Goffman explains *felt identity* as "an individual's subjective sense of [their] own situation and [their] own continuity and character that an individual comes to obtain as a result of [their] various social experiences."[67] Felt identity is how we make sense of ourselves and how our everyday experiences coalesce to shape this understanding. It is who we believe we *really* are. The place identities of the people I met had been forged through an accumulation of life experiences and memories that occurred in other types of places, which shaped their subjective understandings of who they were in relation to where they were.

This process is not unique to the people I talked with. Political scientists have written about how people *feel* place identities in ways that shape political behaviors. People who identify as rural, for instance—even if they currently do not live (or have never lived) in a rural place—align themselves with rural affect and values, exhibiting a group "affinity" and voting in ways that align with rural people and places.[68] Affiliations with rurality and urbanism are powerful forces in signifying identity and orienting our understandings of the social world, regardless of whether we actually live in the place categories with which we identify. This book explores felt identity as an independent variable emergent from a confluence of life experiences that has the power to pattern people's orientations to social life and inform how people engage with the world around them.[69]

Second, I suggest that place identities can be *projects.* A *place-identity project* involves the construction of oneself using place-specific meanings, attributes, and practices, explaining how people both attach their sense of self to certain places and engage in everyday actions to accomplish this aspect of their identity.[70] In modern life, people do not experience some aspects of identity as ascribed features, given to us at birth. They are *projects,* something to be expertly and continually curated over time in an effort to define ourselves and situate our place in the world.[71] It explains the rise of self-help books, the popularity of TV show makeovers, and even the trend of personal branding for social media influencers.[72] This new emphasis on our individuality means we work every day to become who we are and want to be. I explore our relationship to place, *where* we want to be located, as related to this feature of modern life.

Scholars of urban and rural life have been writing about processes akin to place-identity projects for decades.[73] For example, Richard Ocejo finds that first-wave gentrifiers on the Lower East Side in New York City develop identities as the symbolic owners of the neighborhood's distinct bars and nightlife and, to protect this sense of self, fight at community meetings against neighborhood upscaling.[74] Robin Bartram follows building inspectors who come from working-class backgrounds and see themselves as the city's arbiters of justice, using this conception of self to inform their everyday practices—whether they issue an inspection fine, for instance—to make communities more equal for people who have been historically denied housing advantages.[75] People act on behalf of how they understand who they are in relationship to the places where they live. This not only affirms how people view themselves but also shapes the trajectories of the communities around them.

In this book, I extend this research by specifying the mutually constitutive relationship between place identity and social class.[76] First, I show how social class influences place identity by shaping the development and enactment of felt place identities and the relative weight and style of place-identity projects. That the people I met are upper-middle-class propels them to remain in affluent communities for access to value-generating resources, even if they would rather be somewhere else. Yet not everyone who has a felt place identity can act on it, and not everyone has equal abilities to make places more like how they imagine them.[77] I show how the social-class position of the people in this book matters for their ability to turn their felt identity into a project through second homeownership.

It also influences how acute their everyday practices are in their second-home communities. The people I follow in this book may not attend community meetings to fight against upscaling or use their occupational position in a community to advocate for change. Nor can they run for political office or even vote in town or neighborhood municipal meetings to exert their influence in communities, as can permanent residents. However, they have a wealth of social, economic, cultural, and political capital that extends beyond the walls of their high-end real estate investments and even beyond the boundaries of a singular municipality. Their social position enables them to support local nonprofit institutions that serve as their community representatives, ensuring that the places remain how they imagine them—even in their absence.

Second, I explore how place-identity projects influence social-class position. Affiliation with nature in the country and culture in the city provides the people I met with a presentation of their social-class identity that they find legitimate and secure.[78] Much has been written about the different discursive methods and everyday practices elites use to justify their social-class position. Rachel Sherman, for instance, writes about the meanings and morality of upper-middle-class lifestyle choices. The elite people she interviewed frame their basic consumption needs as ordinary, even normal, particularly as they are foiled against the ostentation of the superrich. This discourse works as a way for elites to feel morally deserving of what they do and what they have. It is a "site of legitimation."[79] Places also operate as this "moral preserve."[80] Sociologists like Justin Farrell, Jennifer Sherman, and Michael Bell explore how affiliation with nature and rural people in the country enables some elites to solve their ethical class dilemmas in an age of wealth inequality.[81] I build on this to show how affiliation and engagement with select parts of the country *and* the city can serve as a moral preserve. This affiliation is what Rachel Sherman refers to as a "mode of justification of privilege."[82]

To be sure, social class does not operate in isolation. The people I met are predominantly white, which combines with and creates their social-class position in ways that shape their cultural orientations to the city, the country, and the suburbs. As I will explore in each section of the book, their interpretations of these place categories constitute and are constituted by the *racialization of space*, in which different place categories take on socially constructed, symbolic meanings associated with racial categories, which create hierarchical boundaries among and between locations.[83] These meanings are historically specific, changing across time and place as larger economic and social forces redraw the boundaries of racial inclusion and exclusion. That parts of the city, the country, and the suburbs are racialized as white spaces is a precondition for any of these places to be considered either a source of institutional advantages or a source of place identity for the white upper-middle-class people I talked with. By connecting this process to the everyday practices of the people I talked to for this book, I make a larger point: by critically examining the origins, limits, and implementation of some upper-middle-class suburbanites' place-identity projects, we can see how every place is beholden to people like them.

Studying Second Homeownership

THE CASES: RANGELEY AND BOSTON

I first began thinking about second homeownership as a social problem while reading community studies about amenity-rich rural places. I began questioning how the small rural vacation communities that I frequented while growing up in a small city in central Maine have, for decades, grappled with the seasonal influx and exodus of second homeowners—people I often heard referred to pejoratively as "flatlanders" or "from aways." Second homeowners are intriguing for community scholars because they complicate typical newcomer/old-timer dynamics, place strain on community life, and increase property values for many working-class towns.

I decided to focus this inquiry on Rangeley, a small rural vacation community in northern Maine that I had only visited a handful of times before I began the project. I was intrigued by its long-standing, year-round, highly dense second-home population, drawn to the very remote and isolated corner of western Maine for its abundance of lakes, mountains, and forest. Rangeley is a valuable case for understanding rural second homeownership. Unlike newer and more highly animated second-home communities in the Mountain West that have garnered a great deal of academic attention, the entire state of Maine and northeast region have relied on economic strategies that attract second homeowners since the decline of its agrarian economy throughout the twentieth century.[84] Today, Rangeley maintains a full-time population of a little over one thousand people and at the time of the research, well over half of the nearly two thousand housing units in Rangeley were occupied by second homeowners. Attention to a place like Rangeley could capture the variability in how second homeowners influence communities and how communities react to their in-migration. Second homeowners are not a new or exogenous force in the region.[85] They have a long history tied to the town's development and history.

To study second homeowners in Rangeley, I lived in a one-bedroom apartment on Main Street in Rangeley for nearly a year between 2013 and 2014. I conducted in-depth interviews with thirty-seven second homeowners whom I met through permanent residents I came to know well, through the jobs I worked, and through other second homeowners. For the interviews, many invited me to their second homes, where we often spent all morning or afternoon together, allowing me to see part of their world from their point of view. Most of the participants in my sample worked in professional or managerial positions, had a bachelor's degree or higher, lived permanently in suburbs or exurbs in New England or Florida (which mirrored the primary residences of most second homeowners in Rangeley), and were politically heterogeneous.[86] The average estimated value for their second home in 2021 was $490,187, compared to Rangeley's median home value of $234,400 (see table 1).[87] The estimated value of their permanent residence was $731,240. All second homeowners in my interview sample were white. Drawing from their education levels and occupations, the second homeowners I met in Rangeley were part of the upper middle class.[88] Their collective housing assets also necessarily place them in a category above the middle class.[89]

I also observed nearly every facet of local life where second homeowners might appear: municipal meetings, church events, sporting associations, nonprofit organizations, coffee shops, bars, bakeries, restaurants, museums, bookstores, and community events—fairs, farmer's markets, parades, festivals, lectures, home tours, municipal events, and so on. I held two local jobs while completing fieldwork, working alongside permanent residents and observing their interactions with second homeowners as they occurred (or did not) in everyday life. During the winter I worked at the local recreational mountain, and during the summer I was a server at a restaurant in town. Additionally, I analyzed an array of community documents including newspaper articles, historical texts, municipal records, property tax records, donation databases, and community forums.

Because I am simultaneously a "Mainer" and an out-of-stater, although I do not identify as a local Rangeley resident nor as a second homeowner, I was able to traverse and gain entrée with both diverse groups in town. Aspects of my personal history, such as identifying as a "Mainer," coming from a family of farmers and steelworkers, and having a working knowledge of all of the primary outdoor recreation activities found in this area (including skiing, snowboarding, fishing, hiking, hunting, four-wheeling, and snowmobiling), gave me almost immediate entrée with permanent residents, and working at the mountain and at the restaurant helped me build rapport, despite not being from Rangeley myself. On the other hand, my educational background coupled with living in a large urban area outside of Maine for graduate school enabled me to build rapport with second homeowners who were not from Maine.

As this project unfolded, I considered another important lesson I learned reading about community life: there is a recursive relationship between urban and rural people and places.[90] I began considering what draws people to second homeownership in cities and how, if at all, these processes are similar to patterns in rural parts of the country. The rise of second homeownership in cities is a relatively recent phenomenon, and is most common in highly affluent neighborhoods in global cities.

Boston is a constructive case for understanding urban second homeownership. Although it is a smaller global city, the rise of second homeownership there mirrors the rise in larger cities, as well as in cities of the same size across the United States.[91] Despite making up only a small fraction of the total housing stock in Boston, second homeownership concentrates in core parts of the city, much like it does in larger cities like New York, Chicago, and Los Angeles. Today, Back Bay, Beacon Hill, Downtown, North End/Waterfront—central-city neighborhoods that have been on the front lines of the city's revitalization efforts and are in stages of super-gentrification today—contain the highest density of second homeowners in Boston.[92] In neighborhoods like Back Bay and Downtown, second homeownership has risen from less than 2 percent of the total housing stock to just over 10 percent over a thirty-year period from 1990 to 2019.[93] While still not a huge portion, many of these second-home units are concentrated in clusters of buildings within these neighborhoods.[94] These patterns suggest that the rise of second homeownership has occurred in conjunction with Boston's increased affluence and exclusivity in the central part of the city.

However, deciphering who exactly these owners are is methodologically challenging. Tax records in Boston collect information on who receives the permanent residency tax exemption, but they do not collect information on the intended use of the non-residents' units. It is thus difficult to distinguish units via the Boston tax records between owners who use the property for vacation or leisure, investment, or as a rental unit to tenants or via third-party platforms. There is great variety in who potentially owns these units. Some are exclusively Airbnb owners, some are international wealth elites who use urban real estate as a safe-deposit box, some own a place to be near their children attending college, others are like the second homeowners I talked to for this book, and still others are a combination of these categories. The people I follow in this book are thus one segment of this increasing population.[95]

In Boston, I completed this research between 2014 and 2016 while I lived in Jamaica Plain. I interviewed twenty-four second homeowners. Because of their highly transient lifestyles, the second homeowners I interviewed in Boston were much harder to talk to in person than the people I met in Rangeley. Most would spend a few days a month in their second homes, and many could not be sure about when that might be. Because of this, I spoke with almost all of them over the phone, often from long distances, because they could not guarantee their availability at a specific time to meet me in person. I relied on them to describe their daily activities and the details of their second homes to me. After our conversations, I spent time walking through their neighborhoods to get a sense of the daily routines and practices they relayed. Yet these very methodological problems, I learned, helped me better understand their transient, anonymous, and limited orientation to city life, a theme that weaves throughout the book.[96] My educational position at a well-known university in the Boston area helped me gain entrée with the highly educated second homeowners in Boston I met, many of whom went to college in Boston themselves.

Nearly all of the second homeowners in my sample owned a second home in central-city neighborhoods, except for two who owned second homes in Jamaica Plain. On average, second homeowners from Boston had more wealth in housing than the second homeowners I met in Rangeley. The average value of their second home as of 2021 was $897,030 compared to Boston's median home value $532,700.[97] The average estimated value of their first home was $1,228,290. Most held professional or executive occupations. Many were doctors, lawyers, professors, or CEOs and CFOs of small to midsized corporations. Almost all had a graduate degree. All but one identified as white and were American-born. About half lived permanently in the suburbs or exurbs of Boston and the other half lived in the suburbs of other cities across the United States. Like in Rangeley, they were politically heterogeneous. Drawing from their housing assets, occupations, and education levels, the people I met in Boston sat slightly higher in the upper-middle-class socioeconomic category than the people I interviewed in Rangeley.

In Rangeley, I was immersed in the world of permanent residents and second homeowners, watching how they interacted with each other (or did not) in everyday life. I saw them riding ski lifts together, discussing the best berries to buy at the farmer's market, and, at times, ignoring each other. Yet one cannot see second homeowners in Boston in the same way as one can in Rangeley. Because of the sheer density and anonymity of city life, one is unlikely to know if one passes them on the street or bumps into them at the coffee shop. I knew this going into my project. To then capture a portrait of how certain neighborhoods in Boston understand second homeowners (or do not), I relied on a sampling of different sources of data. I interviewed six community leaders and five real estate agents. I also interviewed an employee at the Boston Symphony Orchestra and an employee from the Boston tax assessor's office. I analyzed an array of community documents, including newspaper articles, tax records, donation databases, community forums, and archival data. I attended ten community meetings in neighborhoods where second homeowners most

TABLE 1. Demographic Characteristics of Sample in Rangeley and Boston

	Rangeley	Boston
Race	all white	predominantly white
Age range	40s–80s	40s–80s
Occupation	managerial and professional	professional and executive
Education	majority BA or higher	majority graduate degree
Mean est. second-home value[1]	$490,187	$897,030
Range est. second-home value	$180,000–$1,490,000	$361,700–$2,823,000
Mean est. first-home value	$731,240	$1,228,290
Range est. first-home value	$288,345–$1,618,894	$200,800–$2,661,210

[1] Home values are derived from July 2021 Zillow Estimates (Zestimates July 2021). These might be higher than typical because of pandemic-induced real estate inflation. However, Zestimates are often the best proxy, as tax assessment is typically much lower than "real" value in marketplace. Not all Rangeley homes have Zestimates. In instances in which they did not, I used comparable homes located on the same roads with similar characteristics (waterfront, square footage, bedrooms/baths, etc.).

heavily concentrate in Boston: the North End/Waterfront, Back Bay, and Downtown. This allowed me to measure the presence and/or absence of second homeowners in Boston's civic sphere and to chart their reception by civic leaders and community stakeholders.

It was this comparison that I set out to explore. I wanted to understand the linkages between urban and rural second homeownership and how affluent people affect these two geographies. However, as my interviews unfolded, I noticed a recurring pattern in how they talked about their second homes: it was always relational with their primary residences. So as my interviews went on, I continued to ask more questions about this relationality. I learned that to fully understand the people I met and their multifaceted influence across local life, I not only had to understand their relationships to their second-home host communities; I also had to understand their social-class position in relation to their hometowns.

THE PEOPLE: UPPER-MIDDLE-CLASS AND MOSTLY SUBURBAN

In my research design, I did not originally set out to study people who were predominantly upper-middle-class and primarily from the suburbs. However, I learned after talking with second homeowners from Rangeley and

Boston that both categories were important for understanding their motivations for and practices associated with second homeownership.

At first glance, this particular group of upper-middle-class people who buy second homes in the city or the country and live permanently in suburban communities may seem unique or niche, especially after years of accounts in major news platforms that focus on international wealth elites who buy real estate as a safe-deposit box in places like the Time Warner Center in Manhattan or jet-setting urbanites who purchase million-dollar views in resort towns like Jackson Hole, Wyoming, or Aspen, Colorado.[98]

However, many second homeowners today are upper-middle-class, a category I use as a heuristic to talk about people who are neither in the middle class nor in the top 1 percent.[99] Upper-middle-class people typically work in upper management or professional occupations, or are small-business owners, they often have a college degree and sometimes a graduate or professional degree, and they make between $150,000 and $500,000 annually. While other demographic data are difficult to obtain for second homeowners, a Zillow analysis of data from the Home Mortgage Disclosure Act in 2019 found that the median income of a second-home buyer with a mortgage was $170,000, and most of these buyers were white, aligning with the broad category of upper middle class.[100]

Upper-middle-class people are an increasingly important subset of elites to study. Shamus Kahn has suggested that elites are people who "[occupy] a position that provides them with access and control or as [those who possess] resources that advantage them."[101] This definition encourages us to look at the heterogeneity of elites, not just those who sit at the top of the socioeconomic hierarchy, to understand the multiple and complex methods by which people maintain control or access to resources in ways that have "transferable value" and disadvantage others.[102] Scholars like Lauren Riviera and Rachel Sherman have built on this by studying the top 20 percent of income earners who hide in the shadows of the hyper-affluent. This social location beneath the top 1 percent enables upper-middle-class people to obscure, minimize, and justify the privileges they secure—inherited wealth, access to quality schools, and robust social capital, to name just a few.[103]

Whereas many accounts of second homeowners follow city dwellers to the countryside or international global jet-setters across city real estate, the vast majority of the people I talked with were from suburban communities.[104] This aligns with recent research that suggests that the majority of second homeowners in New England are, in fact, from the suburbs.[105] If we consider that many second homeowners are upper-middle-class, it should be no surprise that most of those who spoke with me lived permanently in the suburbs and other highly affluent communities because this is where many upper-middle-class people reproduce their social position.[106]

It is important to note, however, that there is no uniform measure that exists to define "suburban."[107] In fact, it is a contested category that can encompass everything from geographic location, transportation, planning type, to culture.[108] Geographically, nearly everyone I spoke with lived in an incorporated municipality in proximity to a small or large city. Whether it was a small city or a small town, most talked about their permanent residence in relation to larger or smaller metropolitan areas nearby, with the vast majority describing their hometown as "outside/north/south/near X city." These interpretive and geographic definitions closely align with contemporary efforts to define *suburban* (table 2).[109]

What unites all the places where my respondents lived is that these types of communities have benefited from America's system of metropolitan division—the incorporation of small towns and cities that are within a metropolitan area but beyond the urban core—that allocates many public services based on the local tax base from this small geographic unit.[110] Nearly uniformly, they lived in predominantly white communities where the average median household income was higher than the median household income for the state in which they live.[111] Within these communities, they lived in large homes and maintained access to top-quality schools, healthcare facilities, job opportunities, and public services. To put it simply, they lived in highly affluent and resource-rich municipalities.

Highly affluent suburban communities have received sustained attention over the course of nearly a century for the ways in which residents within them secure their resources at the expense of other people and places.[112] It is where wealth has been created and inherited through federal programs that provided many white suburban residents with access to home mortgages. It is where zoning restrictions limiting density have continued to make access to these communities a scarce resource.[113] It is where resource-rich schools concentrated after the white middle-class exodus from the cities during the era of school desegregation.[114] And it is where many affluent people continue to develop social capital through ties with each other that sustain these very locational advantages.[115] That the second homeowners I met were predominantly upper-middle-class and suburban is an important theme in this book. This unique social location informed their orientations to the places where they lived and owned second homes, connecting the relationship between place and privilege.

TABLE 2. Second Homeowners' Permanent Residences in Sample by Household

Permanent residence type	Urban second homeowners	Rural second homeowners	Total
Urban	5	3	8
Suburban	18	14	32
Rural	1	5	6
Total	24	22	46

Organization of the Book

Part 1 takes readers to the suburbs, the places where the vast majority of the people I met called home. In these chapters, I explore the origins of their dissatisfaction with their hometowns and explain why these people, who were from the same social class and who lived in the same types of places, experienced them in entirely different ways—either as too urban or too rural. But more than that, these chapters answer fundamental questions. If they did not like the places where they lived, why did they move there in the first place? And why did they stay? In answering these questions, the chapters chart how their relationship to their first home contributed to deepening spatial inequalities between the suburbs and the city and the country.

In Part 2 and Part 3, we travel to Rangeley and Boston, respectively. In these chapters, I explore the place-identity projects of the people I met, how their sense of place guided their everyday actions, how this matched up with Rangeley's and Boston's own place-making projects, and how their place-identity projects relied on and further contributed to deepening enduring inequalities within the city and the country. At the end of each section, I explore how local folks thought about and reacted to second homeowners' presence or absence in community life.

In the conclusion, I discuss the theoretical and empirical contributions of the book—how studying this process can help us understand affluent people's relationship to community, the ways in which privilege lies at the heart of the relationship between place and identity, and how to approach policies made about second homeowner in-migration.

The Suburbs and Everywhere in Between

Cassie's two-story, five-bedroom brick colonial sits on a half-acre lot in a small suburban community outside of Boston. Its backyard is private, lush with tall pine trees and weeping willows. There is a narrow stone path flanked by a flower garden that winds through the property and ends at a private veranda. It also has a playground set, where her kids spend their afternoons when school is out. The house is close to the center of her town. Yet when she walks along the streets, even as she passes grocery stores, cafés, restaurants, and art galleries, she misses the pace and culture of city life. She feels like she lives in the country.

Holly's two-story, three-bedroom, cottage-style cape sits on a highly manicured one-acre lot, separated from neighbors on each side by imposing white birch trees and balsam firs. Her newly renovated kitchen looks out into the completely private backyard where they have a fireplace set up for the winter days and cool summer nights and a brick patio where they host friends and family. Her home is just a mile from the town center, with easy access to grocery stores and restaurants. It is also a short drive from some of the state's best golf courses, a yacht club, and other coastal attractions. But every week as she drives to pick up groceries from the town center, she cannot drown out the clamor of the people or the bumper-to-bumper traffic. Longing for peace and quiet, she cannot tune out the everyday conditions that feel like the city.

If I had not asked, I would have been sure that the second homeowners I met in Rangeley and Boston, like Holly and Cassie, came from entirely different worlds. In Rangeley, I heard countless complaints like Holly's about the noise pollution, crowded streets, and traffic that made it seem like they lived permanently in dense urban centers while they longed for rural places. Waxing poetic about city life, while also lamenting the lack of culture and walkability and expressing dissatisfaction with small-town parochialism, made me think the people I met in Boston like Cassie lived deep in the country. But the people I met in Rangeley were not from the city. And the people I met in Boston were not from the country. They were both mostly from the suburbs.

I was puzzled over these findings. Why do these people, who are relatively similar in terms of race and social class and who are politically heterogeneous, see the same type of place entirely differently? And why do these relatively affluent and mobile people stay in these places when they would rather be somewhere else? Answering these questions became the key to unlocking their distinct relationship to their hometowns, to second homeownership, and to the city and the country.

———

To understand the places called home by the vast majority of the people I met requires a brief history of the relationship between affluence and American suburbanization. The United States has a long history of incorporating small towns and cities outside of major metropolitan areas into what is known as *suburbs*. Municipal incorporation has been a long-standing basic right of self-governance since the early days of colonization in the United States.[1] As American cities began to grow during the late nineteenth and early twentieth century, this method of local control expanded along the outskirts of major metropolitan areas. This type of governance allowed residents direct control and taxation over resources and public services like schools, sewage, and water while freeing them from taxation for urban improvements.[2] It also allowed direct control over land-use policies like zoning, to prevent unwanted housing developments or urban encroachments. Perhaps most fundamentally, municipal incorporation was a mechanism to secure resources and provide distance from the modern city.[3]

The post–World War II period marked the rise of the middle-class suburb as an American ideal. This proliferation was a racialized project, in which the government issued federally backed home loans to families in predominantly white suburban neighborhoods, barring the funding of mortgages to people in predominantly Black, financially "risky" areas typically found in cities, what is known as redlining.[4] Middle-class and upper-middle-class white Americans flocked to the suburban subdivision for single-family homes equipped with modern amenities, privacy, and spacious yards.

Life in the suburbs during this period provided a range of material advantages. First and foremost, it enabled generations of middle-class white families to generate wealth through homeownership. It also provided access to resource-rich institutions. Schools flourished with the infusion of middle-class tax dollars and social capital. Suburban communities saw everything from state-of-the-art buildings to new textbooks to highly credentialed teachers. This wealth of resources became further institutionalized during the era of school desegregation, when a series of Supreme Court rulings barred metropolitan-wide desegregation efforts between the city and the suburbs, creating a material and symbolic wall between the white suburbs and the predominantly Black cities.[5] This all but ensured that white families in the suburbs did not have to share their most valued resources: schools.

The suburbs also provided white middle-class and upper-middle-class people with a range of cultural and natural resources, once located only in the city or the country. Residents found their own bounded site of nature and leisure with trees and green grass and flowers, what used to be found only in proximity to parks in cities and bucolic landscapes in the countryside.[6] Suburban communities also offered the best of both worlds for people who still desired proximity to amenities and cultural institutions not typically found in rural places. Taken together, the suburbs became perceived as the ideal place for such people to raise a family, separated by trains and highways from modern urban life.[7]

But in the decades that followed, several changes complicated these notions of suburban living.[8] Deindustrialization and the flight of industry in the search for cheaper land and labor prompted the emergence of new office parks, highways, and sprawl in some suburban areas. While the suburbs were once free from the hustle and bustle of city life, these new material patterns soon encroached on quaint, white-picket-fence communities, blurring the lines between home/work, city/suburb, industry/leisure, and nature/city.[9]

The civil rights era also altered the cultural meanings associated with suburban life. The suburban subdivision was once considered an American ideal for white families, but as backlash against racially exclusionary policies and practices came to the fore, the suburbs subsumed meanings associated with sterility, uniformity, and racism for many liberal-minded dwellers.[10] It was no longer a source of social distinction for the white habitus.[11] What used to be *the* place to live soon became passé. This rejection of suburbia as an American ideal prompted a wave of migration.[12] Scholars across a range of disciplines have documented the out-migration of people from the sub-urbs into rural towns or urban neighborhoods in search of a lifestyle that matched their ideological orientation to place.[13] For many white and advantaged people, the suburbs were *out* and the city and the country were *in*.

Yet the focus on these patterns of migration overshadows an enduring trend: affluent people are still moving to and staying in low-density suburbs and exurbs.[14] While some suburbs are becoming more racially and economically diverse in recent decades as cities become increasingly unaffordable, suburban places are still by and large segregated along race and class lines.[15] Within these segregated communities, institutions and services are also stratified. White residents still maintain access to the lowest-poverty neighborhoods and access to the best public services, including schools.[16]

Not all white middle-class and upper-middle-class people left the suburbs to gentrify the city, nor did they permanently leave to find the so-called good life in rural places.[17] Many continue to move there. Many continue to stay there. The vast majority of the people I met were part of the enduring trend, in which many white middle-class and upper-middle-class people move to and remain in suburban communities.[18]

It is here where the book begins. The chapters that follow trace why the people I met experienced a dissonance with the places they called home, why they experienced this dissonance differently, and why they continued to stay in their hometown communities when they would rather have been in the city or country.

1

Ennui

In *The Pursuit of Loneliness*, Philip Slater argued that American suburbs, characterized by single-family homes, private backyards, and do-it-yourself culture, undermine innate desires for community and connection. The suburbs erode the "bonds that give [people] a comfortable sense of [self]."[1] What was once thought to be the best of all worlds was soon realized as the worst of all and best of none. On the suburbs he wrote:

> The suburban dweller sought peace, privacy, nature, community, good schools, and a healthy child-rearing environment. Instead, he found neither the beauty and the serenity of the countryside nor the stimulation of the city, nor the stability and sense of community of the small town.[2]

Slater was perhaps the most unsparing in his critique of American suburbs, although other sociologists and public writers have echoed these broader claims.[3] The suburbs were once considered the American dream for many white middle-class families. However, the very thing the suburbs promised— this best of all worlds—proved to undermine its dwellers' relationship to place, home, and community. Critics of the suburbs argue that this is due to a reliance on cars, racial homogeneity, an ideology of individualism, and a preponderance of private spaces, each of which separates us from our connection to place and the bonds that bring us together.[4]

Much has been written about the suburbs before and since Slater's critique. Scholars have highlighted the very real complexity and heterogeneity of suburban places and the meaningful modes of community that can form in these places.[5] Yet the people I talked with expressed the tensions Slater highlighted: their hometowns did not provide them with a coherent sense of place.

A Dissonance

Most of the people I talked to in both Rangeley and Boston permanently resided in places that existed somewhere between distinctly urban and distinctly rural geographies. While some lived on the exurban fringe or in small cities, the vast majority lived in small towns and small cities in the suburbs.

There was an undercurrent of dissonance many articulated when talking about these primary homes. Many viewed their permanent residences as entirely too urban or too rural, despite living in places that were mostly suburban. Suburban communities often contain more outdoor amenities than urban locales, including green space, parks, and spacious yards. But because of their proximity to cities or larger metropolitan areas, the places where they lived were also proximate to resources not typically found in more rural communities, including numerous grocery stores, retail establishments, hospitals, and sometimes even cultural attractions such as art museums and theaters.[6]

Suburban life does contain its own distinct culture and way of life, but the heart of suburban living is that it is an amalgam of urban and rural environments.[7] The suburbs, and many exurbs and small cities, have a little bit of everything. But to the people I talked with, this little bit was *not enough* and *too much* at the same time. For the people in Rangeley I talked with, these areas did not have *enough rural* and had *too much urban*. For the people in Boston I talked with, these same place categories did not have *enough urban* and had *too much rural*. For all, they were entirely *too suburban*—a place typology too diluted.[8]

Although the suburbs can offer its residents the best of both worlds, the people I talked with expressed a personal discordance with these places they called home; it did not provide them with a *place identity*. Places provide us with a vocabulary for interpreting and explaining our place in the world. It is how we understand ourselves within our socio-spatial environment.[9] But most of the people I met did not view their hometowns as places that provided this coherent vocabulary to situate their place in the world—they expressed feeling out of place.

In Rangeley, the people I met viewed their permanent residences as places that have subsumed many distinctly urban qualities of suburban life;

it was too noisy, too dense, and too chaotic. Holly, for instance, described her hometown as "traffic, people, dogs, kids. Just the hubbub. Totally opposite of what we like about here [in Rangeley] is what we don't like about it there . . . the noise is what gets me. Every time I pull in [to Rangeley]. It's like 'oh, I can hear again!' And you get home and it's just so noisy." Holly was a schoolteacher, and her husband, Greg, worked in finance. They lived in an affluent coastal suburb less than ten miles from the city of Portland, Maine. Here, they lived in a two-thousand-square-foot home in a residential neighborhood that sat on an acre of property, with houses separated by trees and fences. The town celebrates its abundance of natural amenities, proximity to Portland, and top educational system in the state, providing its residents with the best of all worlds. From her house, she had access to hiking trails, beaches, and parks. Despite these natural amenities that abound, Holly described urban sprawl in her suburban life. Walking along the beach or hiking in the abutting forest was not enough to drown out the clatter of the people and the cars, to her the noise of city life.

The culture of suburban living was also experienced as too urban. At the beginning of the twentieth century against the backdrop of urbanization, Georg Simmel was among the first to characterize what city life did to individual character. The density and new money economy fueled by rapid industrialization created a new urban personality, someone who was transactional, money oriented, rational, and calculating.[10] Over one hundred years later, this was how Ted described the people who lived in his hometown. Ted was from an affluent suburb of Portland, Maine, where he lived on a four-acre lot in a 2,500-square-foot house worth over half a million dollars. He never went to college but worked his way to becoming an owner of a small manufacturing company. Like Holly, he complained about the density and the noise in this small suburb, but he also described a change in the type of people who surrounded him. He called his community a "briefcase community" in which people come to Maine for job opportunities, but their "intention isn't to stay here, just to move up the ladder for the career." Ted described how this new class of people had altered the kind of community his kids were growing up in. It was no longer a middle-class community in Maine. It was "northern Massachusetts," a community where teenagers drive "Jaguars and Audis" to school each day and were only concerned about getting ahead. For Ted, urban sprawl had crept up the coast all the way from Boston.

The people I met in Boston were from similar kinds of hometowns as the people I interviewed in Rangeley. The majority lived in affluent suburban communities, with few others living in exurban towns and small cities.

However, they did not view these same place categories as too urban or sprawled but as too rural or provincial. Dan, a president of a midsized company, was from a suburb of Boston, what he called a "bedroom community, [where] most people commute north due to work." This community was very similar to Holly's and Ted's—second homeowners in Rangeley. It was a commuter town with ample cultural and natural amenities. At the time of our interview, his 3,000-square-foot home that sat on a three-quarter-acre lot was worth $700,000. He had immediate proximity to parkland and the ocean, and in less than three miles he could find a lively downtown with restaurants, art galleries, cafés, and upscale boutiques. He called it "the country." For Dan, this town lacked high culture and the types of amenities he valued. He explained: "I'm a big foodie. I love to eat. I love to cook. I love any type of ethnic food. I don't care where it's from. . . . Down here in the country, you got your regular Italian, American, Chinese. You know what I mean."

Eva moved from her beloved South End apartment to a 2,500-square-foot home worth nearly three million dollars in one of the wealthiest suburbs outside of Boston when she had children. She and her husband both attended highly selective liberal arts colleges and obtained their master's degrees. As an heir to the president of a major U.S. company, Eva was among the wealthiest people I talked to. She had left her career working in a nonprofit to stay home with her children full-time. Her husband was a computer scientist. In this town she was near ample greenery and open space and was just a short walk from the downtown center, which boasts fine and modern art galleries, a performance hall, restaurants, and retail establishments. She enjoyed the open space and greenery but lamented the distinct lack of culture. She explained, "I have a pull to want our kids to stay engaged with the city and the culture, the things that you don't find [here]. . . . We have wonderful things out here, but there's a lack of culture in terms of art and music and theater." The suburbs were plentiful with amenities but for some I talked with, they lacked high-cultural institutions to enrich children's lives. The suburbs were described as too provincial, too inward-looking, and too void of sophistication.

Tracy was a young lawyer who was the only Boston second homeowner I talked with who lived in a large city proper. Despite being from a city, she still explained her hometown using many of the same descriptors as others I talked with who owned second homes in Boston. "I like the idea that when you actually do talk to people [in Boston], you can talk to them about ideas instead of mind-numbing small talk. I like the history, there's a rich, intellectual environment that you constantly learn things from people everywhere. I like that you can get art-house movies that you can't get down in [southern city]." Depending on the region, the cultures of cities can vary greatly, and Tracy experienced Boston as much more culturally rich than her hometown. She also described her city as quite suburban:

> Having lived [here] for twenty years plus one of the frustrations that I have about it is that you have to get in the car and the traffic is terrible. You could, in theory, go for days without having a substantive communication with someone that you pass on the street. One of the things that I loved when I had been up in our place in Back Bay is that I walk around and I look at people and even if people look at me like I'm crazy when I smile at them and say "Hello," that human face-to-face connection isn't between car windows and glass.

Whether from the actual suburbs or cities that feel suburban, many of the people I met in Boston complained about the lack of walkability in their hometowns, a distinctly suburban characteristic. In Boston, they were free from their cars and all that these motor vehicles represented—environmental degradation, work, inefficiency, and ordinariness. Instead of getting into a car, driving through traffic, and working in an office that sits in the middle of a business park, people like Tracy preferred walking the tree-lined streets of Back Bay, finding an open table at the Boston Athenaeum, and poring over legal briefs among the company of other highly educated strangers.

The people I interviewed in both Rangeley and Boston expressed a dissonance with their permanent residences. However, they differed in that they applied different meanings to similar place-based facts.[11] For some, a commuter town with people coming and going from their homes to their jobs was too cosmopolitan, too city-like; for others this same type of place was too homogeneous, too country-like. For the people I talked with, their hometowns have subsumed the multiple, often contrasting meanings of *the city* and *the country*. Raymond Williams argues that these categories are cultural frames people use to make sense of the world, providing a vocabulary to talk about what is good and moral and what is not, and these meanings change over time.[12] He explains that notions of the city and the country represent "human interests and purposes for which there is no other immediate vocabulary. It is not only an absence or distance of more specific terms and concepts; it is that in the country and the city physically present and substantial, the experience finds material which gives body to the thoughts."[13] The places where the people I met lived permanently are liminal spaces, somewhere between urban and rural places. Even scholars who study these place categories have a difficult time agreeing on vocabularies to define it.[14] When the people I met talked about their primary homes as being too "city-like" or too "country-like," they were using the cultural meanings associated with these place categories to identify their values and commitment to particular kinds of communities.[15] If they valued cosmopolitanism and sophistication, they viewed their hometowns as country-like, characterized by provinciality. If they valued the country's "innocence and embrace of nature," they viewed their hometowns as city-like, characterized by "bourgeois corruption" and "alienation."[16] They used the city and the country as an ideological framework to describe what, to them, the good life entailed and *where* it existed. They used these frameworks in the absence of a coherent suburban vocabulary.[17]

The Making of Felt Place Identities

The people I met developed this dissonance with their hometowns as part of their *felt* place-identity narrative construction, the accumulation of their life experiences that influenced who they felt they were and where they felt they belonged. Place identities are typically conceptualized as dependent on where one lives. Although they lived in suburban or sometimes exurban or small urban places, none of the people I talked with rooted their identities in these place categories. They never once claimed an identity as a "suburban" person, describing their hometowns only as "nice" before enumerating its shortcomings. Their place identities were *felt*. They used locational meaning from other places to situate identities, viewing themselves as fundamentally city or country people.

The second homeowners I met in Rangeley claimed place identities they associated with rural places, describing themselves almost uniformly as "country," "outdoors," or "outdoorsy" people. And Boston second homeowners claimed place identities they associated with urban localities, describing themselves as "urbanites," "city people," or even a "city mouse." These notions of the self were crafted in the places where they lived during formative moments in their lives—where they grew up, where they went to college, or where they met their spouse. However, over time, the people I talked with experienced ruptures that unmoored them from the places they associated with themselves, transforming their place identities from *situated* in where they lived to *felt* as part of their identity narrative construction.

Most of the people I met in Rangeley had either grown up in Maine or spent time at earlier points in their lives on Maine's coast or in Maine's woods, forming memories and self-concepts that would stay with them throughout their lives.[18] When I first met Jeff, a retiree from Florida, I readily noticed his faded New York accent and tried to piece together how someone who grew up in New York City and lived in Florida found their way to Rangeley, Maine. Jeff was born in Maine but moved to New York with his family when he was young. He spent the better part of his childhood summers with his family returning to the lakes of northern Maine. For Jeff, buying a second home was "just a little nostalgia." He explained, "I loved being up here when I was a boy and being up in the lakes." After years of living in New York and an eventual move to Florida for a work opportunity, Jeff longed for the days he spent lakeside in Maine among family and friends. Others I met were like Elsie and Howard, who had never lived in Maine, but visiting Rangeley reminded them of a past they wanted to re-create. They used to live in Montana in a log cabin, loving the "kind of small-town character place." Elsie explained that they "loved skiing. We loved being near a skiing resort. We loved the wilderness, we loved nature, we loved moose roaming all around. All of those things."

Nancy and Jack were the only second homeowners I met who had grown up in Rangeley. Both had left town after high school, going their separate ways for college. After meeting up again years later, they began dating and eventually got married. Together they moved to a town in southern Maine to start their lives. After a while, they missed the quiet pace of life, the outdoor activities, and the family they had left behind. They eventually bought a second home to enjoy during the summer and winter. As Jack put it, "I brought her back."

Ted and Cindy had never moved out of their hometown but experienced a rupture in their ability to identify with the place where they were born and raised. Both Ted and Cindy grew up in a suburb outside of Portland, where both of their parents grew up and went to school. They met in high school, got married, and never moved away. They described how this place used to feel like a small town, quintessential to Maine, but had changed considerably since they were young. They expressed nostalgia for the way it used to be. Cindy explained:

It just isn't what it used to be, like, we grew up there. My parents grew up there. My mother, my grandfather, you know, like it is just kind of been generational. But it's very different now. When we were younger it was more . . . hometown locals . . . and now it is people from other states. They are coming in and they are just changing everything.

These types of changes and ruptures to place attachments often leave people feeling nostalgic for an idealized past—in this case, a small-town, rural Maine life.

The second homeowners I talked with in Boston often had direct ties to the city, typically forged during college, where they developed strong place attachments and identities. Many of them had moved away, and buying a second home functioned to repair the discontinuity that emerged from this relocation.[19] Mark's wife grew up north of Boston. They met in Boston while they were both attending college. It is where they both started their careers before other opportunities pulled them away. They felt a deep connection to the city where they met and began their lives together. After leaving, they always promised themselves they would find a way to live in Boston again.

The same was true for Maggie and her husband, who had met in Boston after graduate school while they were in the early stages of their careers—she was a consultant and he worked in finance. "My husband is from Massachusetts," she explained. "We met when he was working in Boston, and I was living in Cambridge. I lived there about fifteen, sixteen years. . . . Then in the course of our careers we moved away but always either tried to come back or wanted to come back to the Boston area because we knew it and we liked it. That didn't work out during our careers." At the time of our interview, Maggie and her husband lived permanently in a small exurban community in New England but spent nearly twenty years living in a suburb of New York City. They expressed a void in their lives after leaving Boston and living in the suburbs for so many years. They missed the days of dining out, attending the theater, and visiting museums, and they enjoyed being the kind of people they were when they lived in the city.

Boston and Rangeley second homeowners developed deep place attachments to urban and rural places at earlier points in their lives when they crafted narratives about who they were and where they felt they belonged.[20] But these narratives were ruptured by relocation to other communities, undermining their ability to associate themselves with the places where they permanently resided. In this particular social and economic epoch, people move within and across cities, states, regions, and countries, rupturing felt place identities. They do so for school, work, family, opportunity, and refuge.[21] Such movement uproots people from communities that moor their self-concepts, from food, sports teams, recreational activities, social ties, and ways of life. Nostalgia is often used as a method to repair identity discontinuity in the aftermath of a rupture in place attachment, whether from a move across geographies, the destruction of a meaningful place, or a fundamental change to places well known.[22] Nostalgia helps reclaim continuity by re-creating a narrative about relationships to the places that form our self-concepts. Nostalgia is best understood as "a positively toned evocation of a lived past in the context of some negative feeling toward present or impending circumstance."[23]

The people I met felt nostalgic for a time and a place in their lives that they attributed to their felt place identities and used these evocations to explain why they could not align themselves with the places they called home—and why they wanted to reclaim their sense of identity elsewhere. Yet this was a distinctly privileged position. Anyone can have a felt place identity, but few can transform felt identities into projects. The social position of people I talked with enabled them to buy a place identity through second homeownership.

2

A Land of Opportunity

The Limits of Nostalgia

The people I met experienced ruptures in their attachment to rural and urban places at earlier points in their lives, which explains why they did not identify with the mostly suburban communities where they lived and relied on locational meaning from the city and the country to make sense of their place in the world. Yet this rupture and subsequent dissonance with their hometowns were created by design. For many of the people I talked with, unmooring themselves from the city and the country—the places they identified with—was a locational choice made to gain access to resources that the city and the country lacked. It is why this highly mobile and affluent group continued to stay in their hometowns even when they would have rather been somewhere else.

I learned more about this process as I talked to Monica, an artist who splits her time between her primary residence in an affluent coastal community in Massachusetts and her second home in Boston. Monica identified deeply with the city and expressed frustration at having to divide her life between these two places. Exasperated, she elaborated:

> I don't want to do it anymore. I don't want to be here anymore . . .
> I want to be in [Boston] full-time because of the art, the culture, and the
> community . . . I can't explain it. It's just the social interaction and
> the culture and knowing. Having my finger on the pulse of what's hip

and trendy and not being out in the middle of nowhere with a bunch of married people raising kids.

I asked Monica why she continued to live in her permanent residence, given such dissatisfaction with the place she purportedly called home. I was especially curious about this because Monica was the only person I talked with in Rangeley or Boston who felt more connected to community life in the typical sense in her second home than in her primary home. She had many local social ties and involved herself in an array of neighborhood organizations. She responded matter-of-factly, "For the past six years, I've been going back and forth because the money was [in the affluent community] over the summer." Monica's livelihood was in the arts, a precarious form of employment dependent on the whims of wealthy patrons. She continued to live in her permanent residence because this was where she could generate the most income. It was a financial necessity. Monica's economic position was different from most other people I spoke with who occupied professional positions, yet many echoed similar sentiments. Their permanent residences remained important sites of institutional resources and economic opportunity, despite not being a source of place-identity fulfillment. And the places where they owned second homes lacked these valued resources. It is this very access to resources and opportunities that helped explain why they moved to their permanent residence and why they remained.

The educational system is one such valued resource. Although Ted and Cindy had complaints about the affluence that concentrated in the school system in the suburbs of Portland, Maine—the kids driving to school in Jaguars and Audis—they admitted that it was one of the best school systems in the state, a resource they simply could not have given up. Ted and Cindy's high-school aged son, Pete, had broached the idea about moving up to Rangeley full-time to enroll in the public school for his final year of high school. He wanted to be a game warden and thought being in Rangeley might be more amenable to that life goal. But Cindy said no. "'Pete, you can't make it your whole life. I want more from you than that,'" she reflected. Ted added, "You see certain people and you think to yourself 'Oh Jesus! What are you gonna do in another ten years? I mean, you can't stay here and live on ten dollars an hour.'" Going to the school in the suburb of Portland left, in their words, "the doors open" for their children, even though they resented the kind of place they felt their hometown had become. Yet, the affluence that concentrated in their hometown, a feature that undermined their connection to it, had infused the school system with financial and cultural capital that had turned it into one of the most coveted educational systems in the region, ranked among the top fifteen high schools in the state.[1]

Like Ted and Cindy, many of the second homeowners I met in Rangeley criticized the educational system. Jeff, a retiree who no longer had to worry about where his children attended school, complained about paying a lot in taxes to fund Rangeley's school system. He joked: "And for what we pay per student for school, these kids could be going somewhere nice!" He elaborated:

> At least this year [the graduating class] didn't all seem like idiots. We've been up here for fifteen years, and when you read some of the comments the graduating kids have it's heartbreaking to think that the best person in the world [to the students] is "Jay Z." It's like, are you serious? You know, it's like, the kids are all nice, but somehow the education they're getting is . . . this is a great place to be retired. If I was young and single I couldn't be here. There's not the job opportunity. There's not the social opportunities. So, you know I understand why to me this place is paradise, but if I were a kid I would be trying to get as far away as I can. . . . If your graduating class is seven! Pssh. You know, and two of them are probably your cousins. So that kind of leaves the social . . . it's a great place to vacation.

Jeff captured a few themes that emerged after talking with second homeowners in Rangeley. To them, it was a beautiful location to vacation and enjoy in small doses in the winter, in the summer, or on the weekends. Rangeley was not a place most of my interviewees would have considered living full-time, and for similar reasons: to them, the educational system was subpar and the town was devoid of employment opportunities. Rangeley lacked many of the institutions and resources they valued.

Of all the people I spoke with in Rangeley, Holly was perhaps the most willing to consider moving from her suburban community to live in Rangeley full-time. She was a schoolteacher, and her husband was able to work remotely. They had no children and they did not plan to. Holly wished she and her husband *could* have lived in Rangeley, but despite their flexibility, she told me she simply could not—and would not. She explained:

> We actually looked into [living in Rangeley full-time] because my husband is able to work wherever, but the school system here is not where I'm at . . . I went and observed. Really thought about it. Just not my . . . just not where education is right now. That's all. It is what it is. It's an old town with a lot of older people and it's hard to explain to older people

why things cost what they cost and to do what you need to do to get your kids ready to do what they need to do. So . . . when [a job position] came up I really thought about it, and I talked to some people and a couple of the subs, and they just said. . . . "They're not ready for you Holly."

Holly considered moving to Rangeley but could not see herself working in a school system that was not up to her standards. This calculated decision meant living in Rangeley was not for her after all and she decided to finish out her career in her suburban hometown. Over the past few decades, rural places have seen a decline in their productive economies. Jobs like logging, farming, and manufacturing have all but disappeared.[2] In their wake came more precarious, service-sector work. People like Holly, Jeff, and Dan captured the consequences of this for the educational system. As people migrate out of rural areas in search of better job opportunities, they take their economic and social capital with them—capital that is necessary to provide resources for school districts.

The second homeowners I talked with in Boston were even more explicit about education influencing their locational decisions. I asked John, who sat overlooking the cul-de-sac of his residential suburban neighborhood while we talked, what brought him to this community nearly thirty years ago. "The school system," he answered bluntly. For John, Boston "just was not where I wanted to live. When I bought this place [in the suburbs] in town, my kids were still pretty young, and we lived in a nice community, which was, I just think a better environment for them, rather than living in Boston. That just wasn't in the cards at all." And John was not alone. When Eva had children, she and her husband moved out of Boston to the suburbs but kept their apartment in the city. Her home "is nice. It's a quiet place. It's more simple. The life here seems to be easy. There's not a lot of competition for stuff. You have wonderful options for your kids. . . . It seems like there's a lot of really good people around here who are really family focused." Eva's house is an idyllic, large single-family home in the suburbs of Boston, sitting on an acre of pristine lawn, big enough for her children to run around and play. This maps onto long-standing trends, in which opportunities for children often outweigh desires for cultural amenities and lifestyles when choosing where to live.[3]

Betsy is a second homeowner from Boston who was from the same hometown as Eva. She was more unequivocal about her locational decisions. Although she and her husband "love city living," they moved to this particular suburb of Boston "so the child could go to the [suburban] school system."

It was a functional locational choice made to provide her daughter with opportunity. The town's high school was ranked among the top 15 percent of public high schools in Massachusetts.[4]

This migratory flow of second homeowners from the city to the suburbs and back again into the city due to schooling and childrearing was confirmed in an interview I had with Leslie, a luxury real estate agent in Boston, who explained the typical chain of events he has experienced in the second-home market in Boston:

> Usually, you have folks that come here for school. And they oftentimes end up staying in Boston. So those folks end up buying. And when they get married, or they end up having a child, they might upgrade to another property. And I find most of the time, when folks have a second child, or number one gets to be a certain age, they go to the suburbs. It is usually for more space. I think it is easier to have kids in the suburbs, and also for the school systems. But funny enough, after people have their children, and they are finished with all of that. . . . They want to come back. And most of the time, they are not quite ready to give up the house in the suburbs. So they buy something small in town [Boston].

Such migratory patterns for wealthy suburbanites serve as a running joke among real estate agents who work the luxury market in Boston. Leslie ended his explanation of these migratory patterns by confiding: "In fact, we always kind of joke. We hope the Boston school system does not get fixed completely, because then there goes our . . . We are going to lose our flow of business."

This process relates to larger patterns of white flight—reflected in Boston's major population decrease—that occurred in Boston during the latter half of the twentieth century. Many who left Boston for the suburbs in search of a better school district for their children did so during a time of educational and social upheaval in the city—and those who made these decisions later did so because of this very reputation. During the era of school desegregation, busing, and education budget cuts, many middle-class families left Boston in search of affluent and white school districts in the suburbs. As a result, in the 1990s, 90 percent of the Boston school system was made up of minority students and Boston's total population dipped to 575,000.[5] Scholars of education have written extensively about this process. White middle-class and upper-middle-class families, like the people I talked with, have used their mobility to choose high-quality schools for their children for decades, reproducing social inequality and the unequal distribution of resources between the suburbs and the city.[6]

Job opportunities also explain why the people I interviewed continued to live in other places, despite identifying deeply with Rangeley and
Boston. Jack and Nancy grew up in Rangeley, but Jack "couldn't leave fast
enough." To him, the "best view of Rangeley was in the rearview mirror."
His father owned a local business that he wanted Jack to inherit, but Jack
said to himself, "I ain't going to do this. . . . There's nothing here [for me]."
Nancy agreed. She left for college in Massachusetts where she majored in
health care administration. After graduating she came back home for a
period of time but realized that "there are no administration jobs here. . . .
That's when I realized I couldn't come home. There's no jobs." Because of
this, she decided to live permanently in Massachusetts where her pay was
considerably more than what anyone in Rangeley could imagine making. It
was there she raised her young children and started her career.

Even though Boston was rife with job prospects, many still left to pursue
other opportunities elsewhere. Mark had gone to college in Boston and met
his wife in the city. They loved city life, but when Mark was offered a job
opportunity in Michigan, he could not pass it up. He and his wife ended up
purchasing a six-thousand-square-foot home on the outskirts of a major metropolitan area where he raised his three daughters, all of whom attended an
elite college preparatory school located nearby. Bruce was a CEO of a small
construction company in Texas. While he had never lived in Boston, he and
Joyce viewed themselves as urban people. But their rapidly growing suburban
Texas community remained attractive to them because, he argued, it was a
"business-friendly environment." The reason for this was simple: taxes. For
the people I met who split their time between Texas and Boston the choice of
permanent home, legally speaking, was quite clear. Texas does not withhold
personal income tax, and Massachusetts income taxes are comparatively high.[7]

To be sure, the people I talked with *liked* their hometowns. Although the
communities where they lived were not sources of place-identity fulfillment,
they remained vital places of opportunity and privilege. Their hometowns
offered a quality of life they valued, access to a range of institutions, social
ties and networks, amenities, and opportunity. Many saw the suburbs as
good places to live. But forgoing place-identity fulfillment was a locational
choice made at earlier points in their lives to gain and maintain access to
select institutional and lifestyle resources they valued, not typically found in
urban and rural destinations. The suburbs may not have been urban or rural
enough. Yet these places—by design—contained access to some of the best
educational systems and opportunities in the country. While it is not the
place they would have rather been, it is the place they felt they *needed* to be.

Securing the Suburbs through Limited Liability

Access to resources kept the people I met in their hometowns, even when they would rather have been somewhere else. Although they might not have found a sense of place identity in their hometowns, I learned that they still maintained limited liability to these communities, in which they selectively supported the very resources that kept them there.

Morris Janowitz coined the term *community of limited liability* to explain how urban denizens divide associations throughout an entire city in response to a broader debate about the state of contemporary community life in America. At the time, scholars debated whether increased size, density, and heterogeneity, which were characteristic of modern industrial cities, would segment people from primary social ties or foster urban villages and subcultures.[8] Embedded in this debate, however, is a basic assumption that community is bound to a locality—that people live, work, and socialize within a singular ecological unit, like a neighborhood or town. Janowitz and others questioned whether such immediate proximity is a necessary condition for community.[9] In contemporary metropolitan areas, residents are not exclusively tied to the small array of resources proximate to their place of residence. They can choose from a wide array of resources made available to them in the larger municipality, thus making their liability to the smaller ecological community area more limited, and more self-consciously chosen. However, community identities and boundaries can endure without densely knit, neighborhood-bounded, inward-focused residents. Janowitz argued that institutional actors, such as the community press, can operate as "an instrument of cohesion" for communities regardless of individual-level commitment by local residents to the smaller neighborhood area.[10]

The people I talked with were not geographically bound to just one metropolitan area; they had limited liability to multiple communities across the country.[11] They carefully divided an array of community attachments across their first and second homes—social ties, institutional and commercial engagement, and place identity. Their selective institutional engagements reified their hometowns as resource rich, as they used their social, political, and economic capital to support the institutions that cohere community resources and character; they helped maintain the identity and boundaries of the suburbs as privileged places.

Among the second homeowners I met in Boston, many supported the institutions in the suburbs they had eluded in the city through philanthropic and civic participation. Stan had owned his second home in Boston since the 1980s, which was originally his primary residence. Work had taken him away to the Midwest where he had lived permanently ever since. In his hometown, Stan was president of the school board and part of a local educational advocacy organization, spearheading an effort to provide financial opportunities to children in school through a nonprofit foundation. Maggie was heavily involved in an environmental and economic development program aimed at reviving the local downtown economy and conserving the environment. Her most recent involvements included championing an effort to move the town's snow-dumping station to another part of town to restore parkland and provide public access to the river that winds through the community. During our conversation, she was intrigued by the comparative project in Rangeley and wanted to know more about the efforts of the Rangeley Lakes Heritage Trust (RLHT); she said they mirrored her own. And Karl, who consciously opted out of participating in neighborhood life and vowed to let the people who live in Boston make decisions about their own community, was a community leader in his hometown. He had served on the zoning board of appeals, influencing land-use policies and practices in the suburbs north of the city, known for systematically limiting density and height restrictions that might have made the town more affordable and accessible to others.

The second homeowners in Rangeley I interviewed similarly uplifted the very institutions in their hometowns that they bypassed in Rangeley. Holly refused to apply to a school opening in Rangeley because the school system was not up to her standards. Yet in her hometown, she was heavily involved in innovating the school system, leading an advocacy group for children in early education. She had been honored as an educational leader in the school system she worked for, which was ranked among the top ten best schools in the state.[12] Peter was a doctor from an exurban town in Maine who viewed his involvement in Rangeley very narrowly, only recently working to oppose a cement plant that might abut his property. In his hometown, however, he has worked tirelessly to secure grants from the federal government to expand the health-care infrastructure for his region, bringing access to medical care to many rural residents who needed it most. Tony and Michelle, who preferred to keep to themselves in the privacy of their second home, were small business owners in their hometown, where they were civic leaders as part of a vast downtown revitalization effort that transformed once-vacant property into mixed-use developments meant to revive the economy and attract middle-class people. Others were active in ways that aligned with other accounts of upper-middle-class people who aimed to control land use in their communities. James, for instance, spent time fighting against a zoning change that would have allowed a gravel pit to be constructed in his neighborhoods.

This is to say nothing about their vast philanthropic efforts aimed at virtually every dimension of the communities where they permanently resided. Collectively, they supported food banks, community land trusts, affordable-housing infrastructure, economic development projects, councils on aging, religious institutions, educational foundations, health centers, the United Way—the list goes on. These specific community engagements ensured that the suburbs remained a repository of institutional privileges from which they continued to benefit, in effect limiting these opportunities for urban and rural places. The people I interviewed were effective local citizens who gave time, money, and energy to improve their communities' local educational system, health care, nonprofit sector, and economy.

These municipalities furthermore benefited from this division of communal associations, reaping the rewards of the continued institutional and civic engagement of people who may have otherwise moved to places that better aligned with their felt place identities. This is a pattern happening with many middle- and upper-class people today who have moved to urban or rural areas as gentrifiers or amenity migrants to find a sense of place belonging and, in doing so, take their social, political, and economic capital with them to their new destinations.[13] But for the people I met, the second home keeps them in this privileged place. This strategic division of community associations allows them to have a sense of place belonging *and* maintain the majority of their resources in their hometown.

Opportunity Hoarding

The people I talked with had a unique relationship to place. They were mostly upper-middle-class. Upper-middle-class people tend to secure their socioeconomic position through modest wealth, high-earning professions, and access to resources they have by virtue of where they live.[14] Although their hometowns did not serve as a source of place identity, proximity to affluent communities provided the institutional resources and opportunities necessary for the reproduction of their social-class position. It was a place-based resource.

Many scholars have written about this process as *opportunity hoarding*. Charles Tilly defined opportunity hoarding as a method of social closure, or ways of drawing boundaries to secure resources.[15] It is a causal mechanism for inequality in which people secure valuable and renewable resources for themselves and those within their own social networks at the direct expense of others. They are not engaging in overt or explicit forms of exploitation: they often do not set wages for employees, they do not own multinational corporations, they are not elite politicians, nor are they wealthy enough to fund and operate interest groups. They are not extracting anything. They are hoarding opportunity.

Yet opportunity hoarding is not simply a method to secure individual- or group-level advantages. It is intimately tied to place-based inequality, wherein some places are more resource rich than others. The resources made available to us by virtue of where we live are powerful variables in patterning the trajectories of our lives. They govern the food we have access to, the schools we go to, the medical care we receive, the job opportunities we have, the quality of air we breathe, and even how long we can expect to live.

Education provides a compelling and relevant example. Because of the design of the U.S. educational system, the quality of schools is based on the quantity of the local property tax base, making each individual municipality distinct in terms of available capital. Public schools in urban and rural areas have been historically deprived of resources based on this formula. White flight from cities during the era of school desegregation wholly ensured the flight of resources from the city to the suburbs. Rural schools have witnessed a similar resource strain against the backdrop of increased rural poverty and "brain drain."[16] When people move to the suburbs for access to quality schools, they are not just securing these resources for themselves; they are systematically denying these resources to other places.

When opportunity hoarding as a concept is applied to white upper-middle-class people it often refers to the process in which this group, wittingly or unwittingly, disadvantages other people by securing valuable resources for themselves. Richard Reeves has popularized this application in his book *Dream Hoarders*.[17] He suggests that upper-middle-class families help secure advantages for their children through mechanisms such as legacy admissions at universities that give their children a leg up and through resistance to inclusive zoning practices that would allow other people to live in resource-rich places as they do. Others have applied this concept specifically to people who live in the suburbs, who have historically and contemporarily used their mobility to hold a monopoly over educational advantages.[18] The maintenance of value-generating resources is inextricably tied to place.[19]

The people I met and talked with neatly map onto these applications, supporting opportunity hoarding between the city and the country and the suburbs—a key feature of their broader place-identity projects. They remained permanently in places for the resources made available to them in these locations and uplifted the institutions they valued, in effect ensuring that suburban locations continued to be resource rich as they strategically denied other places their social, economic, and political capital. Unlike the upper class whose wealth can be geographically unbound, the type of people I talked to for this book *relied on* opportunity hoarding in places like affluent suburbs to reproduce their social position, even if these places did not provide them with a sense of place identity.[20] These places are essential resources for upper-middle-class social reproduction.[21] However, unlike the middle class, those in the upper middle class have *just enough* time and money to buy second homes in places that satisfy these identity wants without making explicit locational sacrifices.

But the people I met and talked with were also distinct from every other suburban resident who uses geography to secure value-generating resources.[22] The people I met, who had modest levels of wealth and time, did not settle for identity discontinuity. They did not make the choice between access to resources and a quality of life they valued and identity fulfillment. They had both.[23] Buying a second home reconciled this place-identity incongruity while allowing them to still benefit from the resources they had access to in their permanent residences. Most people without time and resources only have the option to use nostalgia to repair such discontinuity.[24] But the people I met were the benefactors of decades of institutional housing policies and practices that have enabled predominantly white middle- and upper-middle-class families to build intergenerational wealth. They had enough time and money to buy a second home, finding their sense of place in the city and the country.[25]

PART II

The Country

It was a weekday evening at the end of May just after Memorial Day, the unofficial start to the summer season. Although the blackflies were swarming, it was nice to walk along Main Street and see the town lively again. Rangeley had just opened up after "mud season," a period when the snow melts and every inch of the town is covered in literal mud. Many people who live on dirt roads cannot access them. Hardly anyone visits. Local families who can afford to do so take their children somewhere warm for April school vacation. And many stores on Main Street hang a sign on the front door, "Closed in April," leaving much of the town temporarily underemployed.[1]

I was walking from my apartment at the far end of Main Street to an event taking place in the center of downtown. Rangeley's Main Street sits between two bodies of water. Behind the businesses on one side is Haley Pond, the smaller of the two, used as an ice-skating rink during the winter and a place to rent kayaks during the summer. On the other side is Rangeley Lake, a larger body of water where people fish and boat and swim and kayak from the landing and park. At the time I lived there, Main Street had a little bit of everything: there were a couple of restaurants with extensive wine and cocktail lists and family-friendly places like the Red Onion, known for its pizza. Sarge's was the local dive bar, open most of the year and a staple for anyone who wanted a beer after 8 p.m. or some place to watch a basketball game. There was a small bookstore, cleverly named Books, Lines, & Thinkers. And there was even a coffee shop, the Inner Eye, in what used to be the town's pharmacy.

My destination was the Rangeley Lakeside Theater, a combination performance art center and cinema, operated by Rangeley Friends of the

Arts, a nonprofit group that provides the community with live theater performances, viewings of independent and big studio films, and a variety of reduced-cost youth programming. They also rent the theater to the town for special events. That evening I was there to attend a meet the candidates event, as four different Rangeley residents ran for the next vacant seat on the select board. There were about forty other people in attendance, most of whom were over the age of fifty. All were white and many were seated in pairs. I sat in the back corner by myself until a familiar face approached and asked to sit next to me. It was Craig, a fifty-something man, wearing khakis and a flyfishing shirt under a Patagonia vest, whom I knew from my time working at the ski resort mountain. A high-ranking member of the Rangeley Lakes Heritage Trust, Craig was attending that evening to represent the interests of the land conservation organization.

The event began and the moderator asked the candidates a series of questions, mostly centering on their economic plans for the town. Their answers were relatively similar, focusing on ways to boost the town's business-friendly environment. Cathy, a forty-something woman who had lived in Rangeley for twenty years, responded that good cell phone service and internet access would be her main priority. Greg, an older retiree, campaigned on the platform that the town needed to welcome businesses and support the 'entrepreneurial spirit.' And three out of the four candidates agreed that some of the nearly $2.5 million of town reserve funds needed to be given back to local taxpayers who, they felt, deserved their fair share. In the middle of these answers, Craig leaned over and whispered to me, 'Did you see that article online about the top-paying jobs in Maine?' I said that I hadn't. 'Logging is the very last,' he continued, 'the very last.'[2] He shook his head, as if to emphasize the gravity of Rangeley's declining productive economy.

Next, it was time for the audience to pose questions, which were all variations on a theme: What would the candidates do about the lack of internet and quality access in town? How could the town expect economic growth without internet? How would the town better take care of the aging sixty-plus population? How would the town address water quality and excess runoff issues? How would the town create strategies to help new businesses grow? There was a lot of urgency in these questions, an undercurrent of worry that not enough was being done to promote the economy and protect the people who lived there.

After the event, we all exited the auditorium and made our way onto the sidewalk. As everyone else got in their cars to leave, Craig hung around for a bit to debrief with me. 'I couldn't believe they were saying they had too much money and needed to give it back to taxpayers,' he said in disbelief. I tilted my head in question, allowing him to continue. 'Seventy percent of that tax revenue comes from people who don't vote in town, from the seasonal residents. They have nothing to complain about . . . the most intense tax hikes are places on the water where locals don't live.'

On my walk home, I contemplated the many tensions I noticed in that hour and a half at the Rangeley Lakeside Theater. Candidates were threading the needle between discussing strategies to attract tourists and seasonal visitors to Rangeley to promote the economy, while ensuring they also appealed to voting residents who begged for more public goods and services. Craig lamented the decline of Rangeley's productive economy. Yet he also defended second homeowners who made up over 80 percent of volunteers and donors for the RLHT, an organization that had, arguably, played a role in limiting Rangeley's economic diversification through its conservation efforts, which had at times prevented potential housing and commercial development across the region.

Rangeley is made up of many different elements. It is a place of economic production, where people work at restaurants and hotels, fix roads, and build homes and offices. It is a place to enjoy outdoor activities, where people go snowmobiling, skiing, hiking, biking, boating, four-wheeling, hunting, and fishing. It is a place for arts and culture, where people attend gallery exhibits, buy tickets for theater performances, and watch independent films. It is a place to go to school, where two hundred schoolchildren grow as learners. It is a place to socialize, where people meet at Sarge's, on the mountain, in homes and businesses, or at the IGA grocery store. It is also a place to age, where many people decide to stay into their retirement years. But to many of the second homeowners I met, Rangeley was not this complex.

———

Every Friday when the bell rings, Holly's bags are already packed. Her husband will pick her up at the school where she works and they drive their dark green Audi, with a "ME: RANGELEY" bumper sticker, two hours north to Rangeley from their suburban hometown outside of Portland. Their Rangeley home is fully stocked with nearly everything they need: Holly's "Rangeley clothes," kitchenware, and other household essentials. They just need to stop to pick up food they will need for the weekend.

If Holly and her husband take Route 17, the long way, they can stop at the RLHT's Height of Land, a protected scenic overlook that makes the pages of travel magazines and Facebook posts to showcase Rangeley's allure, before they settle in for the weekend. The Height of Land is where locals and visitors alike can marvel at Mooselookmeguntic Lake, a large body of water tucked below the vastness of the northern woods.

By taking Route 17, they can also avoid most of Rangeley's Main Street. They won't drive past Parkside and Main, a family-friendly eatery, or Sarge's, the local dive bar. They won't see children playing on the grass and beach at Rangeley's Town Park or lined up at Pine Tree Frosty. And they won't have to stop at the local IGA grocery store to procure the weekend's essentials. They can bypass Rangeley's town center altogether and drive straight to the sleepy neighboring Oquossoc Village to pick up everything they need for their trip. In fact, Holly tries to avoid the "hubbub" of Rangeley whenever she can:

> The reason people come here is to be alone. To be isolated and to not . . . maybe some people. But everyone we know is not really social. The reason we chose here [the lake farther outside of the center of town] is because it's quiet. If I have a choice to go to Oquossoc or Rangeley, I always go to Oquossoc. My post office is in Oquossoc. When the church is open, I prefer that one. I prefer the Farmer's Daughter, I prefer Scottie's. It's just . . . quiet.

Holly had found Rangeley's school system subpar and decided she could never have lived and worked in Rangeley full-time because of it. That was the end of her calculus, and she continued her career in southern Maine. She did not go to Rangeley to work or to socialize or to even *be* in Rangeley. She went there for her quiet reprieve on the lake.

Holly was similar to most other second homeowners I met in Rangeley, who maintained a bounded and narrow orientation to the town. Rangeley was not the quaint local library or new coffee shop that served bubble tea. It was not the service workers who provided them with coffee and freshly made blueberry muffins on the one day a week when they went into town. Nor was Rangeley the loggers whose businesses had been in decline, or the nearly two hundred schoolchildren who populated the town. For the second homeowners I met who could buy remote property on the most valuable real estate and who did not have to rely on Rangeley for work, Rangeley was the quiet, non-productive landscape surrounding their second home. Rangeley allowed them to be their *country selves*, their particular localized place-identity project that employed attributes, meanings, and practices related to rurality to construct their place identity.[3] It was how they found a sense of place that they did not find in their hometowns.

Rural is a material place, often defined by its low population density relative to high-density urbanized areas. It is a spatial arrangement that is a product of the changing means of production in a capitalist society.[4] *Rural* is also a symbolic place, made up of an array of meanings that people have given to aspects of rural life throughout history. It is made up of distinct foods and community and ways of life and types of nature.[5] At times throughout history, rural has been conceptualized as free from capitalist interests, removed from all human intervention.[6] It has been framed in books, movies, and even landscape portraiture as untouched by the contemporary ills of modern urban life. The second homeowners I met, like Holly, untethered themselves from the materiality of ruralness, from Rangeley as being a site of productive labor, where people work and pay rent and mortgages, or reproductive labor, where people raise children and age in place. Rangeley was primarily their isolated refuge set in nature, free from human intervention.

———

The notion of the country as a site of retreat for affluent second homeowners, like Holly, began in earnest in the United States at the turn of the twentieth century. Rural areas across the country lost a large portion of their productive labor force as people migrated to the city for work in factories. The effects of urbanization were significant for the country. As Kevin Loughran argues, during this period and beyond nature in the countryside was racialized as *white*, a symbolic foil against the racialized "ills" of modernity in cities: overcrowded tenement buildings home to working-class Black and immigrant families, the specter of capitalism that transformed once communal social relationships into market transactions, and perceived social disorder emergent from these combined conditions.[7]

To "escape" these conditions, many wealthy white urban families built homes near the suburbs in addition to their urban residences.[8] Such families also extended the reach of their real estate acquisitions to coastal communities far outside metropolitan regions.[9] Weekend and summer estates were commonplace for families who amassed excess wealth on the backs of laborers in industrializing America, normalizing the second home as a central feature of high society for the urban elite.[10]

The second home became not just a functional retreat away from the heat, density, and pollution of industrialized city life but a status symbol, a new way of life, for these newly moneyed families. Proximity to nature, and appreciation for the activities found there like fishing, hiking, and swimming, emerged as a source of cultural capital, a non-economic resource transferable in social relations, conferring social status and distinction. To protect this newfound resource and vision of rurality, wealthy urbanites invested in conservation.[11] Renowned philanthropist and capitalist John Rockefeller provides the most paradigmatic example. He purchased a second home near Bar Harbor, Maine, and spent money and a great deal of effort conserving what is today known as Acadia National Park. This transformed this once-Wabanaki land from a fishing, lumbering, and shipbuilding port into a national tourist and resort destination.

After World War II, many of these established spatial arrangements changed, and second homeownership democratized beyond the urban elite. The advent of federally backed home mortgages and highway construction reconfigured the location of affluent white families as America suburbanized. It was during this period that the average middle-class family simultaneously moved to the suburbs as part of the American dream and began to amass generational wealth through homeownership. The postwar period, then, not only transformed *where* many affluent families lived but altered *who* was able to generate wealth, enabling an entire new cohort of middle-class people to realize a new American dream: the second home.

The rise of dual-income earners, liberal lending policies, low interest rates, new tax incentives, and emergent generational wealth also provided the necessary financial foundations for middle-class families to afford not just one home but two.[12] Throughout the middle part of the twentieth century, the development of highway systems, proliferation of automobiles, and rise of modern technologies also made it possible for families to venture into more affordable locations far outside of typical second-home destinations. Such natural-amenity-rich areas also witnessed a further decline in their productive economies, such as logging and farming, during sweeping deindustrialization across the country. In its wake, many of these communities turned to tourism as a primary economic strategy, marketing and selling rural places as *destinations* for people who were primed to consume rural lifestyles, cultures, and amenities to search for the "good life."[13] As a result, in the latter half of the twentieth century, deep into the Northeast forest and upper Midwest lakes, new pockets of second homeownership emerged as middle-class and upper-middle-class people sought out a range of natural amenities and lifestyles found across rural landscapes.[14]

As extractive industries continued to decline and tourism rose as a primary economic strategy, many small rural towns' longtime local populations at once welcomed and admonished second homeowners' in-migration.[15]

This complicated relationship has endured in both academic and popular discourse today, where questions abound as to whether the advent of second homes serves as a curse or a blessing for the tourism-reliant rural communities that host them. On the one hand, some research has found that second homeowners fill the economic void left by the flight of extractive industries by providing the necessary tax base and consumption practices to keep local services and commercial institutions afloat.[16] On the other hand, other research has found that second homeowners' in-migration contributes to rising property values, environmental degradation, and community and culture clash.[17] Second homeowners' presence has a long, complicated history in these small rural communities, and their influence does not show any signs of abating.

In the chapters that follow, I explore these tensions. In chapter 3, I begin by asking how the second homeowners I met conceived of Rangeley and what it meant for them to have a place identity tied to this small rural community. I next ask how place identity tied to Rangeley provided them with a sense of deservingness and legitimated their social privileges. I end with exploring how their place identity was dependent on limiting resources in Rangeley. In chapter 4, I link the everyday practices of the second homeowners I met to Rangeley's broader place-making project, which increases the town's dependence on tourism. I end by showing how this dependence can come at a cost for rural people and places. In chapter 5, I explore why there is some local acceptance of second homeowners in Rangeley but how this acceptance is mediated by several local conditions. Altogether, these chapters detail how privilege is at the heart of the relationship between rurality, place, and identity.

3

The Way Life Should Be

An Isolated Refuge

The second homeowners I met in Rangeley did not work there. They did not send their children to school there. Many did not even have friends there. This orientation to the community enabled them to view Rangeley only narrowly: as their quiet retreat set in nature.

I learned a lot about this limited understanding of Rangeley during the process of setting up interviews. I always asked if they had a preferred place in town where they would like to meet. I typically offered some of my old haunts: the library, the coffee shop, or a quiet corner at the mountain pub. Almost uniformly, however, they invited me over to their second homes, as did Henry, a wealthy business consultant in his mid-fifties from coastal Florida. Henry's home sat upon a lake known for its spectacular views of the mountains. He insisted I meet him at his place so I could see what the fuss was about.

When I arrived on that warm Saturday in July, he met me at the door in shorts and a T-shirt while still on a conference call with a Bluetooth headset in his ear. He seemed agitated at whoever was on the other end and gestured for me to take a seat in his front room, where I sheepishly waited for him to finish his conversation. After fifteen minutes or so, he put down his headset and asked me if I wanted a drink. I politely declined while he grabbed a Corona out of the refrigerator. Without saying much, he ushered me past his living room, opened the sliding glass door to the back deck, and offered me a seat on an Adirondack chair that faced the lake and mountains.

I watched as he took his first sip of beer and quietly melted into the chair, at once transformed by the breeze coming off from the lake and the scent from the pine trees above. I asked him why he had been drawn to Rangeley. He turned his head toward the view, slowly inhaling the fresh air. "I like what the good Lord did," he reflected. "I like the beautiful surroundings. It's impossible not to notice as you sit and look at the mountains and the lake and the sky." He continued, "I love how quiet it is up here. Not in terms of social life, I mean quiet in terms of decibel levels. I love the fact that I can walk out onto my property and essentially not hear anything." This back porch was his oasis, Henry's favorite spot in town. It was where he puts down his headset and shuts away the noise from the outside world. This experience with Henry was not unique. I interviewed second homeowners on back decks sitting deep in the woods, docks floating on the lake, ski lifts zipping up the mountain, and in living rooms overlooking water or mountain views. To them, this was Rangeley. It was a quiet refuge set in nature, free from the static of everyday life.

This version of Rangeley was rooted in the isolation of their second homes, a bounded understanding of what Rangeley was and should be. Jeff was a gruff retiree who enjoyed a lively social scene at his home, which, like Henry's, was also in Florida. But in Rangeley, he did not know—nor did he want—such a life. He loved that the road where their second home was located was isolated and made of dirt. "We're glad this is a dirt road. If they pave this," he grumbled, "I'll sell the place and go someplace else, it wouldn't be the same. I walk that road almost every day with the dog. I went down to the [end of the dirt road] and back [and] saw three trucks and a car . . . just the way we like it." At the end of my afternoon with Jeff, he poured himself a glass of whiskey and had me follow him through a winding path of tall pine trees to his lakeside dock. We sat there in silence for a moment while Jeff sipped his drink and consumed the view. We couldn't hear cars driving on the road or boats speeding past. All we heard were the waves from the lake splashing into the rocks on the shore. I couldn't help but notice how drastically this life differed from the Rangeley I experienced every day.

I lived on Main Street, mostly among locals and seasonally employed workers. During the day, I heard neither birds nor waves, only a constant buzz of cars, logging trucks, and four-wheelers, depending on the season. At night, I did not hear the loons. I heard boisterous locals as they stepped out for a cigarette at the bar across the street or the clamor of my downstairs neighbors getting home from a night shift. Throughout the course of my year living in Rangeley, I saw many different versions of the town from the window of my second-floor apartment. During the winter, I observed a parade of snowmobilers at the annual Snodeo festival, a fundraising event hosted by the Rangeley Lakes Snowmobile club. During the summer, I watched families walk to eat pizza for dinner at the Red Onion and stroll to get ice cream for dessert at Pine Tree Frosty. And every morning before the sun came up, I would watch the procession of cars drive to work to turn on the town. Yet these versions of the town were nowhere to be found in my interviewees' descriptions of Rangeley. It was primarily their private oasis away from the static of everyday life.

I learned the extent to which this understanding of Rangeley is bound to *particular* notions of nature during my conversation with retirees Ellen and Albert Johnson and their neighbor, Ray. I serendipitously met Ellen at the local IGA grocery store when she struck up a conversation with me while we were both waiting in line to check out. She learned of my project and insisted I come talk with her and her husband, as she scrambled to give me directions to her place. Later that afternoon, after what felt like miles of off-roading deep into the woods and my first moose sighting of the year, I arrived at the Johnsons' quiet retreat on the shores of a small body of water that prohibits motorized boats.

Ellen invited me into her living room where I met her husband, Albert, and neighbor Ray, whom she excitedly invited over as another witness to Rangeley's allure. As we drank coffee and shared blueberry muffins, I became particularly curious about why either the Johnsons or Ray came to a place like Rangeley. Both lived in communities in Massachusetts and New Jersey, respectively, where they lived close to the water in proximity to many of the same amenities found in their second homes. Considering this, I asked what they got from Rangeley that they could not get from their permanent homes. "Total peace," Ray insisted. "Oh, it's heaven up here. It's total peace," he emphasized. Ellen jumped in to add, "Oh totally. You can just go in a kayak, and you know, just put your hands in the water. It's like you know, this is therapy. I'm in therapy." Their hometowns were densely populated, popular tourist destinations attracting hordes of visitors to the beaches and Main Streets annually. For the Johnsons and Ray, these places were hardly experienced as quiet retreats set in nature even though they contained an abundance of natural amenities. Michael Bell refers to this as *pastoralism*, in which people associate nature with a particular type of place. Those in rural areas see themselves as closest to nature, while those in urban areas are the farthest from it, even if these places contain objectively "natural" amenities. Nature is an idea as much as it is a material condition.[1]

In this quiet refuge, the second homeowners I met identified deeply with the non-productive aspects of nature, to the ebbs and flows of the land, animals, and water. So many of my interviews devolved into long, winding, tangential, but incredibly vivid stories about loons, waterfowl, moose, and fox. I met Elsie at her mountainside condo on a Sunday afternoon in July. We sat in her dining room, overlooking Saddleback Lake that sits at the bottom of the mountain. Elsie was a retiree from a golf community in Florida who had begun to develop knee problems. As a result, she thought her time in Rangeley was soon ending. While admitting they had talked recently about selling their second home, she conceded, "How could I ever leave this place?" She sat back, reflecting on why it would be hard to give up her daily life at the mountain:

> First we go kayaking or canoeing. Howard said, "Let's go sit in the canoe, the kayaks have backs." So, we go down and we just passed the island, which you can see from here, and a bald eagle flies right up! We must've startled him. He was on a tree. He didn't have a nest in that tree, but he must have been maybe eating a fish or something. I can't believe it! Our first journey down there and a bald eagle flies up. And even when we went out with our daughter on Sunday it was so rough and there were whitecaps. I thought, "Where do the loons go on a day like today?" All of a sudden, we were passing along the coast. And all of a sudden, she said, "Are those two buoys?" She goes, "Mom, it's two big loons." They were so big they were actually bouncing at the top of the waves. And there's the loons there. That's another thing we do. Wildlife watching. My husband gets up really early and tends to say: "C'mon Elsie. It's five o'clock. Want to go moose hunting?" And he sees some moose and deer and fox and porcupine. And a bald eagle and a loon. So that's the other joy of managing our time.

At first, I felt like these types of highly detailed stories about eagles, fish, loons, moose, deer, fox, and porcupines were off topic to my questions at hand: how they were involved in Rangeley and why. However, I soon learned that this deep connection to the outdoors told a story about who they were and how they understood what nature is. These elaborate narratives served to locate the people I met close to nature that is left untouched by human intervention.

Implicit in such narratives was a definition of what nature is and should be and where it was to be found—in Rangeley. These narratives were imbued with particular cultural meanings of rurality. Rural places are isolated. Rural places are plentiful with nature. Nature is the birds, animals, land, and water. And this is only found in Rangeley. It was their therapy, their inspiration, their heaven. This was what gave them the sense of place they longed for.

The Natural Conscience

Affiliation with Rangeley was more than a series of abstractions. Being in Rangeley defined the contours of their social-class position, giving clarity to who they were as upper-middle-class people. It helped them distinguish themselves from other people they knew from their same social position who engaged in what they perceived to be more garish or conspicuous displays of wealth. It provided them with a sense of deservingness, and it legitimated their privileges.

Proximity to nature in Rangeley was a *moral* position for the people I met, who expressed a misalignment between their hometowns that felt too city-like and their cultural tastes and values.[2] Michael Bell wrote extensively about this process in his analysis of a country village in exurban England, where people make distinctions between themselves as "country people," who are a "highly valued social group," and others on the outside of this boundary who are "city people." Being a country person is an "identity [regarded] as morally good" because of its proximity to nature and notions of community, which enables upper-middle-class people to distance themselves from morally questionable social-class identities.[3] He finds that Childerleyans "use this sense of their difference as a source of identity, motivation, and social power—a source they find secure and legitimate."[4]

As Michael Bell found with Childerleyans, I found that the *country self* in Rangeley provided the people I met with a legitimate way to express their social class and corresponding practices. Bob and Jane Stevenson distinguished themselves from family members who owned a second home in a vacation community in upstate New York. Jane's grandparents originally purchased the summer home that has been passed down through the generations. Jane marveled at its grandiosity. At the time her grandparents bought it, it was among the largest houses in the bay of the lake because it was the only one to have a third floor: a private room and bathroom, her grandmother's "maid's quarters." Jane highlighted the differences between her daily life and the daily life her grandparents fashioned there. "Basically," she explained, "people in the bay partied. There were tennis courts, there was a golf course and that's who you socialized with. . . . Most of the homes had maids, and most of the maids were the help, were Black people."

In Rangeley, Bob and Jane did not spend their days partying or segregating themselves in exclusive social spheres, nor did they hire in-home seasonal "help," which for them epitomized the extreme vulgarity that throws in stark relief racial and class inequality that emerges from second homeownership. Instead, they spent their days hiking mountains, weeding a newly planted garden, and canoeing in the lake. Michael Bell articulates the power of affiliating one's self with nature. Nature, he writes, is perceived to be "free from social interests—something that stands apart from the selfishness, greed, power, and domination [seen] in social life." Nature is used as a "moral preserve in the landscape of materialist desires, an alternative region of moral thinking . . . the *natural conscience.*"[5] The country self positioned the people I met closer to the natural conscience, foiled against conspicuous consumption and social-class interest, what they saw as more morally dubious projects. It provided them with an expression of their social-class location they found legitimate and deserving.[6]

This affiliation served as a source of deservingness to justify their immigration in Rangeley. Ray was a white man in his early sixties with a thick New Jersey accent, who could often be found wearing khaki cargo shorts and an old, hooded sweatshirt. He spent his days puttering around his lakeside cottage, occasionally canoeing in the lake with his dog by his side. I never would have met Ray if not for his neighbor who introduced us. He did not like to go into town, he did not attend many cultural or sporting events, and he did not do much socializing. He mostly kept to himself in the privacy of his beautiful four-season second home set deep in the woods on the shores of one of Rangeley's many lakes that was valued in 2021 at around half a million dollars. Ray lived permanently in a small suburban town on the Jersey Shore, a highly populated second-home destination in the mid-Atlantic region, in a home worth nearly $700,000. Ray spent a good part of our interview grumbling about what his hometown had become in his time living there: too dense, too loud, and too full of New Yorkers. These New Yorkers, who were second homeowners much like himself, "take over the Jersey Shore." They build large, beautiful oceanside houses, fill the restaurants, and flood the streets and beaches. Feeling the palpable irony after making this claim, he shifted in his seat and hedged, "But the difference [here] is that the people that come here, they want to blend in, not take over."

I heard this narrative over and over again in my interviews with second homeowners in Rangeley. Nearly all of them made attempts to distance themselves from the more conspicuous social-class practices of other similarly classed people they knew. They saw themselves as significantly more ordinary, even classless. Jeff, who lived across the Rangeley region from Ray, venerated the types of second homeowners found in Rangeley, including himself. During his search for a second home, he toured various lake communities across Maine. Rangeley stood out to him because it was the only place where, to him, second homeowners appeared to be more inconspicuous despite their local density. "Everybody up here isn't really a vacationer," Jeff explained. "Everyone up here is a second homeowner. It was a good mix, a good relationship. The townies weren't hostile toward us, and we weren't superior to them and so there was none of that. You walk down the road, and you can't tell who's who. And so, it's sort of an egalitarian kind of thing." As proof, he got up and grabbed a few pictures of the previous year's lake association summer gathering, pointing to the doctors and professors, who looked as if they had just stepped out of an L.L. Bean catalogue—to him, classless. The narrative Jeff told me aligns with what Jennifer Sherman refers to as "class blindness." This is the "tendency for those with privilege to be blind both to their own advantages and to their impacts on less-advantaged populations around them."[7] Sherman found that newcomers in an amenity-rich destination often emphasized their positive impact on communities, ignoring the ways in which their presence altered community life for those around them. Such narratives that focused on their classlessness and neutral impact on the community allowed the people I met to similarly ignore their social location, justifying their in-migration into Rangeley.

There were interactional measures that some of the people I met took to enact this "classlessness," a particular kind of presentation of wealth in everyday life.[8] I learned about this process during my first encounter with Elsie. I met Elsie and her husband, Howard, at their two-bedroom mountainside condo, which overlooks Saddleback Lake. Elsie greeted me at the door unadorned, wearing an old sweatshirt, casual cargo shorts, and tennis shoes. Howard wore a plain, untucked T-shirt and jeans. They invited me in for lunch, and we sat down to eat sandwiches on paper plates in their dining room, which was sparsely decorated with simple family portraits hanging on the walls.

Elsie talked at length about her style of dress. When she was in her hometown in Florida, she enjoyed wearing "gold sandals" and "fancy beach dresses" but admitted that she would never dare to wear such things in Rangeley. She elaborated that "[in Florida], everyone dresses well, and I can get a pedicure and I can't get one up here! So, I kind of like that, you know I like to dress up, and I like to wear nice clothes. Up here, you know, like you look like an idiot. No one is wearing heels." Elsie described swapping her gold sandals for her tennis shoes as her "schizoid existence," a separation of her existences between these two differently classed social spheres.

Second homeowners I met in Rangeley also relied on a particular script when describing their summer or winter home. Most I met, regardless of the actual structure and quality of the home, call their second home a "camp." This is a term I am quite familiar with. Almost everyone I know from Maine who owns a second home refers to it as a "camp." Its origins come from the abundance of hunting or fishing camps germane to many lake and mountain communities across the region that emerged at the turn of the twentieth century, denoting a small, one- or two-season cabin with basic plumbing necessities and sometimes hot water.[9] It has since been co-opted to describe any such seasonal residence, but with an important implication that it is unadorned, basic, and unpretentious. However, I found that the people I talked with used this word to downplay their class status.

I noticed this tendency in particular with Ted, who owned a small manufacturing company in southern Maine and whose work often brought him to the Rangeley region. Because of his work, he was embedded in local social circles of manual labor, which heightened his visibility and class status. Ted's so-called camp was a beautiful two-story log cabin, a four-season home fully equipped with indoor plumbing, heat, and electricity. It was not, by definition, a camp, even though Ted positioned his second home close to this category that is locally framed as morally deserving. He recounted an interaction he had with someone in Rangeley that forced him to confront his everyday terminology to describe his second home:

> The first time he came here, we were outside at the little campfire going and he looked at me, and he says, "I thought you were building a camp." And I said, "We did! This is our camp." He goes, "Dude! That is a house." [Laughter] And I chuckled, like "No, it is just a camp." He goes, "No, that is a house."

Ted's insistence that his beautiful log cabin was "just a camp" was an insistence on his class position, his closer affiliation with a working-class identity. For Ted, *camp* was a more class-neutral, generic term for a house built in the woods or on the water that conjured notions of roughing it, living in the woods with only life's basic necessities. Calling his four-season home a camp instead of a vacation home, a lake house, or a cottage was an effort to downplay its luxuries and make it appear more everyday to the people around him.[10] It was a script that helped him navigate the tensions between being elite for owning a second home and wanting to blend in with working-class rurality.

I noticed this desire to downplay class status beyond just what people said to themselves, to others, and to me. Some of the second homeowners I met changed the interactional props they used while navigating daily routines in Rangeley to downplay their social-class status. Henry, a highly successful consultant and philanthropist from Florida, was the wealthiest second homeowner I met during my time in Rangeley. He owned a nearly four-thousand-square-foot, three-story, lakeside second home, valued in 2021 at over a million dollars, that was adorned with highly valuable modern art. But when I saw Henry driving around town, he drove an old, beat-up, maroon-colored Buick. He said that it was "more practical," that it was his "Rangeley car."

These everyday practices to minimize their visibility in Rangeley can be understood as strategies that justified and obscured privileges. Over the past few decades, elites have become more diverse.[11] Power and wealth are not just in the hands of the aristocratic elites. Yet with this shift in *who* elites are comes new methods of justification.[12] When scholars write about elites, they typically consider the methods they engage in to secure and possess resources by excluding others—either materially or symbolically. This can mean, for instance, people like those I interviewed who move to the suburbs and deny others access to these resources by limiting housing development. Sociologists also consider that people who are in the upper middle class engage in what Rachel Sherman refers to as "aspiring to the symbolic middle," in which they position themselves closer to a different symbolic social class group than their social one.[13] Situating one's self closer to the boundary of middle-ness both "[justifies] their possession of . . . social resources and [denies] their own advantages."

The place-identity projects of the people I met in Rangeley did more than realign their felt place identities or emplace themselves in a rural area that aligned with their feelings of who they really were. While they saw Rangeley as free from economic activity and social-class interests, affiliation with Rangeley reproduced, defined, and justified their own social-class practices. Proximity to Rangeley and nature and working-classness provided a moral grounding, a sense of deservingness, relative to other upper- or upper-middle-class people they knew whom they perceived as engaging in far more conspicuous displays of consumption. The narratives they constructed about themselves allowed them to obscure privilege.

Disconnected

I learned that the meanings the people I met gave to nature and rurality in Rangeley were not necessarily neutral. These meanings were dependent on conditions that limited resources for permanent residents. The second homeowners I met in Rangeley expressed not being able to live there full-time because it lacked the institutional resources that were abundant in their hometowns. Yet, paradoxically, their sense of place would be undermined if the very resources they found unacceptably deficient improved or if they supported these resources. If Rangeley became a hub of economic activity, if it attracted new young families to the region for its innovative school system, if it had more operable internet service from towers atop their beloved mountains, if a new local hospital attracted retirees from all over, then Rangeley would not be *un*populated. It would not be their quiet refuge set in nature. And supporting these qualities would necessarily compromise their vision of Rangeley and themselves within it.

Most people I talked to mentioned Rangeley's limited access to health care as a deterrent to living there full-time. I heard this explanation in nearly all interviews with retired second homeowners. But something deeper than that came to the fore during my conversation with Elsie. Rangeley's lack of medical care explained why she would likely have to stop coming to Rangeley in the near future. Elsie concluded:

> It's not an easy place to live. It's hard living. And I'm also older. . . . But you know, I think about that. And if you can't get out there and do all the things that are offered here . . . I don't know; if I make it to eighty-five, I think probably then I would be content to hop on a train and go to museums and plays and orchestras in New York City and maybe I could enrich myself that way.

The same was true for Paul and Carol, who were at the time quite active. Every day they did laborious chores around their house and spent their downtime paddling their canoe on the lake to check for invasive species on behalf of the RLHT or meeting up with other RLHT members to go for a hike. This was what they loved about Rangeley and their time there. They could be active, outdoorsy people. But they reported that they knew there would come a time when they could no longer do this and would have to leave. When they are no longer ambulatory—when they can no longer prune shrubs, garden, hike, or patrol the lake—they expressed they will no longer have the same connection to their second home. It will no longer provide them with a sense of place because their version of rurality is intimately tied to their everyday practices embedded in these place categories.

I also listened to many talk at length about the struggles of Rangeley's undiversified economy, a deterrent for many who might consider living there permanently. Henry agreed that "the Rangeley area is in deep, deep trouble." He had noticed that the high school seniors "that work hard and play by the rules and have the brightest futures can't possibly wait to get out of here to find an opportunity for an interesting life or a promising career somewhere else." He suggested that this was a "fairly serious indictment of the economic fabric of the town." Henry, himself, had tried to do something about Rangeley's struggling economy. While he admitted that he was "not at all involved with anything local and political, [and he can't] name one member of the board of selectmen," he wanted to do his part to try to create some economic opportunity in the region. Henry was from considerable means, and owned a great deal of art. He wanted to create an art museum on Main Street in one of the vacant buildings. He would loan his art to the museum, and he asked other wealthy second homeowners to do the same. He explained that he got two responses:

> One is, "Sure, happy to help," two is "Don't bother me." And I said: "Why not?" And they said, "Look, when we're home, you know it's about art and restaurants and culture and all of that stuff. You know, if you ask me will I lend something to the gallery up here? Probably, but honestly, just leave me alone. You know, we come up here to dip our toes in the lake and be left alone. I don't want to go to the art gallery, I don't want to talk about whether my art or your art is in the art gallery. We want to be left alone!" I thought that was a very interesting reaction.

Henry's anecdote captures several themes. Many of the second homeowners I met do not view Rangeley as a place of economic activity. They don't see Rangeley as a place of art or culture. It is their refuge set in nature. For them, it is free from economic activity and from "the grind" of daily life. They prefer to keep to themselves in the privacy of their own second homes. Henry is the only second homeowner I interviewed who discussed plans to intervene in Rangeley's economic future. Most others felt it was none of their business, or not part of why they came to Rangeley. Those are the kinds of concerns they must deal with in their hometowns. Henry concluded, "While there are obviously many people of means who come up here, many of them are invisible in the community itself. They come up here to relax or fish or be left alone."

Yet, if the amenities, institutions, and resources that second homeowners ignore or deride began to flourish, it would undermine their relationship to Rangeley altogether. When Ted and Cindy told their son that he couldn't attend Rangeley's public school for his senior year, they made a calculated decision. They felt that the school in their hometown in the suburbs of Portland left the doors open for his future job prospects. And Rangeley did not. When they first presented me with this story, the decision appeared to be exclusively about resource access and opportunities found in their hometown—resources they wanted to take advantage of and hold onto. However after I learned more about how they thought and felt about Rangeley I began to understand that there was more to the story. They did not want to live in Rangeley full-time because they felt it lacked the opportunities that their suburban hometown had in abundance. But supporting the very institutions and resources would puncture the carefully curated image they had of Rangeley and their place within it. This paradox was inherent to their place-identity projects.

Rangeley's poor internet connection highlights this contradiction. There were many mornings in Rangeley when I sat at the kitchen table in my small apartment on Main Street trying to do work. I was teaching a course at a nearby college at the time, so I often had to check and respond to emails, prepare for classes, and use Blackboard (an online course management site). On most days, however, I found this impossible to do. Despite living directly in town on Main Street, my internet connection was choppy at best. I often could not access my course materials online or respond to my students via email. Sometimes I walked to the town library or to the coffee shop in the hopes that their connections would be better. But it never was. I often sat among other frustrated patrons just trying to check email.

The slow, unreliable internet was a significant source of frustration for many business owners and permanent residents in town. Many could not rely on newer technologies to improve their services because they could not rely on working internet access. This was also a topic that came up quite often at municipal meetings I observed, with residents often begging community leaders to do something to remedy the town's poor access, and the topic was a frequent gripe on Rangeley's local community forum. However, many of the second homeowners I spoke with explained that bad internet connectivity was *precisely* Rangeley's appeal.

Although Ted cited the lack of employment opportunities as what prevented him from living in Rangeley permanently, he relished the very things that prevented businesses from flourishing, things like high-speed internet.

He explained that his children "truly get the whole concept of what Rangeley is and offers. They come up here and they can barely use their iPhones." Although Ted and Cindy could have had internet access at their camp, they would never have hooked it up. They liked that their kids could not connect to the internet and that their cell service was spotty at best. This meant more time for their family, and there was more incentive to enjoy outdoor activities. Ted even felt that it was part of the local charm. "When you come here," he explained, "you step out of that [talking about his experiences living in a fast-paced society]. As you know, a lot of these people barely have the capabilities of technology to run. . . . They still have the old slide-board, for the credit card. It's like, 'That's cool!'"

Ellen, too, admitted that "we are here for peace and quiet. . . . You love the peace and quiet but once in a while you miss the Wi-Fi." While she would have liked a reliable and fast internet connection every now and then, she confirmed that her "first choice is to see the loons." Some of her friends could access a (somewhat) working internet connection in Rangeley, but these friends were not as remote as Ellen and her husband were. Their entertainment revolved around sitting on the dock watching the lake's loon mother and chicks, not browsing Facebook or watching Netflix. Second homeowners in Rangeley placed their preferences for the quiet, unpopulated landscape above local amenities that could have increased the town's connectivity.

The second homeowners I talked to in Rangeley wished to enjoy it only in small doses because they perceived that it could not offer them everything they needed: employment, a social life, health care, and an educational system. Because of the lack of these resources, they would never have considered living in Rangeley permanently. But the amenities the people I talked with ignored were also amenities that would have undermined their relationship to the town. They built their sense of place on the very conditions that limit opportunities and disadvantage permanent residents in Rangeley.

4

My Vacationland

As you drive from Farmington to Rangeley on Route 4, you can steadily feel the elevation rising. The pine trees get smaller and closer together. The road gets windier. You can feel the anticipation building that something is just over the bend. And when you eventually reach the top of a hill you can pull off the road before you enter Rangeley's Main Street. From Whip Willow Farm Scenic Overlook, a privately owned conservation easement, you can take a moment to see how the sun and mountains reflect off Rangeley Lake and watch the slow-moving waves crash against Doctor's Island, a small island in the middle of the lake, privately owned by second homeowners.[1]

At the edge of the overlook is a golden-framed placard attached to a rock, which dedicates the attraction to a founding member of the RLHT, a second homeowner turned permanent resident after retirement. It reads: "In recognition of his wise and generous spirit, his enduring commitment to the Rangeley community and his tireless efforts in support of the Rangeley Lakes National Scenic Byway and Rangeley Lakes Heritage Trust."[2] Here, before you see the houses, restaurants, coffee shops, or people, you see and feel the tremendous weight of the RLHT and the people behind it, patterning the topography and carefully curating the image of Rangeley for the world to see.

In what follows, I explore how the second homeowners I met support this organization, selectively involving themselves in this aspect of associational life in Rangeley because it supports their sense of rurality. As part-time residents, the second homeowners I talked with could not vote in town meetings or run for political office as could permanent residents. They relied on the RLHT to act as their community representative to protect their vision of Rangeley, and the trust relied on their philanthropic and voluntaristic practices to support their vast conservation efforts in the region. I connect this to Rangeley's broader place-making project that relied on the trust to sell itself as a natural-amenity-rich destination. Together, this process all but ensures that the town will be increasingly reliant on tourism and the in-migration of second homeowners for decades to come.

Proprietors of the Country

Jeff and Bonnie spent their winters in a gated golf community in a coastal town in Florida and their summer in Rangeley. I asked whether during their few months in town they involved themselves in any community organizations in Rangeley—civic groups, municipal meetings, or religious institutions. In response, Jeff rebuffed, "Not really. Four months isn't really enough to get involved."

Most of the second homeowners I met in Rangeley echoed this sentiment; they avoided most aspects of Rangeley typically associated with "community" because they were only part-time residents. Ted and Cindy had school-aged children and frequented Rangeley every weekend year-round. During the winters, their children worked at the ski school and during the summers, they passed their days canoeing and hiking. But when it came to other forms of local involvement, Ted admitted:

I am just here part-time, so to me, it's, "Don't disrupt the local flavor per se." You know, as you have mentioned about the school board [I had previously told him I attended a meeting] . . . I just don't want to be part of that. I don't want someone saying: "Well, you know, you did it and the guy you chose was wrong." So, I would just say, "Let them figure it out and I'll support them and let me know how much it is, and we'll pay our fair share, and that will be it."

Ted did not want to attend municipal meetings. Others I met could not name one member from the board of selectmen. And some even drove miles out of their way just to avoid "the hubbub" of the IGA grocery store.

Many also opted out of making local social ties, instead choosing to bring their social ties with them from their permanent residences to Rangeley. Ted elaborated, "I wouldn't say that we have established any real friendships, you know, as part of just being up here." Holly even had a group of friends she met with in Rangeley who were from her hometown in a suburb of Portland:

> We are actually very quiet. We don't have a lot of friends. A lot of our friends from where we live have places here. So, it's that . . . our group of friends, all of our friends [from home] have places up here. So, this is really where we socialize, but it's usually with our friends.

This was a recurring theme I observed in both my interviews and my observations. The second homeowners I met in Rangeley knew permanent residents casually but preferred not to make local social ties, instead using the second home in Rangeley to foster primary ties from their first homes and within their families. What ties second homeowners did make in Rangeley were often with each other, if at all. They avoided most aspects of Rangeley typically associated with a geographically bound "community." They did not attend most municipal or civic meetings. They did not make strong local social ties. And they did not feel liable for most institutional resources in town.

But they *were* involved, albeit selectively. The people I met did more than feel a certain way about Rangeley. Many of the activities they did in Rangeley helped protect their vision of it. Their liability to the town was primarily limited to supporting institutions they associated with their sense of place, upholding that which ensured Rangeley remained, for them, an isolated refuge set in nature. Almost everyone I talked to donated to and participated in organizations that helped protect the environment. They also used their private practices and financial investments to prevent development on the land surrounding their second homes and selectively engaged in local political issues that directly affected their individual consumption of the landscape. Their limited liability to the community was driven by their narrow vision for what Rangeley—and rural life—should be and how their place-identity projects were tied to this vision. They reserved most other forms of community engagement for their hometowns.

Almost all second homeowners I spoke with in Rangeley were either directly or indirectly involved with the RLHT, which many of the people I met became involved with through their lake associations or through the RLHT's outreach programs. Holly was a member of the RLHT and in charge of the patrol of her lake. Biweekly, she went out onto the lake in a non-motorized boat with her neighbor, another second homeowner, to "scan the whole lake for invasive plants and write a report on it." Twice a month on another lake, Bob and Jane Stevenson took out their boat on behalf of the RLHT to monitor for invasive plants and collect samples to check water quality in a cove nearby. Across town from Holly and the Stevensons was Carol, the amateur botanist. She has expertise on land plants but had begun to dedicate a great deal of time studying water plants so she could become more involved with the lake-monitoring programs of the RLHT. During the late summer when water plants begin to flower, she and Paul would take out their canoe to survey the invasive species along the shorelines.

The second homeowners I interviewed volunteered a great deal of their time to the RLHT. Almost all, whether they volunteered or not, donated money to this organization. In fact, the RLHT is in large part made up of volunteers, 82 percent of whom at the time of my research were second homeowners. A high-ranking employee from the RLHT at the time I was conducting my research confirmed that the majority of donations to their organization came from second homeowners themselves.[3] They helped sustain this organization through both the physical labor necessary to monitor the designated scenic land and lakes in Rangeley and the monetary contributions that enabled this organization's geographically vast conservation efforts. As stewards of the land, the RLHT has since its inception purchased and continued to conserve fourteen thousand acres of land including fifty miles of lake and river frontage, fifteen islands, and the 2,443-foot Bald Mountain.[4] Second homeowners have been on the front lines of these extensive conservation efforts sweeping across the Rangeley Lakes region.

It was not enough to donate to the RLHT and monitor the lakes. Some took private action to ensure the preservation of the property surrounding their homes, becoming private stewards of the land. Carol hoped that more people would come to Rangeley so that the town and people of Rangeley would be economically successful. However, she confessed, "I don't want them down here though! [Laughs] Isn't that awful?" Carol and Paul purchased thirty-two acres of property adjacent to their property. Unsatisfied with simply owning this property, Paul and Carol donated it as a conservation easement to the RLHT to safeguard the land for decades to come. Jeff, the gruff second homeowner from Florida, admitted that his "consternation comes when somebody wants to change things . . . because we want it just the way it is." To prevent change and preserve the quiet unpopulated land around his second home, Jeff and his wife, Bonnie, purchased an acre of woodland across the road from their property. Having done so, Jeff could be sure that no developments would disrupt his rural retreat on the lake.

While second homeowners I spoke with did not involve themselves in the day-to-day bureaucratic decision making in Rangeley, they selectively involved themselves in regulatory decisions that affected their relationship to the land around their second home. They became actively involved when local political decisions and problems abutted their private property, threatening their sense of place.

In a follow-up interview with Peter, I learned about a conflict in the town over the location of new industry. Peter lived part-time in a subdivision that sat next to an empty lot where a construction company was trying to start a cement plant. Others in Peter's homeowners' association were against the plant's construction, arguing that it would be "heavy industry," for which the lot was not zoned. Peter relayed to me that many in the association were concerned about the noise and the potential pollution that the plant would generate. It would also infringe on a protected scenic area. He explained:

> There's the association that has, maybe twenty-five members and there's maybe ten landowners around us that are really going to be impacted by the cement plant that's just up the hill from a nature preserve. The Hatchery Brook Nature Preserve right there and any accidents with the cement plant are going to drain right into the stream and Rangeley Lake, so it's a crazy place to put a cement plant.

Peter, who had been a second homeowner for over twenty-five years, expressed feeling particularly frustrated with the process. He and the other homeowners, many of whom were second homeowners, were fighting the plant at board of selectmen meetings and planned to take the construction company to court. The homeowners' association agreed to give $1,000 to lawyers to begin working on the case.

Peter had never really involved himself with local politics in Rangeley before. In his twenty-five years there, he mostly kept to himself. Working at the mountain during the winter as a ski instructor was his greatest involvement. However, when the cement plant threatened to disrupt his second-home property and the scenic byway nearby, he quickly reacted, rallying the homeowners' association to hire lawyers and attending board meetings to have his voice heard.

The Stevensons, too, preferred to keep to themselves. They volunteered for the RLHT but never felt the need to attend local municipal meetings. However, this changed when a development near their second home was causing increased runoff into the lake. They tried to contact the builders themselves to fix the problem, but the Stevensons were not able to make any headway and escalated the issue directly to the state. Jane explained:

> Oh yeah, when they put that development in, "Oh, we know how to build roads. We know how to control things." Well, they didn't, and the runoff was incredible! We have nice blue water out there after a storm and a brown line, just brown, right on the shore, all the silt that came down! "Oh, well, we'll take care of it." Well, finally after the state came in [at their request], they recommended they put some punch pools in, which I don't think they did. By then most of the damage was done and all its runoff is probably finally held in place by growth.

As self-designated proprietors of the lake, the Stevensons took it upon themselves to contact the state to regulate and inspect the development near their second home.

Holly, too, explained that the origin of her involvement with the RLHT dates back to when developers wanted to build a summer camp on the pond where her second home is located. The RLHT was organizing the "no summer camp" campaign, and Holly jumped on board. "It was a huge huge issue for the town," she explained. "Five years ago, there were two hundred campers, you know, we're talking huge and no more boats are allowed on [the] pond, so all of the motorized boats would be here. Everyone was all up in arms. So that's when we became part of the Heritage Trust because they were organizing this drive of 'no.'" Moreover, Holly explained that her involvement with this organization was driven primarily because they were not permanent residents. They did not have the ability to vote for or against its development. Through donations of time and money to the RLHT, she could have her voice and political will heard. In the end, no summer camp was built on the pond.

This is an important nuance of second homeownership. Second homeowners are not permanent residents, which makes their territorial claims distinct from those of other types of wealthy in-migrants who can influence places by running for political office or using their voting power to direct municipal expenditures and zoning and land use. The people I met did not want to be part of local life, preferring instead to use philanthropy to support institutions they valued instead of engaging with the community in other ways.[5] Yet, the people I met also could not vote in local decision-making processes, nor could they run for office or make change through typical governmental means. To influence change, and to protect their vision of Rangeley's rurality, the second homeowners I met donated time and money to local nonprofits. The RLHT became their non-elected representative in community decision making, protecting the interests of second homeowners in municipal processes.[6] Jeremy Levine has written about this process in urban neighborhoods, in which local community-based nonprofit organizations take on a non-elected representative role in community decision making—political representation thus becomes privatized. I found that the second homeowners I met were conscious of this process, strategically supporting the RLHT as they knew it would represent their interests within and outside of municipal processes. And in times they deemed necessary, they also could harness economic and social capital to control local land-use policies and practices outside the municipal sphere in Rangeley—a place where they did not live full-time. While they were not knowingly unified in these pursuits, their patchwork practices came to dominate Rangeley's landscape.

Selling Nature

The institutions that the second homeowners I met supported buoyed Rangeley's place-making project, a broader coalition of business and civic leaders who directed the future of the town's economy and culture.[7] Against the backdrop of declining productive industries like logging and farming, the town relies on the RLHT to protect its natural amenities, which they used to package and sell Rangeley as a tourist destination. Therefore, second homeowners' support of the trust was vital to how Rangeley was defined, packaged, and sold to the world.

When I first moved to Rangeley, the town had recently adopted a comprehensive plan. A comprehensive plan is a "public document" developed by an appointed group of local citizens who, through a series of community discussions and research, defined "what makes Rangeley such a special place and what needs to be done in the future to keep it that way."[8] Comprehensive plans help communities define their needs and plan for the future. They are a strategy to control local growth created by a coalition of stakeholders.[9]

The plan was clear about the kind of place that Rangeley was and what best helped it grow and flourish. Rangeley was framed as a tourist destination, dependent on its vast idyllic landscape and the unique bundle of camps, cabins, and cottages that are spread throughout the area, to sell itself as an amenity-rich tourist destination. The plan articulated this strategy:

> The greatest asset that Rangeley has is its natural setting. The pristine
> lakes and mountain environment [have] drawn sportsmen, tourists and

families alike for well over 150 years. The lore of Rangeley has been pack-aged and sold, capturing the minds of many. . . . The camps, cabins, cot-tages and village centers also define the region, and it is the way that development occurred, and will occur in the future, that is of great inter-est and concern at this juncture. The Rangeley Brand was not invented by L.L. Bean, and likewise the community cannot rely on others to protect, promote and enhance its identity: the issue of the future of Rangeley must be taken on here.[10]

In the document, Rangeley's natural setting was understood as central to Rangeley's economic future. It was what attracts tourists, visitors, and sec-ond homeowners to the region year in and year out, supporting the economy as other forms of economic production have all but disappeared.[11] The lakes, rivers, and ponds that pepper Rangeley's topology have "attracted visitors for nearly two centuries" and "support businesses that employ over 85 percent of the local workforce, while sustaining and growing the region's world-class fisheries, its wildlife, its second home market, and its public services. They are the primary reason that people live here, own second homes, and visit all 12 months of the year."[12] Such natural resources were framed as vital to Rangeley's economic growth.

These bodies of water had been facing challenges related to pollution and invasive plant species, potentially undermining Rangeley's most important economic, environmental, and cultural asset. But municipal officials alone did not have the money, tools, or specific environmental knowledge to moni-tor and conserve these bodies of water to protect Rangeley's future. They relied on a series of extra-local stakeholders for conservation. The Rangeley Lakes Heritage Trust was central to coordinating these efforts. And its value to the town had been substantial:

> To help coordinate and educate the public, Rangeley Lakes Heritage Trust implements its award-winning Headwaters Lake Protection program. Created in 1998, and supported in part by the Town, RLHT's program utilizes it[s] staff and more than 80 volunteers to 1) monitor water clarity and chemistry, 2) teach boaters how to inspect their watercraft, trailers, anchors and fishing gear for invasive species, and 3) survey more than 100 miles of shoreline on 10 or more water bodies to identify and docu-ment all the plant species they find. If an invasive aquatic species is found, RLHT will work with the Town, Maine DEP, UMF and several regional organizations to implement a cost-effective management plan that will address the invasive infestation with minimal ecological impacts.[13]

The RLHT was framed as a vital resource for the town to ensure its economic vitality. The town's place-making strategy relied on its natural-amenity-rich landscape to sell itself to the region and the world, which contributed to employing nearly the entire local workforce. The RLHT is a nonprofit that relied almost exclusively on donations of time, land, and money to meet its conservation goals and secure Rangeley's character. It needed people to monitor the land and lakes, educate the public, opt into conservation easements, and write checks. Second homeowners have been the near sole contributors to this process, helping the RLHT meet these goals and ultimately helping Rangeley "retain its brand . . . outstanding clean air and water, large remote areas, scenic views of lakes and mountains, a sky that is dark at night, peace and quiet, wild brook trout, and bountiful wildlife."[14]

Nonprofit organizations have become increasingly common community actors that influence municipal policies and land use. Along with other local institutions, including the Rangeley Lakes Regional School, the Rangeley Historical Society, the Rangeley Public Library, the Rangeley Friends of Art, the Rangeley Sportsman's Association, and "caring neighbors," the RLHT "[helps] define the social and cultural character of Rangeley."[15] The people I met were essential to crafting this definition. Supporting the Rangeley Lakes Heritage Trust thus bolstered its ability to direct the future of Rangeley.

Rural People and Places Left Behind

As people like those I met work to ensure that places like Rangeley remain isolated refuges set in nature, free from economic activity and connection to the modern world, rural people and places get left behind. Permanent residents living in tourism-dependent economies navigate precarious and low-wage work, a lack of affordable housing, poor internet coverage, and a dearth of health-care services. This is in part because places like Rangeley are largely dependent on private actors to fuel local growth, and many of the people with the most economic and social capital in town—second homeowners—direct much of their efforts toward conservation, which has the effect of *supplanting* other local needs.

Economies remain undiversified and precarious. Rangeley's economy and others like it tend to fare better than their neighboring rural communities that lack an amenity- and tourism-based economy.[16] However, local residents stretch themselves thin, making ends meet by working multiple jobs in the tourism industry year-round in places where median housing prices are often exorbitant.[17] Jobs available in rural tourist destinations are often economically insecure, dependent on the whims of the seasons and visitors' preferences, and rarely offer health insurance, retirement, or other benefits. My coworker at the restaurant where I worked, Tanya, a single mom, highlighted these tensions. She constantly fretted that she worked only one job during the summer months, which was rarely enough to support her three kids. During the school year she worked three jobs: as a substitute teacher, a varsity coach, and a waitress at the restaurant. She had to plan her year and her savings around having only one job during the summer months so that she could care for her children while they were out of school. This often led to the summer months being stressful for Tanya. The summer we worked together, she suffered from a toothache. But she did not have dental insurance, and she had no wiggle room in her tight budget to pay for dental work out of pocket. Her tooth would have to wait until she had saved enough money to fix it, which required picking up extra shifts to do so. A slow day at the restaurant could be devastating. Our nightly tip income varied that summer between $30 and $200 on any given night, and it was often impossible to predict what kind of night it would be. After a few weeks of agonizing pain and slow nights at the restaurant, Tanya decided to have her entire tooth pulled because she could not afford to get the root canal she needed.

As wages remain stagnant and precarious and real estate prices rise, finding affordable housing becomes a material concern for rural people. Many rural, natural-amenity-rich communities are among the most highly segregated parts of America. People who live and play part-time in rural places tend to occupy the most highly valued land, often with water frontage or mountain views. People who work in these places tend to live far outside of them, enduring long commutes and sometimes relegated to hazardous living conditions.[18] In Rangeley, this process is not very different. According to the Maine State Housing Authority, "The average two-bedroom rent is unaffordable to renter households with the medium income in Rangeley."[19] Affordable monthly rental housing has become increasingly rare in the age of Airbnbs and summer sublets, where property owners can make a premium on daily or weekly rentals. Houses that are rented at a fair-market rate (or lower) are often done so because of the goodwill of the landlord, hardly a sustainable solution to this structural problem. Land itself is also expensive and inflated.[20] During my time in Rangeley I watched my downstairs neighbors, Ron and Debbie, work multiple jobs during each season throughout the year, picking up every extra shift they could, to afford a down payment on a house in Rangeley. I would often wake up to the noise of their truck pulling into the driveway late at night and the clamor as they entered the house after working a night shift. Nearly ten years after I left the field, I learned that Ron and Debbie did buy a home. But not in Rangeley. They bought a three-bed, two-bath single-story home for $150,000 in a very small rural town, one hour south of Rangeley.

It is difficult to find land that is not priced in such a way as to be accessible only to second homeowners or those locals whose jobs fall outside of the precarious service sector. Affordable housing is a top priority for the town as it plans for its future.[21] However, attracting second homeowners to support the economy can complicate these goals, as second homeownership drives up real estate costs and as second homeowners purchase and conserve land. Furthermore, affordable housing is often better in communities with a robust nonprofit infrastructure to support and fund these efforts.[22] But in Rangeley, a large portion of the philanthropic support from the most affluent residents goes toward supporting the Rangeley Lakes Heritage Trust.[23] This all but ensures that the local population will be continually dependent on the in-migration and consumption practices of second homeowners, who constitute nearly 70 percent of the local tax base, for decades to come.[24]

As rural economies remain dependent on natural amenities as a primary economic strategy, other resources can fall by the wayside. Rural places still lag far behind suburban and urban places in terms of internet coverage and use.[25] Attention to larger economic structures clarifies why places like Rangeley still suffer spotty internet coverage and why the coverage that is available remains slow. Internet coverage is market-based and thus subject to capitalist interests of supply and demand. There is not enough diffusion of technological infrastructure or competition in rural regions for companies to want to invest in these spaces.[26] It's just not profitable. And this lack of competition means that rural people lack higher-quality services. Access to high-speed broadband coverage in rural areas under market-based conditions then requires political and economic capital. It requires the will of local civic leaders to fight for resources and municipalities' own abilities to finance or subsidize these endeavors.[27] Places that do not have this type of capital often lag behind. In Rangeley, residents and business owners often implore municipal officials to act on the region's poor internet access and municipal officials often discuss the lack of access as a major local social problem, themes I have detailed above. Yet many of the people in Rangeley who have the most economic resources and political capital, like the second homeowners I talked with, do not prioritize reliable and speedy internet access. Many of their efforts instead go toward expanding amenities they value, such as the RLHT. This can lead to what sociologists refer to as the digital divide, which includes both unequal access to broadband coverage and unequal methods of use, all of which influences the resources people have access to, the development of social networks, the ability to upgrade and update business practices, and access to online or remote education.[28]

Rural places are also medical deserts. This is particularly disadvantageous for older rural residents, who tend to have higher rates of heart disease, cancer, and chronic conditions and need more medical attention. Yet because health access in the United States is market driven and because local care or transportation services in rural places are costly, rural places are less likely to have this sort of medical infrastructure available. Rural people are then doubly disadvantaged, by higher rates of health problems and lack of care.[29] Many rural communities are also affected by lack of health-care access and inadequate broadband access, limiting access to health information and opportunities for telehealth options found in other parts of the country.[30] In Rangeley, the closest hospital and many medical and pharmaceutical services are in Farmington, nearly a two-hour drive down and back. On Rangeley's community forum, older residents who could not drive themselves or did not want to make the trip to Farmington would often post pleas to other residents to help them pick up their prescriptions or to drive them to a doctor's visit. Doctors in Maine urge better broadband connection to rural places like Rangeley that need services like telehealth most.[31]

This is not to say that permanent residents do not value and appreciate natural amenities, nor is this to say that conserving natural resources is detrimental to the local area. Communities with high concentrations of second homeownership often experience an increase in environmental quality. But they also experience a decrease in economic well-being for permanent populations.[32] In Rangeley, the permanent residents I lived and worked with would romanticize how lucky they felt to live in such a beautiful place and realized how important conservation was in maintaining what they valued. In fact, many I met lived and stayed there because of the outdoor amenities they could access year-round and saw the value in protecting their community, themes I turn to in the next chapter. But living and working in a rural community means that you have to think about local conditions other than nature—how you will pay for rent and fuel if it rains for a week and the mountain you work at as an hourly employee is closed, or how your children will access their remote schooling if your internet service remains intermittent at best, or where you will go and how you will get there if you have a medical emergency.

Rural places like Rangeley are highly dependent on private investments to uplift local institutional resources, such as housing trusts that provide affordable housing, philanthropists who fund hospitals and health-care infrastructure, and local leaders who use their political capital to advocate for high-speed internet access. When people in rural communities who have the most economic, social, and political capital funnel much of their efforts into conserving the environment, other important resources can fall by the wayside: hospitals, affordable housing, and internet access.[33] The place-identity projects of the people I met do not just uplift the institutions that they associate with themselves in rural communities. Such singular invest-ments can simultaneously support broader trends that limit the resources of rural people and places.

5

Open for Business

In an astute, but clearly tongue-in-cheek, commentary on what it means to be a true Mainer, Maine humorist Edmund Smith managed to capture some of the complex dynamics I observed between many permanent residents and the so-called "from aways" in Rangeley:

> The subject of the natives of Maine versus the summer people and the tourists is so complicated that it can be approached only by a gymnast or preferably a trapeze artist of eccentric talent. . . . For unless you were born in the State and can prove it, there is no such thing as total acceptance. If you entered life only ten feet short of the State line while your mother was being rushed by ambulance toward a Maine maternity hospital, you're still "from away." But while the natives form a fraternity you may never quite join, they offer you—tacitly—a series of steps toward the achievement of their trust and affection. The first step is marked "tourist." Here you could remain under scrutiny for years . . . if you keep coming back each season, it proves you must like them, so there must be some good in you. And therefore you advance to "Summer Visitor" or "Summer Person." Try to make it the former. It's nearer to the native's heart.[1]

After my time living and working in Rangeley, it became clear to me that there would never be full acceptance of the types of people I talked to for this book. But there was some, and a bit of truth that the presence of second homeowners and their continued return to Rangeley offered them tacit approval by a portion of permanent residents and civic leaders—but only under certain conditions.

Work, Decline, and Dignity

Rangeley's total population is just over 1,000 full-time residents.[2] Its housing stock is made up of over 60 percent second homes. During the summer months when second-homeowner in-migration is at its peak, the town balloons to over 5,000 residents.[3] Given the pervasiveness of second homeowners in the region, permanent residents across a range of venues are forced to confront these in-migrants. In many places with an influx of second homeowners, this kind of population can be met with contempt.[4] Second homeowners come in for a few days, weeks, or months out of the year and often occupy the most valuable land, monopolizing the scarce mountain and water views. Their purchases inflate property values and contribute to affordable-housing problems. They crowd the sidewalks and parking lots, fill up the restaurants, and overburden local services like the town transfer station. But I learned that some second homeowners' in-migration, their support of the Rangeley Lakes Heritage Trust, and the trust's dependence on second homeowners are not always in conflict with many permanent residents. To understand this, it is first important to understand some permanent residents' own everyday experiences living under these conditions.

Many permanent residents in Rangeley work multiple jobs throughout the year in the entertainment, accommodations, and food service industries to make ends meet in an increasingly tourism-dependent destination. Working multiple jobs is both a source of stress and a source of pride for many of the permanent residents I encountered. It did not take long to learn that they often work multiple jobs, which vary seasonally, to make a livable income. This means that some will work up to as many as six different jobs or more per year. These jobs are often economically insecure and are dependent on the influx of tourists and second homeowners. I myself worked three jobs to make ends meet during my unfunded time doing fieldwork. In addition to working at the ski resort as an instructor for children and as a server at a restaurant, I also worked as an adjunct instructor at a nearby college. My adjunct teaching position at the college was my most dependable source of income that year.

There was a palpable sense of imminent economic decline rippling through the community while I lived in Rangeley. Rumors spread that the ski resort was in economic peril and many worried about what would happen to the economic and social fabric of the town and those who worked within it if it closed. This fear loomed over most interactions that year. One morning inside the lodge at the mountain, Andy, a permanent resident, arrived at work in the break room where Ed, another permanent resident, and I were waiting for our ski lesson assignments for the day. Andy sat down, and without pause he asked if we had seen the email going around about the 'Rangeley visioning meeting.' Looking bewildered, he asked if we had seen one of its stated goals, 'to become less dependent on tourism.' 'What?' he rebuffed. 'That's all we've got here. People need to embrace tourism. There's no more logging, there's no more industry. It's vacationland, it's all tourism.' In agreement, Ed turned to me to elaborate: 'Some people around here get it. They get that all we have is tourism. And people coming up here is good for everyone. It puts money in everyone's pocket.'

This worry that the mountain would close came true in the years after I left the field. The mountain was owned by a wealthy family who had been second homeowners in the region for a long time. They invested millions in expanding operations and keeping it relatively affordable for the community. Yet for the mountain to remain operational, they needed to make major capital improvements, for which they said they lacked financing. As a result, they put it up for sale. The right buyer never came along and they closed the ski resort entirely for almost five years, confirming many people's worst fear. After a series of complicated almost-sales, the mountain was sold to a Boston-based investment firm and finally opened again in 2020.[5]

This sense of economic change and uncertainty operated concurrently with many permanent residents' lived experiences of precarity in a region dependent on tourism. One Sunday evening in mid-July at the restaurant where I worked, Sandra, a local resident in her mid-thirties, walked in and sat at the bar. Kerry, who was bartending, seemed to know her, and they exchanged pleasantries while Kerry poured her a beer. Kerry asked her about her summer. Sandra leaned forward onto the bar to grab her beer, took a sip, and exhaled before responding. She recounted the three jobs she worked that summer: at two different restaurants in the evenings and at a real estate company during the day. She said the day she came in was her 'only night off in weeks.' She slumped back in her chair and said to Kerry with resignation: 'But it pays the bills. That's why we all do it.'

Kerry, herself a manager with a stable income, gave Sandra an all-knowing nod. It wasn't long ago that Kerry was in Sandra's position working multiple server jobs and cobbling together what she could throughout the year while her kids were young. Even once she felt more established with one full-time job, she could not let go of this sense of precarity. Kerry still worked nearly seven days a week and would take a shift in the kitchen, at the bar, or as a server if things got tight to make sure the restaurant was profitable for the owners, to ensure she and the rest of the staff continued to be employed.

Work was a constant source of stress under the context of this uncertainty. However, I found that talking about work functioned as an organizing logic for daily life and as a source of pride for many who lived in Rangeley. This precarity was reframed as a local virtue. Working *hard* and working *often* was a source of dignity for working permanent residents.[6] Hard work was part of the local moral order, the standard against which one was judged. Similar to sociologist Michèle Lamont's study of working-class men, permanent residents I encountered on a daily basis in Rangeley used hard work to "maintain a sense of self-worth, to affirm their dignity independently of their relatively low social status, and to locate themselves above others."[7] Sociologists like Jennifer Sherman find this process to be particularly salient in rural areas that experience economic decline, where people use discourses of hard work to create norms, values, and social hierarchies as they resist and react to larger social and economic forces.[8]

My neighbor, Ron, best embodied this process. Ron and his wife, Debbie, rented an apartment near mine in the center of town while they worked to save enough money to buy a house. Ron worked at night as a custodian and during the day at a grocery store. Debbie worked at the mountain and at a grocery store as a cashier. My daily interactions with Ron and Debbie took only one form: discussing work.

Daily, I would run into Ron and Debbie at the mountain where we worked together or on our front doorsteps as we would come home from our respective shifts. On a dark and cold February evening I had just returned home and was walking up the outside steps to my apartment above Ron and Debbie's. Ron pulled into the driveway in his pickup. As he stepped out of his truck, he hollered up to say hello with his thick Maine accent. I yelled back down to say hi and ask him how things were going. 'Just got back from a double shift. Put in 'bout a hundred hours this week,' he shouted incredulously, but also a bit proudly. His response was not to tell me about his granddaughter who was waiting for him inside or about what he and Debbie were going to do together over the weekend. His response was about work—as it always was. How *much* he worked. How *little* he worked. How much he was *going* to work.

Ron never thought it was enough that I worked just one job in Rangeley during the summer and would frequently knock on my door to offer me jobs that he had heard of through the grapevine—catering jobs, more waitressing jobs, or retail jobs. At first this seemed like either judgment or pestering, but I soon learned that this was Ron's way of connecting with me, knowing the financial ups and downs of working in the restaurant industry in town.

I ran into Ron one day at the IGA while he was stocking eggs on the shelves. After we exchanged pleasantries, he began recounting the long list of odd jobs and total number of hours he had worked that week: during the day he stocked shelves, at night he worked as a custodian, and on weekends he picked up another side job painting houses for a friend. Chuck, a permanent resident I worked with at the mountain, was also working at the IGA that day. He overheard Ron's long list of work and sauntered over to chime in with his own list, which he counted on his fingers: working at the IGA, working at the mountain, helping his wife start her own business, working as a bartender at a restaurant down the road, and occasionally working at the town transfer station. Chuck's various list of odd jobs was a running joke in town—you could see Chuck at every stop you made in a day running errands in Rangeley.

Yet in this interaction, neither lamented the hours worked per se. Instead, they used it as a source of pride and as a method to exert a hierarchy among themselves. They reframed the precarity of their employment into a source of local power. The permanent residents in Rangeley I met were much like Chuck and Ron. Many lived in a state of economic instability, which was a source of daily stress. However, they used pride in work as a strategy to resist this precarity.

"Lifeblood"

The central importance of work to everyday life in Rangeley was why on a macro-level, second homeowners' in-migration was viewed, generally, as an economic good. Some second homeowners shopped at the IGA and skied at the mountain. Some went out to eat at the restaurants on Main Street and brought their trash to the transfer station. The town had developed a discourse that second homeowners were understood as the "lifeblood" of the local economy, a resource the town depended on to ensure its economic future.[9] A confluence of economic, historic, and cultural conditions elevated this frame over others.

I observed this theme in political, civic, nonprofit, parochial, and commercial organizations in town, where a coalition of business owners, upper-level managers, and nonprofit leaders would evangelize the importance of second homeowners for the economy. I attended Rangeley's town meeting, a form of governance in which residents gather once a year to publicly debate and vote on how best to appropriate local governmental funds.[10] Attracting second homeowners to the region was used as a guiding logic to support the appropriation of money. During a discussion about the allocation of funds to the chamber of commerce, a local business manager declared that he wanted the community to invest in marketing strategies that would attract second-home buyers, who were '68 percent of the local tax base.' This helped the whole region and 'pays for itself,' he asserted.

One by one, people took to the microphone to voice their support; one even pronounced: 'The economic landscape has changed. We're at war trying to get tourists. It's our lifeblood.' Finally, a man walked to the microphone and declared, 'These are not donations, these are investments.' After this, a handful of people in the audience clapped and the article passed without further discussion. Second homeowners in this instance were framed as a resource worth investing in and pursuing. Their presence in town was viewed as the element of the economy that could prevent the region from decline, and local municipal decisions and resource allocation were thus based on this premise.

Local businesses I observed similarly framed second homeowners as the resource on which they were dependent, and they ultimately pursued the in-migration of second homeowners because of this very frame. For instance, while working at the restaurant, an owner of a neighboring restaurant came in to discuss with Kerry, the bartender and manager, the problems he was experiencing in his own restaurant nearby. After having a beer, he divulged that local permanent residents had complained that his menu did not have options that catered to them. Then, unapologetically, he told us that he did not care what the locals thought of his menu. He cared only about what the second homeowners and tourists thought because they were his moneymakers—they ordered the drinks, appetizers, and desserts.

Greg, an administrator at the local ski mountain, similarly used this frame to interpret and direct the future of their business practices. He asked if the ski instructors could brainstorm a way to come up with $75,000 by the end of the winter. Steve, a young ski instructor, suggested appealing to the 21+ crowd by having events that would draw in these customers (e.g., concerts, beer festivals, and even keeping the bar open later at night). Greg dismissed the idea. He explained: 'It's important we create a place where families want to come because families are the ones that will come up and buy condos someday. They're the repeat customers we want.'

And indeed, the activities that took place at the mountain the rest of the winter reflected this family-friendly logic. The mountain had an Easter egg hunt, a cardboard box sled contest for kids, and the bar always shut down before it could get too rowdy. In these cases, both managers highlighted precarity in their businesses and positioned second homeowners as the resource that could save them.

Yet I noticed this pattern even outside the municipal or economic realm. On one balmy Sunday morning during early spring, my observations led me to a pew in the back corner of the town's Catholic church. I sat there quietly, watching parishioners make their way into the building, sitting in clusters of family units waiting for mass to begin. The priest processed to the nave, offered an opening prayer, and began his sermon reflecting on Rangeley's seasonal residents. He moralized the generosity of second homeowners, whom he thanked for their monetary contributions. Without these contributions, the church would not have been able to afford the exorbitant heating bill throughout the cold winter months. He paused, gesturing to a family of four sitting in the middle pews: the Kennedys, second homeowners who owned a condo at the ski mountain and lived permanently in southern Maine. The parents sat there quietly and nodded their heads in deference to the priest. In the priest's weekly letter to the parishioners, he even wrote:

> I trust that we are all happy to see such a good attendance at Mass, especially at the 9:00 a.m. Mass in Rangeley at a time of the year when we are sometimes very few. Families with children have certainly made a big difference. . . . In a Parish with few children, our seasonal children are a special blessing.

A special blessing. There was no objective measure found in a survey or data set that could have captured what I had seen and heard: a waning Catholic church's subjective experience of seasonal in-migrants, who filled the pews and financed operational utilities. The second homeowners were moralized for their generosity, a symbol of benevolence for the common good of the community. While few other people or institutions in town explicitly drew upon this sacred language to describe seasonal visitors, many echoed these sentiments.

Nearly every nonprofit organization I observed in town mirrored this pattern: the library board relied on donations from second homeowners; the RLHT was dependent on second homeowners' donation of time and money to preserve land in Rangeley; and even the Rangeley fitness center came to fruition in large part because of donations from second homeowners. There was a palpable awareness in town that second homeowners were the hand that fed them.

Yet it is not just that second homeowners helped business owners pay the bills and support workers in their daily efforts to make rent. Instead, the arrival of second homeowners to the region throughout history had also helped the town articulate its distinct qualities to others.[11] The arrival of second homeowners to the region served as what Charles Cooley referred to as the *looking-glass self*, a theory of social identity construction that suggests that our *perceptions* of how other people view us are central to identity formation.[12] Second homeowners' continued commitment to Rangeley affirmed the town's perception of itself that it was special and distinct, a place worth visiting.

The arrival of second homeowners to the region helped construct the town's unique place character. Rangeley's historical texts and museum exhibits commemorated the migration of second homeowners to the region. Historical texts of Rangeley pointed to critical moments that marked the emergence and economic expansion of the town, celebrating second homeowners as central to its origin story.[13] For example, in 1876, Rangeley, Maine, appeared in the *New York Times*. A New York City angler wrote to tell the tale of the superior fishing and sporting he found in the north woods of the Rangeley Lakes region. Articles such as this were said to have spurred the in-migration of curious fishermen from all over the Northeast, which led to the eventual formation of the Oquossoc Angling Association in the 1800s and the in-migration of hunters, fishermen, and those seeking leisure in the woods of northern Maine.[14] This narrative, according to local historians, was what "put Rangeley on the map."[15] These histories of Rangeley emphasized the inception of hunting and fishing camps and the eventual arrival of second homeowners as central to the town's economic, social, and cultural history.[16]

This history was so central to Rangeley's past that it was commemorated in the historical society's Outdoor Sporting and Heritage Museum, which was built around an old sporting camp and honors the Rangeley region's long history as a popular hunting and fishing destination for both local residents and summer vacationers.[17] This is what makes Rangeley distinct from more rapidly changing destinations in the Mountain West, where shifts to a post-productive landscape are more recent and animated and where a new reliance on tourism abuts and conflicts with extractive industries.[18] In Rangeley, second homeowners and vacationers have a long legacy, visiting Rangeley's "fishing camps" to enjoy the outdoors and catch "award-winning" trout.[19]

Even in mundane interactions in town I saw permanent residents use second homeowners to articulate Rangeley's distinctiveness. One evening during my shift at the restaurant, I overheard a conversation between that night's bartender, Kerry, and a patron of the restaurant. He was doing some traveling and asked her advice about visiting Moosehead Lake in Greenville, a lake town northeast of the Rangeley area. Kerry encouraged him to travel there because that area of Maine is 'a lot like Rangeley.' She justified this comparison by claiming that 'the second homeowners in Moosehead are a lot like people in Rangeley. . . . [They] actually care for the area's community and landscape.' She made it a point to note that they were different from the second homeowners in the Sebago Lake region in southern Maine, a lake community known for its highly affluent, primarily Massachusetts second-home population. She ended their conversation by cautioning him to avoid that area. Kerry could have chosen many other elements to celebrate the distinct qualities of Rangeley: the lakes and mountains, the longtime local families who have stayed in the area, or even the downtown businesses. But she chose second homeowners to help frame Rangeley's distinct character.

Given all I had read about second homeowners in the sociological literature that suggested at times a fraught relationship between newcomers and old-timers, and even my own understandings, as someone who grew up in Maine, of "from aways," I had expected to hear and see frustration with affluent second homeowners coming into Rangeley. But I learned that second homeowners were tacitly woven into the fabric of the town. They were framed both as an economic necessity as the town was increasingly reliant on tourism and as a symbol of Rangeley's place distinctiveness.

The Boundaries of Acceptance

I learned, however, that there were boundaries to this relatively diffuse acceptance. Second homeowners were viewed less favorably when they obstructed permanent residents' other production pursuits or made noticeable the social-class divisions between themselves and permanent residents.

During one of my many conversations with Chuck and Andy in the break room during slow periods at the mountain, I asked how they would describe the relationship between permanent residents and second homeowners. Andy, a forty-something chef and part-time ski instructor, explained that there was a 'divide' between 'the locals' and the second homeowners, although Chuck was quick to mention that he felt that it was the 'locals who actually imposed this very divide.' Chuck, a free-spirited outdoorsman who worked multiple different jobs throughout the year, insisted that he did not entirely resent second homeowners. They had come to Rangeley, he argued, for the very reasons he did seventeen years ago: to enjoy the beauty of the area. Andy shook his head in disagreement with Chuck. 'Why is there a divide?' I asked. 'They don't live here,' he responded emphatically. 'It isn't just vacationland. This is our livelihood.' The divide stems from his perception that second homeowners were unable to relate to people like him because 'they don't work three jobs [like we do] to support their vacation lifestyle.'

This sense that second homeowners could not relate to their economic pursuits was indeed a source of tension, unearthing the social divides between second homeowners and permanent residents. Chuck explained that he became frustrated only when second homeowners asked him, 'What do you do?' Each time, Chuck would coyly respond, 'I ski, and I fish.' Chuck explained that second homeowners always followed up with, 'But what do you *do*?' This was a point of frustration for Chuck. 'They're all lawyers from southern Maine who want to know what I do for work,' he said. While working hard and often was a virtue, work did not define his entire identity.

Working in the restaurant, I encountered this question almost daily. Asking what someone does for a living is relatively innocuous and tends to be part of casual conversation and routine pleasantries in American culture. But this question was not always innocuous, and I watched firsthand how this divide materialized in interaction. One evening, Tanya waited on a table of two couples who were second homeowners. They were regulars, and I knew one of the couples from my time working at the mountain. I watched as Tanya chatted with the group, and she left the table with a noticeably uncomfortable laugh. After her back was turned to the patrons, her smile disappeared, and she stormed over to the servers' station with tears in her eyes. I asked her urgently what had happened. 'They asked me, "What do you do?" I told them, "I work here, at the restaurant,"' she said as a tear rolled down her face. 'Then they asked, "but what do you *do*?"' as her tears turned into rage. '*This* is what I *do*,' she said through gritted teeth. Tanya fumed about this interaction for the remainder of our shift. I watched her develop warm, even convivial, bounded friendships with seasonal regulars during my time at the restaurant. However, this interaction, set against the backdrop of Tanya's near constant financial worries, made the class divide between them palpable.

These interactional moments helped clarify the impact of affluent people's migration into rural communities beyond rising housing costs and economic insecurity as places become more dependent on amenity migration. Jennifer

Sherman articulates this nuance in her analysis of an amenity-rich town in the Mountain West. These manifest social divides—different orientations to work, capital, and community given one's social location—can alienate long-time residents from their communities as newcomers devalue their moral worth.[20] In this case, moral worth was tied to hard work in an increasingly tourism dependent region, which was inextricably connected to the very precarious economic conditions that second homeowners helped create and sustain.

Some second homeowners' attempted displays of classlessness were indeed a source of derision for some permanent residents. For instance, Chuck chided the second homeowners who came up to Rangeley and 'pretend like they don't have money. They drive around in their beat-up truck, but they have a lot of money.' He explained that Kennebago, for instance, one of the more geographically isolated lakes in the region, was 'like a gated community.' The types of people who lived there, he said, were not the kind of second homeowners you can 'stop by and say hi to. . . . They aren't interested in social events. They're just interested in their private little getaway.' Andy agreed with these sentiments. He called them 'the New Jersey types,' who came into Rangeley in their 'expensive cars' and 'want to be left alone. . . . They don't give anything to their community.' The conspicuousness of some second homeowners' displays of class, even if they try to "downplay" them through their choice of vehicle, and their perceived distance from the community enhance this divide.

Second homeowners' acceptance was also limited if they *materially* challenged permanent residents' economic livelihoods. At the ski mountain where permanent residents and some second homeowners worked side by side providing ski lessons, I observed only one instance in which tensions mounted: if second homeowners were scheduled to provide ski lessons in lieu of permanent residents. There were two very different orientations to working at the mountain. Permanent residents viewed working there as mostly an economic necessity. Second homeowners viewed working there as mostly a hobby. Tensions arose when permanent residents felt that their weekly income was threatened by second homeowners. This manifested on a particularly slow week, when we all rarely worked more than one lesson a day, if at all, which translated into roughly forty dollars total for the week. Ed, a local farmer who made ends meet by working at the mountain during the day and grooming cross-country trails in the early mornings, showed up to work and found that his name was not on the board to work that shift. He began pacing back and forth until he turned to me and to Chuck. He mumbled in frustration that Phillip, a retired second homeowner whose name was listed on the work board to give a lesson, 'doesn't need the money' like he did. Typically, Phillip and Ed had a congenial relationship. They often skied together in their down time and chatted every morning in the break room. But on this particular day, a symbolic wall emerged between them. Phillip knew that Ed was upset and quickly offered to let him take his place.

Most permanent residents did not take issue with many second homeowners' appreciation of nature—as Kerry noted earlier, she appreciated that second homeowners cared about Rangeley's natural beauty—because second homeowners' value of the landscape was part of what made Rangeley distinctive. Rangeley's beauty also influenced how busy the grocery store was, how many diners frequented the many restaurants in town, and how many tickets were bought at the ski mountain. So too did second homeowners' donations help protect the environment, which attracted more tourists and second homeowners to the region. However, there were instances in which preserving the environment rubbed up against permanent residents' *other* production processes.

Let's return to Peter from chapter 4, a second homeowner who was fighting the development of the cement plant behind his vacation home. For Peter, this was the first instance where he felt like he was a true outsider in Rangeley, pushed to the category "from away." At the board of selectmen meeting, Peter and his fellow homeowners were called "flatlanders," an even more pejorative term used to denote an out-of-stater or simply a non-local. He explained, "Sometimes we're referred to as flatlanders and that's okay. We're not equal to a true native of Rangeley; they're voting residents here, even though we pay the same taxes . . . I'm not upset at that. I mean, that's okay. That's the way it goes. It's sort of interesting, I was not aware of that until the cement plant came up. It's a whole new aspect." When I asked if he had ever felt like that before, he revealed, "It was the first time I felt like an outsider at all. I've always felt really welcome, especially since I worked at the mountain. I really felt accepted as one of the locals." The dynamic of the cement plant decision made clear the boundaries that people like Peter were not, in fact, considered locals.

After months of back and forth between the homeowners' association, the select board, and the construction company looking to expand their operations, the town held a special town meeting to decide the fate of the cement plant. Rangeley has a town-meeting style governance, a form of direct democracy wherein permanent residents vote on the town's tax expenditures and zoning ordinances. Special town meetings are often called at times deemed necessary about issues of immediate importance, which allows voting town members to make decisions without having to wait until the annual town meeting held typically in late spring. At this special town meeting, nearly 150 Rangeley residents participated in the vote. For a town of about a thousand permanent residents, this was a significant number for an impromptu in-person meeting. This signaled that many people cared deeply about the future of the cement plant in town. In a 116–31 vote, the voting town members rejected a moratorium on industrial zoning that would have allowed the zoning board of appeals to rezone the proposed property and prevent the construction of the proposed cement plant.[21] This offered the construction company resounding local support for their new commercial enterprise, and in doing so, a statement on the town's limits of conservation.

Although the place-identity projects of the second homeowners I met were not entirely misaligned with Rangeley's broader place-making project, and their presence was, generally, viewed favorably in many spheres in town, there were limits to this tacit acceptance. Boundaries emerged when they pursued their sense of place in ways that abutted permanent residents' other production pursuits. The moments I detailed in this chapter shed light on the sometimes-fraught social relationships that emerge within amenity-rich destinations with an abundance of in-migrants that rural sociologists have captured across the country.[22] It is not simply that the in-migration of second homeowners into rural communities altered the housing market and economic conditions for permanent residents in ways that made their lives more precarious. Their orientations to land use, community, and work created a palpable social divide with longtime residents, whom I observed feeling at times estranged from their own communities.[23] In the case of the cement plant, however, permanent residents used their voting power—a tool that second homeowners did not have by virtue of being part-time residents—to resist the norms imposed by some second homeowners and demonstrate the boundaries between themselves and "from aways." And in the end, this dynamic makes second homeowners' reliance on nonprofit actors, like the Rangeley Lakes Heritage Trust, to serve as their community representative that much more critical in ensuring their vision of Rangeley for decades to come.

PART III

The City

It was one of those crisp sunny evenings in early September in Boston that tells you summer has finally passed and fall is just around the corner. I was on my way to the Nazzarro Community Center to attend a North End/Waterfront Neighborhood Council meeting. I got off the T at Haymarket, the orange line MBTA station just on the other side of the highway from the North End. As I walked, I watched mostly young twenty- and thirty-something women toting their yoga mats to the Rose Kennedy Greenway, where nearly a hundred other people scattered throughout the park for an evening outdoor yoga class. After passing the park, I continued walking to the North End's world-renowned Hanover Street, the heart of Little Italy, where I saw hordes of tourists with backpacks and cameras lining the streets waiting to get into some of the most famous Italian restaurants and pastry shops in the city.

The North End has gone through dramatic transformations over the past few decades. At different times, it had been home to African Americans and various first-generation immigrants, but by the mid-twentieth century, the North End was predominantly known as an ethnic enclave for Italian immigrants, an identity that remains today.[1] This was one of the neighborhoods that Jane Jacobs famously captured in *The Death and Life of Great American Cities*, her 1961 treatise on community in urban life. Jacobs lauded neighborhoods like the North End—highly dense, multiuse residential and commercial neighborhoods—for their ability to foster public safety. In these neighborhoods, she celebrated people who would peer out their windows to check on passersby, shop owners who would guard the sidewalks and clean up the streets, and neighborhood characters of all sorts who would stroll through the streets from sunup until sundown. Together, they performed a "sidewalk ballet," a choreographed dance of daily public life. To Jacobs, the community flourishes because of this ballet that keeps residents' eyes on their neighborhood.

But as I passed through the very street that Jacobs celebrated, I could not help but think about how different it seemed from her depictions decades ago. Many of the homes that line the North End are not owner occupied but are occupied by second homeowners, multiple-property owners, Airbnb owners, or some combination of those three. The Waterfront is lined with luxury hotels and with condos whose lights are off most of the year. The proprietors of the street are no longer only the people who live there; they are also the concierge. The North End has become an entertainment machine, a world-renowned tourist destination that glorifies its working-class Italian American history and capitalizes on its proximity to cultural institutions and historic landmarks. The cast of characters there changes daily. I saw tourists lined up at Mike's Pastry. I listened to passersby pull suitcases that rumbled across the streets. And I watched visitors stand on the curb, waiting for their Uber to take them to their next destination. The sidewalk ballet has transformed into a cacophony of transience.

The Nazzaro Community Center is located in a beautiful brick building that hosts a range of the North End's community services and programming for children and elderly alike. When I made it to the center, I shut the door and the noise of the busy street quieted as I walked into the lobby, stepping into the backstage world of the North End. Here, I waited for the meeting to begin shoulder to shoulder with twenty or so neighborhood residents who were talking familiarly with one another. As we bumped shoulders, I struck up a conversation with a white woman in her seventies named Terry, dressed in a simple blue sweater and jeans, face adorned with only a muted shade of red lipstick. She was surprised and excited to see such a young face at the meeting (at the time, I was twenty-seven) and asked if I lived in the neighborhood. I explained to her that I did not, that I lived in Jamaica Plain and was doing a project on second homeowners, who I knew concentrated in pockets of the North End. She didn't know much about second homeowners but relayed a great deal of neighborhood concern about the North End's waterfront, where, she noted, 'luxury buildings are being built without regard for the community or sea-level rise.'

Our conversation was interrupted as the doors to the meeting hall opened. I followed Terry inside, and we sat down together at one of the many tables spread throughout the room. She introduced me to Margaret, also a white woman in her early seventies wearing jeans and a plain crewneck sweatshirt, who was already seated. Margaret had lived in the North End since the 1970s. Terry filled her in on my project, and Margaret told me that there was a big 'symbolic divide' between the North End and the Waterfront, even though they are part of the same ward and technically considered the same neighborhood. Terry and Margaret turned to each other, reminiscing about life in the North End in the 1970s. Neither could believe that anyone would want to build or buy a condo on an old fish pier, and neither could believe the exorbitant cost of these new developments that were increasing prices everywhere for families who wanted to move or stay in the neighborhood. Turning back to me, Margaret said, with some urgency, 'You need to know about the Lewis Wharf developments. With each new hotel that goes up on the Waterfront, they skirt the zoning laws that prohibit residences from being on the wharfs by including condos as part of their hotels.' Margaret was referring to places like Battery Wharf, a combination hotel/residence luxury development project built in the early 2000s, now proximate to the harbor walk, waterfront taxi service, and outdoor dining.

No sooner had Margaret mentioned the wharf than another woman sat at our table wearing a button with an X though "Lewis Wharf." Carrie, in her forties and smartly dressed in slacks and an oxford shirt, had brought three clipboards with a petition to sign protesting the Lewis Wharf Hotel construction. 'They may need to open Gillette Stadium with all of the push-back against it,' she said of an upcoming Boston Redevelopment Authority meeting on the matter.[2] Terry and Margaret signed the petition and nodded in agreement.

The meeting began and Margaret, Terry, and Carrie quieted. The most contentious agenda item was over a property owner who wanted to tear down his building and rebuild it into five new rental apartment units. One abutter was particularly upset about this. They were not objecting to new buildings in general but to this absentee property owner specifically. She brought pictures of trash piled on the owner's roof deck and the graffiti that splashed across the exterior walls. 'If they can't keep up with the property they had, how could they be expected to keep up the new property?' she demanded. At another point in time, residents were troubled over the potential closure of a nursing home that would displace longtime residents to Brighton, a neighborhood on the western edge of the city. State Representative Aaron Michlewitz attended the meeting. He committed to doing whatever he could to prevent the displacement of 'lifelong North End residents, the lifeblood of the community.' Angrily, he told the residents in attendance, 'I don't want a high-priced condo building' taking its place. There were cheers from the audience.

This small glimpse of civic life in the North End captured a lot of its complexity. People like Terry and Margaret were proud to call the North End their home but resented many of the changes they saw every day, particularly as the neighborhood upscaled. Many properties were no longer owner occupied. The waterfront had become partially privatized for tourist consumption. And fears of displacement loomed. The neighborhood was their home, not just a place to visit a few times a year and buy cannoli at Mike's Pastry or ravioli at Giacomo's. It was where people dragged their trash and recycling cans to the curb every week, where parents picked up their children from the after-school program at the community center, and where people decided to age in place. But to many of the second homeowners I met, places like the North End were not really characterized by any of these qualities.

———

A few weekends throughout the year Barbara and her husband will pack their bags and jump on a plane to Boston from their hometown outside of a major metropolitan area in Texas. If their bags are light, when they land at Logan airport they can take the MBTA to Aquarium Station and walk the remaining half mile to their twelve-hundred-square-foot one-bed, one-and-a-half bath $1.2 million condo on the North End waterfront.

Once they get to their condo, they don't like to do much. They prefer to spend a day or two just there, enjoying the view of the water from their living room. "I love the waterfront. . . . We actually just enjoy being in our condo because it's right on the waterfront. We look out and we kind of kick back and relax there. I love being able to look out on the water and see the boats going by. I can sit at my desk and be on my computer looking out the window." When they decide they want to venture out, they can go to dinner in the North End, visit the Institute for Contemporary Art in the Seaport District, or hop on the train to a theater performance downtown.

I asked if she was part of any neighborhood associations. Matter-of-factly, she responded, "No. I really haven't joined any neighborhood associations. Just haven't had time or occasion to." Only recently had Barbara started thinking about neighborhood issues in the North End. Like Margaret and Terry, she objected to the construction of the Lewis Wharf Hotel development project, which she found to be "ill conceived." But she was not really concerned about what the development meant for the neighborhood. If constructed, she said it would have obstructed her view of the harbor. I asked if she had signed the petitions going around. She told me she had not signed the petition but kept a "No Lewis Wharf" sign hung in her window—a window that remained dark for most of the year.

Academics have called into question how best to define *the city*, debating whether size, density, and heterogeneity constitute distinctly urban forms, or whether there is a set of urban processes like globalization and gentrification that make cities of all sizes distinct.[3] Others even question whether such distinctions are relevant in the twenty-first century.[4] The people I met and talked with in Boston made one thing clear: there were only select places that could be called *a city*, and there were distinct features of this *city life*. Yet their definitions of urban life, I learned, were narrow. For the second homeowners in Boston I talked with, the city was not defined by the dive bars, community centers, coffee shops, locally owned businesses, longtime residents, nursing homes, or schools. It was narrowly defined by Matisse's *Carmelina*, the cellos at the Boston Symphony Orchestra, and the roses at the Public Garden. It was primarily high culture. This notion of city life gave them a sense of place they did not find in their hometowns.

———

Understanding how people like Barbara come to understand the city today as a site of high culture and prestige requires tracing the broader transformations of urban life throughout the twentieth century.

During the era of rapid industrialization at the turn of the century, cities in the United States quickly subsumed racialized notions of modernity's "ills," a symbolic and material foil to the white, "pristine," countryside places like Rangeley. As cities grew from mudholes to boundless metropolises, they were characterized by academics and journalists alike as dense, unwieldy, dangerous, and polluted.[5] Cities were also home to a diverse and dense assemblage of new people: capitalists, rural and southern Black migrants, and waves of European immigrants. This heterogeneous mix of people meant new forms of communal life, spatial arrangements, and methods of social differentiation.

In an effort to control and regulate a growing urban population in the early twentieth century, powerful local stakeholders carved out select areas of the city into exclusive spaces of white affluence, high culture, and social prestige.[6] Industrialists and government officials invested in the development of downtowns and universities across the United States, infusing spaces in the central part of the city with ample educational and commercial resources while systematically ignoring poor, non-white neighborhoods. Networks of wealthy, highly educated white families invested in the expansion of high-culture institutions like the symphony and fine arts museums, making access to high culture and this form of social distinction racially and economically exclusionary.[7] And even the development of private parks and other public spaces became a mechanism of spatial divisions, as resident groups and civic leaders excluded poor and minority groups to enhance the value of these spaces for residents in the proximate neighborhoods.[8] Taken together, these neighborhoods in cities, like Beacon Hill in Boston or the Gold Coast in Chicago, served as a spatialized status symbol and a site of institutionalized advantages for the predominantly white urban elite.[9]

The post–World War II period ushered in a reorganization of the spatialization of affluence. This was caused by a confluence of conditions. The federal government provided middle-class white families with access to federally backed home mortgages in the suburbs, which solidified racial segregation between the cities and the suburbs.[10] Cities furthermore lost their economic base as an emergent deregulatory political climate caused factories to find cheaper labor elsewhere to compete in a newly globalizing world, fueling widespread joblessness, a large-scale financial crisis, and an economic vacuum in cities across the United States.[11] In response, federal and city governments made huge cuts to public spending, quickly eroding the social safety net for the predominantly Black and low-income Americans segregated in the city. In the wake of this residential and economic exclusion, the city became *re*-racialized as a Black space, subsuming connotations of crime, disorder, and poverty for the decades that followed.[12]

These changes created a vacuum that municipalities scrambled to fill with other forms of revenue to solve the financial and "image" crisis.[13] Throughout the 1970s and beyond, instead of solving the actual urban crisis of poverty, joblessness, and homelessness, many places tried to rebrand themselves in an attempt to attract white middle-class tourists, consumers, and homeowners back to the city.[14] Local governments created tourism departments, funneled money into advertisements and branding agencies, and encouraged private-public partnerships in an attempt to brand and sell a city as a *destination*. And these efforts were effective. As a result of this intensive rebranding effort, cities became viewed as a valued authentic experience for middle- and upper-class consumers—places where they could dine and shop and enjoy a show for a day or weekend.[15]

These strategies were so effective that toward the latter part of the twentieth century, white middle-class and upper-class people not only started to visit the city; they wanted to live there again.[16] Scholars and journalists alike have tried to capture the variety of cultural and economic reasons behind the out-migration of affluent white people from the suburbs back to the city, a process linked to gentrification. Some wish to live a lifestyle they perceive to be more authentic. Others want proximity to work and affordable housing.[17] The result was that cities became revalued by middle-class and upper-middle-class people, prompting decades of neighborhood change and churn.

These broader transformations have altered the available location of retreat and financial gain for those with extra time and money to spend. While many financially comfortable middle- and upper-class Americans continue to spend their vacations on the lakes or coast, many now opt for urban areas for leisure.[18] They can attend art museums, experience historic districts, shop along commercial streets and avenues, stroll through lively parks, and dine at an array of trendy restaurants. This is because cities have strategically tried to harness the consumption practices of white upper and middle classes. That the city became re-racialized as white is a precondition for the people I met to see it as a site of leisure and consumption.[19] These changes foreground the urban second home as not just a financial transaction in real estate but a cultural endeavor. It allows its owners to seek out a specific kind of culture, and a distinctly urban lifestyle they value.[20] The pursuit of this lifestyle was enabled by the economic and cultural transformations of the twenty-first century that made the city a *destination*, a place made for and by white upper-middle-class consumption.

In the chapters that follow, I explore how the people I met are tied to these transformations. In chapter 6, I first ask what it means for the people I met to have a place identity tied to the city, how this place identity provides them with a justification for their social-class practices, and how their notions of place are dependent on spatial inequalities in Boston. In chapter 7, I trace how the everyday and philanthropic practices of the people I met are linked to Boston's broader place-making project reliant on high-culture institutions, which have a heavy hand in shaping neighborhood character in the city. In chapter 8, I explore how the second homeowners I met contribute to what city leaders call high-end blight, a process that exacerbates housing unaffordability and undermines neighborhood cohesion. Altogether, these chapters capture how privilege mediates urbanism, place, and identity.

6

City Mouse

A High-Cultural Milieu

In my interview with Doris Flynn, she acknowledged that she and Richard would likely be spending more time in Boston since Richard's retirement. "I'm a city mouse," she declared. "More and more we're feeling very attached to the city place." I was at once intrigued by her identification as a "city mouse." The idiom derives from Aesop's fable about two cousin mice who lead diametrically opposed lives in the city and the country. When the town mouse visits the country mouse, he turns up his nose at his cousin's simple country lifestyle. He insists the country mouse follow him back to the city to experience a world of refinement and opulence, how he ought to live. Their urban dinner is quickly interrupted by the house cat who chases them away. After this encounter, the country mouse decides to leave, declaring "better beans and bacon in peace than cakes and ale in fear."[1] While this fable is meant to highlight the morality of simplicity and precarity of abundance, "town mouse" and "country mouse" have come to serve as analogies for place identity in everyday life. As with idioms, such identification has shed much of its original meaning. However, for the second homeowners I talked to in Boston, fragments of this original story have endured.

Others did not explicitly draw on Aesop's fable; however, Doris was not alone in employing the city to describe herself. Karen and her husband were recent empty nesters, giving them more time on their hands. I asked why they chose a second home in a city. She explained, "At this point in our life, [owning a second home in Boston] gives us access to things that we are interested in. We are both urbanites to begin with." Others located part of themselves in city life. Eva moved out of the city when she got married and had children but could not let go of her two-bedroom Boston apartment in the South End. She kept it "to stay connected to the city . . . to keep at least one toe in the city." Holding onto an apartment was a way to hold onto city life.

At its core, proximity to certain parts of urban places allowed the people I talked with to accomplish their *city selves,* a localized place-identity project that draws on attributes, meanings, and practices they associated with the city. Although cities are material places with transit access, jobs, and housing, the personally held, cultural notions of cities are always contested and multiple given one's social location. Being a "city mouse" for the people I met meant to live a life of high-culture refinement. And the sense of place that the people I talked to seek was tied to particular notions of what a city lifestyle entails, rooted in affiliation with high-culture institutions, cosmopolitanism, and proximity to socially prestigious, super-gentrified neighborhoods.

This orientation to city life became evident as I set up interviews. I had hoped to interview Boston second homeowners in their actual second homes to get a sense of their daily routines, practices, and lifestyles, like I had done in Rangeley. But this proved to be quite challenging. In my initial email exchange with Richard and Doris Flynn, for instance, they asked if I could interview them over the phone or FaceTime. They told me they had a lot of upcoming travel and likely would not be able to meet me in Boston until months later. For expediency's sake, I agreed to talk with them over the phone.

I learned over the course of our interview that, to my surprise, Doris was actually in Boston that day. She had decided on a whim to go into the city after attending a friend's birthday party in Rhode Island, before taking off to visit her daughter for a week in Florida. On the one day she was in Boston, she planned to sneak in a quick trip to the Museum of Fine Arts to attend the lecture course she had been taking for the past month. Given this tight schedule, she simply did not have time to have me over to her home.

Second homeowners I met in Rangeley readily invited me into their homes, offered baked goods, and often blocked off entire afternoons for my visits so we could sit together on their back porches enjoying the view. The second homeowners I talked to in Boston, however, not only were much more difficult to find but, once I found them, were much more difficult to talk to in person. Their lives seemed much more hurried and their schedules full of cultural events and activities. My experiences with the Flynns were characteristic of my interactions with nearly all second homeowners in Boston. I spoke with almost all of them over the phone, often from long distances, because they could not be sure about setting a time to meet me in person. Dan, a top-level executive of a tech firm from the South Shore, only blocked off select holidays or sporadic weekends to spend time in Boston. Eva, a busy stay-at-home mom from a Boston suburb, dipped her toe in the city when a show at the theater or art exhibit at the MFA caught her eye. And when they were in Boston, their agendas were full. On the day I interviewed Thomas, a real estate tycoon from Arizona, he was hosting friends from out of town, spending the day touring Boston's iconic sites before dinner at Island Creek Oyster.

Yet these very methodological problems were revealing for the ways they understood themselves in the city and defined city life. When I asked Karen what drew her to the city, her response was brief and rapid—almost staccato: "Our lifestyle revolves around the arts. Theater. Museums. Lecture. Travel. The city life is great for us." The style and content of her answer aligned with many of my informants' understanding of their *city selves*—being an urban person meant they were fast-paced, high-cultured, and cosmopolitan. Their days in Boston were not slow, leisurely, or relaxed, and they did not have time for a long, detailed conversation as did the people I met in Rangeley. Many would often visit Boston for a few days at a time, so they spent their time expeditiously, floating between neighborhoods in the central part of the city, touching down to consume as many high-cultural spaces as they could during their limited time in town.

These very engagements furthermore informed how many conceptualized the city. For instance, Doris relayed that there is "something about the city that just speaks to [her]."[2] However, when I asked her to elaborate, she explained that the "cultural institutions . . . museums, plays, art exhibits, music, theater" were what spoke to her. To many of the people I talked with, the city was Culture. It was large-scale, elite, high-cultural institutions like the Museum of Fine Arts and the symphony. And being in the city meant primarily engaging with these spheres of social life.

The choice of where to buy a second home within Boston clarified their bounded definitions of the city. Boston is typically understood as a city of neighborhoods, a mosaic in which each area of the city contains its own distinct style, milieu, and reputation. It is also highly racially segregated. Thus, to experience *city life* means something different in different neighborhoods.

Allston is known for its density of college students and hipster scene; its buildings and overpasses are peppered with graffiti as a signal of its "grittiness."[3] Jamaica Plain is known for its artists and longtime Hispanic community and as a LGBTQ enclave; its main streets are known for its bodegas like Pimentel Market and bars like the Brendan Behan and Bella Luna.[4] Roxbury is known as the heart of Black culture and community in Boston; it has a long history of community activism and boasts a density of minority-owned local businesses.[5] The people I met, who had enough capital to live wherever they wanted among Boston's distinct neighborhoods, called upon past, archetypal knowledge of what the city was and which neighborhoods best represented this memory to decide where they wanted to be within this mosaic. The neighborhoods they ultimately chose had reputations as affluent, predominantly white, and prestigious. Tracy elaborated:

> To me, Back Bay and Beacon Hill is sort of quintessential Boston. When I was in college, which was the last time I lived there, that was always the big fun thing to me, was to go into the city and that's what I thought of as the city . . . I love the Common and going and sitting on the benches and . . . getting that sense of history and place.

For Tracy, the decision of where she and her husband would purchase a second home fell squarely upon their idea of which neighborhoods best represented Boston and gave her a "sense of place." In the end, they purchased an 1,800-square-foot duplex in a brownstone built in the 1900s, which sits upon a picturesque tree-lined street in Back Bay. It had been completely gutted and renovated, preserving original moldings while adding new upgrades like stainless steel appliances and a wine bar. Bruce was a bit more direct about the lure of particular neighborhoods in Boston:

> I guess Back Bay was always our first choice just because of the neighborhood feel, the charm, and the central location. I think, at least our perception, that crime is less of an issue there. . . . It's hard to point to one specific thing. I guess if we're thinking of one thing over everything else . . . it would be just the prestige of living in Back Bay.

Bruce and Joyce bought a renovated condo in a full-service brownstone on Back Bay's Beacon Street, outfitted with classic bay windows that overlook the street and a roof deck with views of Prudential Tower. To them, this neighborhood was *prestigious*. It was not trendy, gritty, bohemian, diverse, authentic, or gentrifying, neighborhood characteristics that sociologists have found attract some affluent in-migrants to neighborhoods across the country.[6] Back Bay is known for its unique architecture and ties to Boston's upper class.[7] It is also a destination, an iconic place in Boston where visitors and residents alike stroll along the Charles River esplanade and shop at stores like Chanel and Cartier on Newbury Street.

Bridget, too, sought out a specific milieu in Boston for her second home: "[Beacon Hill] was the feeling of Boston that we wanted: the brick town home feeling and the most residential streets." She explained the process of finding a second home in the central part of the city. She first looked in parts of Back Bay: "We did look at some properties over by the symphony area," she reasoned, "because that's really becoming more gentrified." I learned that most of the people I met were like Bridget. The sense of place they valued was found in neighborhoods that they perceived to be gentri*fied*, not gentri*fying*.

Bridget eventually settled on a small one-bedroom condo on a narrow street in Beacon Hill, one of the most highly affluent and prestigious already-gentrified neighborhoods in the city lined with cobblestones and gas lamps. While only five hundred square feet and a quarter of the price of Tracy's duplex, the unit came equipped with a roof deck that overlooked the downtown skyline. Beacon Hill is known for its exclusiveness as a home for Boston's political and cultural elites. Its history celebrates its claim to being home to famous literary writers of the early twentieth century like Robert Frost, Sylvia Plath, and Robert Lowell, the Boston Brahmins, and present-day global elites like former U.S. secretary of state John Kerry.[8]

Some urban researchers refer to the different waves of gentrification to understand and explain how it unfolds differently over time and place and the degree to which different actors, including private developers, the state, everyday in-migrants, and finance, influence the pace and scale of the process.[9] The people I met were clear that the sense of place they desired was found only in neighborhoods characterized by what Loretta Lees refers to as *super-gentrification*. This is typically defined by the replacement of the middle classes by affluent professionals or the super-rich in already-gentrified neighborhoods.[10]

Super-gentrification happens when already-renovated condos are upgraded with top-of-the-line features, when luxury condominium towers replace multifamily housing, or when new cocktail lounges buy out neighborhood pubs. The neighborhood upscales; its housing, commercial establishments, and amenities change to match the new upper-class milieu. There is a corresponding change in the social class of people who populate the neighborhood and the amount of money they are willing to pay for housing.

Populations change from the middle class to the upper middle class and superrich. This upscaling pushes middle-class and even some upper-middle-class people deeper into other neighborhoods in search of more affordable housing or preferred lifestyles. This churn spurs gentrification in previously disinvested neighborhoods, where the cycle of displacement begins again.[11]

For the people I talked with, who were oriented toward high-culture institutions, Boston was Beacon Hill's gas lamps and brick sidewalks, Back Bay's brownstones, and downtown's proximity to iconic cultural sites, such as the Boston Common.[12] To them, Boston was defined by the affluent, prestigious neighborhoods that have "charm." The second homeowners I talked with sought out the city's most historic, prestigious, and archetypical super-gentrified neighborhoods, which were proximate to sites of high culture. This is what they associated with the city, and ultimately what they associated with themselves.

High Culture as a Moral Preserve

Buying a second home in a neighborhood with a prestigious and affluent reputation did more than provide the people I met with proximity to cultural institutions and an urban milieu they valued. Affiliation with high culture in the city served as a site of social-class legitimation; it placed distance between themselves and more ostentatious elites, whose practices they perceived to be less morally deserving than their own. High culture in the city was their *moral preserve*, a social landscape they framed as more authentic than the conspicuous social-class interests of other urban elites.[13]

Many of the people I met talked about how much they valued the high-culture lifestyles they fashioned in Boston, particularly compared to the lifestyles they had in their hometowns.[14] For instance, Jonathan was clear that when he retired, he "wanted to complement the lifestyle that I had in Texas. I'm not in a rural area, but I'm about thirty miles north of a large city and I have a house on the river with a fifteen-mile unobstructed view to the north. I wanted something to complement that and to experience city life . . . the clear differentiation in lifestyles that I was looking for." I asked for him to elaborate what these different lifestyles entailed. He explained:

> Our place in Texas, if I want to go to the nearest grocery store, it's a thirteen-mile drive. . . . We live in an eighty-seven-hundred-acre golf club community, so when we're there, we tend to go up to the country club and spend some time once or twice a week with friends there or participate in

the country club. For example, in Texas where you get up and decide, "Am I going to go out to eat tonight or am I going to go down to a local market and buy something and fix it at my place?" . . . And for example [in Boston] we got here on Saturday. We went to a concert at the hatch shell last night. We go to the Boston Symphony Tuesday night. We go to a play over on Washington Street on Wednesday night. We go to a hockey game with her sister on Saturday night and then mid next week, we fly back to Texas.

Jonathan's life in Texas was, to him, more suburban, mundane, and predictable. His days revolved around a long drive to the country club, a round of golf, and dinner at home or at a restaurant. But in Boston, his life was more fast-paced and varied. Each day of the week he experienced something new and different; he experienced more *culture*. The pursuit of this sort of lifestyle distinction is often understood to be a method of social closure for elites, a way to solidify and maintain social-class boundaries as people generate exclusive forms of knowledge as they traverse museums, theater, and the symphony.[15] But I found that affiliation with the city and culture also provided the people in Boston I met with a tool to justify their social class and assuage their class consciousness. It was a source of identity they found legitimate.[16]

Many of the people I met like Jonathan used the city as a playground, a place where they could enact their city selves and escape the perceived banality of suburban life. Yet at the same time, they used this high-culture lifestyle to distance themselves from people they viewed as real elites who engaged in more dubious lifestyle choices. This was most evident during my interview with Dan, when he and I engaged in a conversation about my broader project comparing Rangeley and Boston. He had been to Rangeley before and noted that he had heard the term "from away" to describe some of the second homeowners there. He pivoted to discuss the types of "from aways" that he had observed in Boston. He explained, chidingly,

> There are a number of people, especially in the upper unit of our building, the penthouses and stuff where these people have. . . . That's their Boston house. They have a Paris house. They have places in Mexico. You get a little bit of that too, where the people are there for a month or two. There's some people out there with a lot of money.

Dan lived permanently in the South Shore and did not conceive of himself as a "from away" in Boston, nor did he place himself in the category of someone "out there with a lot of money." Instead, Dan spent his vacation days in Boston, where he would meander through the Museum of Fine Arts, attend a theater performance, or dine out in the North End. He framed his connection to Boston as more authentic compared to people who jet-set around the world to and from their multiple penthouse suites. Others I met similarly pointed to multimillion-dollar condominium transactions or purchases of parking spaces that cost more than most of their own second homes as an example of a new sort of urban ostentation. The superrich provided a foil for the people in Boston I talked with, helping them articulate their everyday practices in the city as comparably *respectable*.

I noticed this boundary work in particular with people who owned a second home in Boston and lived permanently in other second-home destinations. Beth lived in a wealthy coastal town in Massachusetts and derided the types of highly affluent second homeowners and vacationers who increasingly dominated her hometown. She explained:

> [It] has exploded. . . . It's gotten to be a place of mega mansions and people come to party. It's kind of funny because when you read some of the reviews in the *New York Times* or something it's about the restaurants or the social scene. Someone wrote an article in the paper saying it's not about the history or the museums. . . . They're still there and they're still important, but you don't have it as a focus as why people come there now. The restaurants, the partying, the wannabe scene, and the capability to say, "I have a home [in the wealthy community]." I don't like a lot of them . . . [it] goes with that a lot of self-importance.

These garish displays of wealth and self-importance were set in stark contrast to Beth's own everyday practices. Proximity to culture provided moral grounding, distance from other more dubious forms of second homeownership by the superrich, like those motivated by conspicuous consumption or exclusive financial gain. Such "class-blind" narratives allowed them to ignore and justify their own privileged lifestyle choices, in which they used the city as their high-cultural playground.[17]

Much has been written about elites' proximity to nature as a moral position, a way to feel better about wealth and to provide some distance from social-class interests. Nature conjures up notions of community and hard work.[18] Justin Farrell has written extensively about this process with regard to the world's superrich. They use proximity to nature and rural people in Teton County, Wyoming, to solve their ethical dilemmas in a world of extreme wealth inequality. Even the second homeowners I met in Rangeley used affiliation with nature to assuage their class conscience. Nature has long been constructed by white elites as removed from the interests of capitalism, framed as a more morally conscionable affiliation.[19] The second homeowners I talked to in Boston highlighted the multiple places elites use to solve these dilemmas. The people I met found proximity to high culture in the city as a source of legitimate identity.[20] It was their moral preserve, a place and social location they viewed as removed from egregious forms of capitalist interests. It was used as a source of *deservingness* about wealth and consumption patterns of second homeownership if set in contrast to the lifestyles of other elites whom they viewed as more ostentatious. It was a site of legitimation for social-class power.[21]

On Neighborhood Valuation and Spatial Inequalities

This sense of place identity—the value the people I met gave to and took from certain neighborhoods—was not neutral or benign. For some neighborhoods in Boston to be socially prestigious, high-cultured, and super-gentrified *depended* on processes that have deepened spatial inequality in Boston. Their identity projects were reliant on both the strategic revaluation of the central part of the city that has made it a place for white middle-class and upper-middle-class consumption *and* the simultaneous devaluation of majority-Black neighborhoods. Taken together, their sense of place was connected to processes that have made Boston one of the most economically bifurcated and racially segregated cities in the country.[22]

First, a note on neighborhoods and valuation. In recent years, there has been a push among sociologists to explicitly theorize neighborhood change as a process of racial capitalism.[23] This involves analyzing how *race* defines the symbolic and material value of any *place*, in which capital investments in a given neighborhood depend on how it is defined within the racial hierarchy. Racial capitalism helps explain the uneven development of neighborhoods within cities; neighborhoods that are racialized as white have witnessed decades of investments from the state and private actors, while neighborhoods racialized as Black have witnessed decades of *dis*investment. For the people I talked with, the sense of place they find in super-gentrified neighborhoods relied on historic and contemporary processes of neighborhood valuation that have funneled money and resources into central-city neighborhoods racialized as white, in which state- and private-sector-led efforts strategically divested these areas from associations as poor, non-white, and disorderly. This is simultaneously reliant on the devaluation of areas of the city racialized as Black, in which state and private interests denied these areas access to the very resources the central city secured.

Central-city neighborhoods are where the people I met, and second homeowners as a whole, are more likely to buy second homes.[24] The people I talked with valued these areas of the city for their proximity to high-culture institutions and social prestige. For these neighborhoods to have these social meanings required decades of state and private interests altering the area's place reputation to attract people like them: middle- and upper-middle-class consumers. These areas are where the city focused its most intensive urban renewal efforts to alter its culture, demographics, and topography—demolishing the tenement buildings that housed poor immigrants in the West End to build new condominium units, razing downtown's Scully Square that was home to Boston's diverse red-light district to make way for the new Government Center, and bulldozing "blighted" streets in Boston's South End to fashion a superblock for new commerce.[25] These areas are where, in the aftermath of these "renewal" efforts, the city allocated a significant portion of its budget to encourage further development projects.[26] And these are the areas where the middle class and private developers followed, converting apartments to condominium units and older retail spaces into luxury hotels and upscale dining. Together, these processes have propelled the area into late stages of gentrification today.[27]

Mark, a second homeowner in the South End, provided a paradigmatic case of how these changes have created the type of urban place he valued. Mark lived in Boston during his college years and was excited to return as a second homeowner, watching from afar Boston change drastically over the past twenty years. He and his wife had originally intended to look at homes in Back Bay, a highly affluent neighborhood proximate to downtown they had lived in originally, until his daughter convinced him to look at parts of the South End that have undergone significant changes over the past few decades.[28] "We had intended to be in Back Bay, which is where we lived," he elaborated. "We left in the early 1980s. The South End was really a bad neighborhood, and our daughter convinced us after we visited her that we should look at real estate in the South End." After he toured the neighborhood, they changed their minds, and the rest is history. "The South End continues to get better and better," he noticed. "More restaurants keep opening. It gets safer. More buildings turn over. There's real gentrification going on still." I asked Mark to elaborate what changes he has seen:

> The city is doing remarkably well. The development . . . has just been incredible for the city I thought. I'm sure there are always things that could be done better but the city of Boston, when we left town, the

elevated southeast expressway came through the waterfront. We watched that happen. We watched the new garden go up. The explosion of hotels has been crazy. We didn't buy really for an investment because this is a retirement. It's always good that you buy something that appreciates as opposed to going backward but the appreciation has been phenomenal. The city focuses on neighborhoods . . . even that Washington Street corridor downtown Boston, which is finally starting to improve. That was bad for so long. That's even started to look good finally. I think they pay attention to architecture, they pay attention to the neighborhoods, to walking. Love how the city has maintained for what, a couple hundred years now, the [Boston] Common and the Public Garden.

Many of the people in Boston I spoke with mentioned gentrification when describing how they chose certain neighborhoods, yet this meant something very specific: they expressed value for the strategic public-private efforts that rebranded certain central-city neighborhoods into spaces for upper-middle-class consumption.

Others pointed to the turnover in people as what makes parts of Boston the city that it is to them. Stan bought his home in Jamaica Plain (JP) in the 1980s as a primary residence and hung onto it as a second home when work took him elsewhere. He has watched it change from afar and has kept the second home as a "cultural investment." This cultural investment for him, however, relied on the out-migration of working-class and non-white residents from the neighborhood. He noted that JP

> has been completely reformed and we have a different culture, a different group of people living in it. It's still quite highly diverse, but we have a much better income mix than we had thirty years ago [when he first lived in Boston]. . . . What we've noticed is our street has gone from old residents, generally speaking, working class to a mix of undergraduate student renters, to highly professional, relative upper-income people working in the medical programs and the universities in a variety of activities.

The cultural value of the neighborhood was linked to who occupied it and processes that have spurred residential turnover have increased this value for the people I talked with. Divesting these areas from their connotations as non-white, disorderly, and poor, and subsequently upscaling it, is what has crafted the type of neighborhood that the people I met valued and considered "quintessential" Boston. It was what had provided them with a sense of place.

However, I learned that this process of valuing only certain neighborhoods is necessarily relational with devaluing others. As Sarah Mayorga and colleagues argue, "To choose to invest in one space is, by definition, a decision to not invest elsewhere."[29] The upscaling of central-city neighborhoods came at the direct expense of majority-Black neighborhoods in Boston that have been subjected to decades of institutional neglect and state-led policies that denied access to home and commercial mortgages, to connected transportation routes, and to vital educational resources.[30] While state and private actors concentrated resources in majority-white neighborhoods proximate to downtown, majority-Black and majority-brown neighborhoods have had to fight for access to resources like transit, affordable housing, and investments in businesses.[31]

The identity projects of the people I talked with mapped onto these processes that continue to both financially and symbolically devalue majority-Black neighborhoods. Many people cited pull factors that have made certain neighborhoods in Boston places they valued, themes I covered above. But some were more explicit about the push factors that kept them away from certain areas of the city. They strategically forwent investment potential in gentrifying areas to *avoid* neighborhoods racialized as Black.[32]

The people I met were willing to pay more to buy into neighborhoods in late stages of gentrification to place distance between themselves and majority-Black neighborhoods like Dorchester and Roxbury. Bruce, for instance, a self-identified conservative from Texas, didn't know much about the reputations of Boston neighborhoods. However, he quickly learned by reading newspaper articles and online forums that tracked crime statistics. He did not consider any neighborhoods in South Boston near Dorchester or parts of the South End below Tremont Street near Roxbury that were gentrifying because of his perception of crime in the area—even if it were economically advantageous to do so. He ultimately decided to spend more money purchasing a second home in Back Bay. He mused, "It seemed like just . . . you pay more in Back Bay, and you get more."

Even though Patricia, a liberal, former teacher, lived in the Boston suburbs, she also was not too familiar with Boston's distinct neighborhoods. But she knew where she didn't want to be:

We were also looking at the South End, but I think . . . There are a lot of bargains there but sometimes they're in an area that's not as desirable or close to other areas that are not, that are kind of sketchy, so I just kind of looked on the map where it was and how close to like Dorchester and

I don't know what else, East Roxbury, and . . . there are parts of [the South End] that are just really beautiful and charming and so I thought it might be a nice area, but maybe, if it's kind of closer to Back Bay and that section.

Eventually, Patricia decided to spend more money to purchase a second home in Beacon Hill, one of the city's most expensive, majority-white, and upscale neighborhoods, rather than what she considered to be a bargain near majority-Black Dorchester.

This aligns with a great deal of research that shows that more-affluent urban in-migrants tend to purchase in neighborhoods in later stages of gentrification, as opposed to middle-class in-migrants who are more likely to buy homes in more racially and economically diverse areas of the city.[33] I found, however, that it is not only that the upper-middle-class residents I talked with valued upscale neighborhoods and had the money to buy into them. In this case, it was that they simultaneously devalued non-white neighborhoods and used their capital to express this. They would rather pay more to avoid majority-Black neighborhoods, making calculated decisions to steer their searches away from more racially and economically diverse neighborhoods even if they could capitalize on investment potential. Instead, they concentrated their capital in already-upscale parts of the city. This contributes to our understanding of how and why super-gentrification happens. Super-gentrification is not simply about the social meanings that upper-middle-class people give to neighborhoods with reputations as high-cultural, upscale, and socially prestigious—it is more than proximity to amenities and luxury housing. For some affluent in-migrants, the social meanings they give to *other* neighborhoods also explain where they fall within a given urban mosaic: *avoiding* areas racialized as Black.

In the end, to think of Beacon Hill or Back Bay as prestigious and Roxbury or Dorchester as sketchy, or to celebrate razing entire neighborhoods to pave the way for new development projects, or to explain neighborhood progress as the displacement of Black and brown people, means that the identity projects of the people I met were dependent on the historic and contemporary processes that funneled money and resources into only certain parts of the city while simultaneously denying it to other places. The source of their place identity—the value they *gave to* and *got from* neighborhoods that shaped how they situated themselves in a socio-spatial environment— derived from processes that have deepened spatial inequality in Boston.

7

A Brahmin Ethos

Boston's Public Garden is a National Historic Landmark located downtown, just west of the Boston Common and flanked by some of the city's most iconic streets: Beacon, Charles, Arlington, and Boylston.[1] Visitors to the garden can stroll through the rows of lush elm trees, marvel at the statue of George Washington, take a swan-boat ride through the park's lagoon, or take a picture next to the duckling statues, a tribute to Robert McCloskey's famous children's book *Make Way for Ducklings*. The garden is public but cared for through a private-public partnership between the city and Friends of the Public Garden, an organization that has become a steward of the public spaces downtown: the Public Garden, the Common, and the Commonwealth Mall.[2]

From the Public Garden, you can walk or take the T a short trip down Huntington Avenue to Symphony Hall, home to the Boston Symphony Orchestra (BSO). Built in the early 1900s with a brick facade and imposing columns, the hall serves as the eastern bookend for Boston's Avenue of the Arts. Just a short walk down Huntington Avenue is the Museum of Fine Arts (MFA), a large granite building that stretches across the middle of the Fenway Cultural District. The walk between the BSO and the MFA has changed in recent years. The sidewalks have been expanded, more trees have been planted, and T stations have improved. These efforts are the product of the Fenway Alliance, a public-private partnership, made up of institutions like the MFA and BSO, committed to the beautification and cultural enhancement of the avenue and surrounding neighborhoods.[3]

These are the places where Joyce volunteered helping to plant roses, where Tracy sat alone quietly on a park bench taking in a sense of place, and where Richard and Doris strolled on their way to an evening theater performance or a morning lecture at the MFA. And these are the institutions they helped support. In this chapter, I move from the everyday practices of the people I met to the broader patterns of change in Boston. I first explore their liability to the community, in which they expressed a disconnect with most aspects of community life not associated with their sense of place—high culture. I then connect their support of high-culture institutions to Boston's broader place-making strategy that relies on using art and culture to sell itself to the world. I end by exploring the consequences for urban people and places when high-culture institutions are empowered in a city's place-making project.

Proprietors of Culture

Living less than an hour away from Boston in a suburb just north of the city, John liked to "pop in every now and then" to his home in the city. I asked if he involved himself in aspects of neighborhood or city life—local politics, community projects, and so on. He abruptly responded, "No because I don't live there. And I let the people that live there make those decisions. Basically, I live up here in [the suburb north of the city], so I'm more connected to this area." This was an underlying theme across all the people I talked with in Rangeley and Boston. They did not see themselves as being part of community in the typical sense in the places where they owned second homes. By and large, they did not attend community meetings, participate in the PTA, vote in local elections, or build local social ties. In fact, maintaining limited liability to most aspects of community life in Boston was a central feature of the practices associated with their place-identity projects, primarily investing in the parts of Boston they associated with their sense of place—high-culture institutions. Such community engagements build on a long-standing place-making project in which affluent people fund cultural institutions to help construct their image of city life and themselves.

The lifestyles the people I met craft in the city did not allow them the time to engage in most aspects of community life in Boston. Dan, who owned a condo in a professionally managed building in the Financial District, quite succinctly summed up their general relationship with Boston's civic and political life: "[I'm] not really [involved] . . . I'm not there. It's not easy for me to make a Tuesday night meeting in the city. I don't do a lot." Like Dan, many acknowledged the difficulties of living between two, or sometimes three, different places. The lifestyle simply did not afford them the time to keep up with, let alone engage with, Boston's civic and political sphere.

Because of their highly transient lifestyles, most of the second homeowners I spoke with in Boston did not develop locally based social ties. What ties they did maintain in the city itself tended to be instrumental in nature. Many cited knowing their neighbors minimally through condo associations, maybe having a glass of wine on the roof deck if they happened to be in town; some noted developing a relationship with the concierge of their building to keep an eye on things while they are away. However, most reported no strong social connections in Boston. Or as Maggie explained, "We have no friends in the city."

Rather than developing ties *within* the city, the second homeowners I talked to in Boston, like second homeowners in Rangeley, brought their ties from their personal networks with them to Boston, and often from their permanent residence. For instance, Dan had started the tradition of renting out units in the hotel next to his second home during holidays so friends and family can visit and enjoy the city with him and his family. Jonathan had his neighbors from his first home in Texas stay with him and his wife to join them in the activities they typically participated in, like going to the theater, visiting museums, and dining out. They invited people to join them as they curated their city self.

Yet I learned that it was not only that the people I met did not feel they had the time to engage in more community-based activities; their limited orientation was a central feature of the sense of place they find and construct in Boston. Some relished not having social ties or community obligations. Doris explained that "a big strong factor, particularly . . . for Richard [her husband] is anonymity. He finds that anonymity in the city. Some people . . . find it out in the remote countryside but we find it in the city." Dan elaborated on this idea: "When you're home, there's always something that you feel obligated to be doing. When you're in the condo, there's nothing . . . we go out on the Greenway, read a book, read a magazine." Boston was not a place where most of the people I met went to work, sent their children to school, or even made friends. Boston was where they expressed feeling freed from civic responsibility, from liability to community life. It was where they could indulge in the kind of lifestyles they did not have in their hometowns.

Despite their not being involved in community life in the typical sense, like developing local social ties or participating in community institutions and organizations, they nonetheless expressed liability to selective parts of

Boston. They participated in, consumed, and donated to high-culture institutions, reifying the images they held of the city—a site of social prestige
and high culture.[4] This was best captured by Doris:

> We'll go to a movie, we'll go to the theater, maybe the Huntington The-
> atre, and see a play, we'll go out to dinner, have friends into the city.
> [We're members] of the Museum of Fine Arts, so I've been taking a
> [lecture] course this past month. Tomorrow I'm going to a lecture on
> the new exhibit that just opened on the Japanese painter Hokusai. I'll do
> a couple of errands in the Back Bay, and then I'll either drive or hop on
> the T up to the Museum of Fine Arts, make my way back.

These engagements at first seemed mundane. But in interview after interview, I listened to people like Doris explain similar overlapping rounds of
activities: the Museum of Fine Arts by day, the symphony or Huntington
Theatre by night. Jonathan similarly detailed his week: "We got here on Saturday. We went to a concert at the Wilbur last night. We go to the Boston
Symphony Tuesday night. We got to a play over on Washington Street on
Wednesday night . . . and then mid next week, we fly back to Texas." They
often talked about these engagements quite casually as well. Most relayed to
me, as Maggie noted, "There's no methodical schedule to [when they visit
Boston] whatsoever." But, as she explained further, her local engagements
were similarly quite patterned:

> We sometimes go down for specific events. Particularly theater . . .
> Lyric Stage, the Huntington, the BCA. . . . We'll go out to restaurants;
> we became members of the MFA. . . . We like concerts, we were at the
> Boston Book Festival recently, and sometimes we don't have any agenda
> whatsoever. We just go down to see what's going on. We really enjoy
> walking, so we'll walk all over the city, we'll walk across the Mass Ave.
> bridge or the Longfellow to Cambridge. Just kind of enjoying whatever
> happens to be going on.

While no one I talked with expressed maintaining more traditional ties to
community in Boston, they spent their time in cultural institutions that
spanned a group of neighborhoods across the central part of the city.

Some enjoyed volunteering for historic sites when they had time. Joyce,
a master gardener, planned to volunteer at the rose beds in the Public Garden, an important historic cultural destination nestled next to the Boston
Common in the heart of downtown.[5] Others volunteered for the Freedom
Trail Foundation; the Freedom Trail is a historic walking tour that traces

Boston's quintessential revolutionary history. Many were members of different organizations and societies, such as the MFA, the BSO, and the Handel and Haydn Society. There were other people I talked with who could work remotely, like Tracy, a young lawyer, and paid for the $460 membership to join Boston's Athenaeum, an exclusive private library founded by the Boston Brahmins.

Their footprints were mostly the same. They spent their days traversing these sites of high culture, collecting stamps on their urban passports: they bought tickets to the theater, signed up to be members of the MFA and BSO, and walked the Freedom Trail until the sun set, waking up to do it all again the next day. High-culture institutions were central to what attracted them to Boston. And these were the institutions they helped support.

When describing the difference between his hometown in the Midwest and Boston, Stan articulated matter-of-factly, "Obviously Boston is what it is. . . . There's much more culture I would say in Boston than we have here. . . . We pack a lot of culture in when we're [in Boston], especially theater." Stan was one of the few second homeowners I spoke with who purchased his second home in the 1980s. He struck while the iron was hot and made a small fortune on the investment of his second home in what he said was an "up-and-coming" Jamaica Plain. In 2021, his home was valued at over a million dollars. In fact, Stan was on the front lines of the first wave of gentrification that swept across the neighborhood, actively fighting zoning laws and challenging developments that might impact his investment. Although he still attended neighborhood meetings, his local efforts had fundamentally evolved. Instead of fighting city hall, he now spent his days attending the theater, watching art-house films, or listening to performances of the Handel and Haydn Society. While he first bought the home as a financial investment, he has kept it for over thirty years for its cultural potential.[6]

The people I met in Boston also actively donated to institutions of high culture, ensuring the vitality and longevity of these organizations for years to come. Unlike the people I met in Rangeley, the people in Boston I spoke with did not singularly support one institution. However, they supported the same *types* of institutions. Collectively, they donated to the Museum of Fine Arts, Boston Symphony Orchestra, Lyrica Opera House, Handel and Haydn Society, Boston Historical Society, Freedom Trail Foundation, JFK Library, Friends of the Public Garden, Landmarks Orchestra, Boston Athenaeum, and Boston Youth Moves.[7] Charitable giving is not as conspicuous as objecting to new high-rise developments at a community meeting or even as subtle as buying a penthouse and leaving the skyline dark and lifeless. Such philanthropic practices are perhaps the most discreet form of city building, funding the future of Boston's high-culture institutions that concentrate across an array of affluent neighborhoods.[8]

This builds on a long-standing place-making strategy of urban elites in Boston. Throughout the nineteenth and early twentieth centuries, the city was dominated by the Boston Brahmins, a highly educated, culturally anchored group of white Anglo-Saxon Protestant wealth-elites whose concentrated political and social power likened them to an aristocracy.[9] The Brahmins poured money and resources into developing and sustaining the city's most renowned cultural institutions to define themselves as elites: the Museum of Fine Arts, the Boston Symphony Orchestra, the Isabella Steward Gardner Museum, WGBH, Peabody Essex, and the Boston Athenaeum.[10] These institutions "reinforce[d] the taste culture of Boston's upper class . . . [and shaped and reproduced] the shared tastes and values that gave the upper class its strong sense of identity and solidarity."[11]

Ownership over institutions like the Museum of Fine Arts and the Boston Symphony Orchestra through private philanthropic support was a method of social closure, a way to create and take ownership over valued institutions and experiences in Boston. Drawing on Pierre Bourdieu, Paul DiMaggio argues that the Brahmins were

> collectors of . . . "cultural capital," knowledge and familiarity with styles and genres that are socially valued and that confer prestige upon those who have mastered them. It was the vision of the founders of the institutions that have become, in effect, the treasuries of cultural capital upon which their descendants have drawn that defined the nature of cultural capital in American society.[12]

The creation and support of high-cultural institutions like the Boston Symphony Orchestra and the Museum of Fine Arts defined the Brahmins as a social class, and support of these institutions defined the meaning of cultural capital and social prestige across the city, for them and for the generations that followed.[13] The people I met were not engaging in such explicit forms of institution building and social exclusion; however, their singular community engagements were reinforcing these patterns, as they used high-culture institutions not only to reflect their social-class tastes but also to ensure their vision of what the city means to them.

While the financial investments of the people I met in urban property were significant, they were not simply buying property and leaving it vacant. They strategically engaged with the city in ways that reified their sense of place—the city as a site of high culture. They built on a Brahmin *ethos*, using cultural institutions to define the city and themselves. To be sure, they were not the singular supporters of high-culture institutions in Boston. The endurance of these institutions since the Brahmin era relies on the support of many other residents and visitors. However, the people I met are part of what Harvey Molotch and colleagues have called a "rolling inertia," where cumulative actions over time from a series of people and institutions combine to form a place's character.[14] Their selective community engagements helped reinforce this inertia that makes parts of Boston a place they value.

Selling Culture

After talking with second homeowners in Boston about their practices supporting high-culture institutions, I wanted to know more about the role of private donations and revenue support for keeping these institutions afloat. And I wanted to understand how this all fit into Boston's broader place-making project. These questions led me to talk with Jenny, an employee from the Boston Symphony Orchestra, about how they fund their operations. I asked how much their organization depended on donations, revenue, and volunteers to keep its doors open. "Right now," Jenny responded, "50 percent of our income is earned, and the other 50 percent is donated." I followed up by asking if they received any support from the government—federal, state, or local. "We get about a million dollars in grants," she mused, "but what percentage of government aid? I don't really know. . . . Usually, our [grant] goals are hit, but that's [by] private foundations. Government support . . . oh man. It's little, *little*. . . . It represents such a small part of our overall budget." Jenny confirmed an emergent trend: compared to other cities of the same size, the city of Boston has historically funneled little of its own funds into supporting cultural institutions. Yet paradoxically, the city has relied on these institutions for its own place-making project, *selling culture*.

Place-making involves both the ordinary people who invest localities with meaning and value and the "upstream forces that drive the creation of place with power and wealth."[15] Boston's municipal place-making project, the upstream forces, relies in part on packaging the city as a world-class arts and culture destination. This includes promoting large, big-C cultural institutions like the Museum of Fine Arts, the Boston Symphony Orchestra, the Institute of Contemporary Art, the Isabella Stewart Gardner Museum, and the Boston Opera House, as well as a range of historic sites that celebrate Boston's revolutionary past, such as Faneuil Hall, the Boston Common, and the Old North Church that weave throughout Boston's commercial spaces. The names of these landmarks and institutions are plastered across Boston's transportation systems and media platforms, meant to remind visitors and residents alike to experience and consume a curated slice of what Boston has to offer.[16]

These arts and cultural strategies are meant to lure visitors into the city, where they will spend money on museums and tours, exorbitant parking rates, restaurants and bakeries, and souvenirs of all kinds at gift shops and locally owned businesses to remember their time in the city.[17] This is a near universal strategy for local economies that are now more dependent on the influx of money into service industries as most manufacturing and other productive industries have declined across the country over the past half century. In Boston, these strategies are effective. Estimates suggest that arts and culture industries and institutions infuse $2 billion into the local economy annually, with roughly $675 million of that amount funneled into the restaurants, parking structures, and local businesses adjacent to arts consumption.[18]

Although the city of Boston relies on arts and culture for its economic growth, it spends little of its own money supporting the institutions it uses to sell itself to the world. In fact, compared to other cities of the same size and with the same density of cultural institutions, "Boston receives the lowest amount of government funding per capita" and "the primary driver of this low public support is the limited funding from the City of Boston. Boston is the only metro area . . . where federal support outweighs state and local funding."[19] Arts advocates across the city have sounded the alarm about the effects of this lack of public support. This leaves a vacuum, in which private support directs the meaning of culture, leading to uneven arts and cultural representation across the city.

The institutions that flourish and become most visible are those that are infused with private philanthropic support and high participation-based earned revenue (e.g., sales from tickets).[20] But those who have the time and money to fund cultural institutions are like the second homeowners in Boston I met. They are often affluent white donors who funnel their capital into large-scale cultural institutions like the Museum of Fine Arts and the Boston Symphony Orchestra, which has the effect of supplanting other forms of local culture.[21] As a result, large-scale, exclusive cultural institutions in the city thrive. Meanwhile, mid- and small-scale diverse cultural institutions struggle to find footing. These types of institutions—theater, dance, performing arts, and institutions that show new art—often value "issues of social justice, equality, and diversity through their work."[22] Critics suggest that culture in the city is thus more homogeneous and exclusive than it otherwise could be.[23]

It is in this way that the people I met were connected to Boston's broader place-making project. Although the city does not provide robust financial support for cultural institutions, it still relies on these institutions to enhance the city's revenue stream. The result of this paradox is that the institutions in the city that thrive are those that receive the most private support, typically world-renowned, high-culture institutions. Under these conditions, the donation and consumption practices of everyday people matter for which institutions are empowered in a city's culture and economy.

Private Control of Public Culture

With philanthropic and revenue-based support and resources, dominant high-culture institutions can extend the breadth of their influence beyond the walls of their institutions. To become more attractive to residents and visitors—to earn yet even more revenue and support—high-culture institutions often turn to improving the neighborhoods surrounding them, becoming stewards of neighborhood character and growth.[24]

In Boston, the Museum of Fine Arts, Boston Symphony Orchestra, Huntington Theatre Company, and Isabella Stewart Gardner Museum, among other institutions, extend the reach of their influence through participation in the *Fenway Alliance*. This alliance is a consortium of institutions whose aim is to work with the city of Boston and the state of Massachusetts to support neighborhood improvements to cohere the district's "cultural identity."[25] In an effort to do this, the alliance encouraged the development of the Fenway Cultural District, an established district in the city of Boston. Central to the district's mission is to provide cultural programming, brand and market the neighborhood to the city and the world, and "increase livability."[26] Materially, this includes the alliance's institutions infusing over $1 billion on capital projects in Boston between 1997 and 2011.[27] It also includes securing $20 million in grants for the beautification of Huntington Avenue. It has improved nearly every aesthetic and functional element of the avenue— sidewalks, transit stations, traffic flow, and greenscape.[28]

These types of improvements made by private-public partnerships at first seem mundane—planting trees, installing acorn lighting, improving transit stations, adding park benches, hanging district signage, cleaning up parks, creating community cultural programming. However, urban scholars have documented the broader implications of these processes for urban people and places. In what follows, I broaden the scope of this chapter to show how the everyday practices of private-public partnerships—which are empowered by the philanthropic and consumptive practices of those like the people I met—can play a central role in directing the futures of cities, curating the type of urban place the people I met value. They do so by controlling a neighborhood's image, contributing to neighborhood upscaling, and unevenly distributing resources across city neighborhoods. I will begin with the former.

As cities and neighborhoods depend on public-private partnerships to maintain a neighborhood's identity and streetscape, the result is often that public culture is privately controlled. Sharon Zukin has written extensively about this in her treatises on culture and urban change.[29] She argues that urban culture is something that has been carefully crafted and controlled by elite boosters and stakeholders against the backdrop of a new urban economy more dependent on money brought in by tourists and visitors. As government funding receded throughout the latter part of the twentieth century—unable to plant flowers, clean up parks, or fix sidewalks—stakeholders like business owners, museums and other cultural nonprofits, residents, and civic leaders started to voluntarily tax themselves through Business Improvement Districts or neighborhood alliances to fund the upkeep of city streets, parks, and neighborhoods and the production of cultural programming like art shows and movie nights. This was done in an effort to boost local revenue by making cities feel safe and vibrant for middle- and upper-middle-class consumers, the valued consumer in the new economy. Yet through this new structure, these private entities became proprietors of public space. They hired private security guards to ensure that no one was loitering, sleeping on benches, or digging through trash cans. Parks developed new rules and new hours and gates that lock before sundown.[30] The result was that public space became privatized and homogenized, constructed singularly and narrowly for select people—white middle-class and upper-middle-class consumers—pushing people who did not fit this new aesthetic far out of sight.[31]

The improvements made by public-private partnerships furthermore do more than control public culture in ways that unite and brand cultural institutions and the surrounding neighborhood as an economic strategy. The improvements can brand an *entire* neighborhood and mark it for growth, spurring revitalization efforts and a neighborhood's upscaling.[32] This very process is described by the Museum of Fine Arts itself:

The MFA has contributed to improvements in the Fenway. . . . The Fenway neighborhood is in the middle of a development boom . . . with many new housing and commercial developments under construction or being planned. As developers seek to market these new properties, realtors have noted that the proximity to the MFA is a key selling point, particularly in efforts to attract empty nesters to the community.[33]

As institutions work to improve the neighborhood through beautification and greenscape projects, transportation improvements, and historic restoration, new forms of housing and commercial development often follow. Neighborhood branding strategies often operate as a mechanism of gentrification.[34] Every aesthetic and functional improvement made to a neighborhood has the potential to both increase property values and rents and attract interest from new residents, developers, and commercial establishments.[35] These improvements thus work in conjunction with other social forces to spur neighborhood change and churn in any given city.

Finally, the improvements made by public-private partnerships have implications beyond the neighborhood in which these partnerships are embedded. They also contribute to uneven resource distribution across the city. Scholars have been writing about this process for decades against the backdrop of urban neoliberalism, or the increased dependence on private actors and the market for city and community growth.[36] As public financing for community development has receded over time, private and institutional actors' willingness to invest time and money in select neighborhoods plays a key role in determining which areas of the city see an infusion of resources and which do not.[37] In practice, this means that some neighborhoods receive grants to improve road and transportation infrastructure, create community cultural programming, or fund beautification projects because of the mobilization efforts of local coalitions, like the Fenway Alliance, who have a stake in a neighborhood's growth. These neighborhoods experience a surge in investments and resources because institutional actors are committed to using their networks and capital to improve neighborhood conditions to fortify their own institutional growth. Such institutional coalitions thus secure valuable resources for the neighborhoods in which their institutions are embedded, in effect leaving behind other parts of the city without the same attention from private interests.[38]

The city's property tax structure also influences how high-cultural institutions contribute to this uneven distribution of resources between neighborhoods. Large-scale cultural institutions occupy huge swaths of land in the city—in Boston the MFA controls over fifteen acres in the city—but do not pay property taxes on them.[39] However, they are encouraged to make donations of money or community programs through Boston's PILOT (pay in lieu of taxes) program.[40] These institutions typically make PILOT donations based on "community benefits."[41] In 2020, the city valued all the tax-exempt cultural institutions across Boston at almost $650 million and received cash contributions of only $445,549. While the city, in theory, received "community benefits" of about $2 million, there is a material deficit of just under $650 million.[42] The addition of these property taxes would have increased Boston's entire operating budget in 2020 by almost a fifth.[43] This means that these institutions not only have a heavy hand in controlling public culture and infusing resources in the neighborhoods they occupy but also simultaneously limit public revenue that might have gone to improving other parts of the city, particularly in underserved and historically disinvested communities—funds to expand transit access or improve transit stations, for example, or to fund public schools, improve public parks and recreational services, or subsidize affordable housing. PILOT contributions in effect limit public revenue for other local needs, reifying the place-making power of high-culture institutions across the city.

When the people I met contributed, both philanthropically and through their consumption practices, to these types of institutions, they were not just ensuring that the Museum of Fine Arts would be able to curate a new exhibit on Degas or that the Boston Symphony Orchestra would be able to bring in world-renowned violinist Ray Chen. With philanthropic and revenue-based support, these institutions become stewards of the neighborhoods they occupy and are empowered to play a key role in processes affecting cities today: the private control of public culture, neighborhood upscaling, and uneven resource distribution in the city. Yet these very processes are part of what creates and maintains a neighborhood's image that the people I met valued—a place that is "safe," "vibrant," and "prestigious" for people like them.

8

High-End Blight

As rural communities deal every day with the presence of second home-owners populating their streets, lakes, mountains, and beaches, urban neighborhoods have started grappling with their *absence*. Typically, when sociologists think about the problems of vacancy in cities, they think about heavily disinvested and neglected neighborhoods and the effects this has on community efficacy. Sociologists write about high-poverty neighborhoods like Park Heights in Baltimore, whose people and infrastructure have been subjected to decades of institutionalized neglect, or entire cities like Detroit, whose residents and neighborhoods still reel from the effects of deindustrialization and the flight of the automobile industry.[1] But in highly affluent urban neighborhoods across the country, like Beacon Hill, Downtown, and the North End—the neighborhoods in Boston where the people I met bought second homes—vacancy has taken on an entirely new meaning. Blight is high-end.

In 2019, Boston city councilors Ed Flynn, Lydia Edwards, Matt O'Malley, and Andrea Campbell held a public hearing on the state of vacant properties in the city. The order for the hearing framed the problem of vacancy as a problem of "high-end blight," in which

> the growth in the number of residential units in large, luxury buildings over 50,000 square feet that are purchased for investment and left empty, or only occasionally inhabited, has challenged the city's efforts to house a growing population and create a vibrant neighborhood.[2]

The people we followed in this book were not the sole contributors to high-end blight in Boston, but they were part of it. Most of the people I talked with only used their second home sporadically, a few full weeks throughout the year, a few days scattered throughout every month, or every weekend. A few people I talked with rented their homes on Airbnb when they were not using them, but most left their homes vacant a large portion of the year. And they were willing to pay the price for this occasional access to the city. What does this *absence* mean for cities?

In this chapter, I trace the two fundamental problems with the rise of "high-end blight" in Boston neighborhoods that city councilors highlight: the increasing problem of housing affordability for the people who live in the city full-time and the meaning of community as homes are purchased and left vacant. I end by discussing the public discourse that frames *who* causes high-end blight in the city and how this discourse upholds the narratives the people I met construct about themselves.

The Problem of Housing Affordability

In the past decade, Boston has witnessed a growth in housing construction thought to help with the problem of affordability across the city, the increased demand with limited supply, and soaring real estate prices.[3] However, city councilors, community leaders, and critics argued that much of this housing boom has been geared toward the luxury market, magnifying the already tenuous problems of affordability and access, as part-time residents buy up and leave unused some of the city's new real estate.[4] To get a sense of this housing crisis, policy analysts Chuck Collins and Emma de Goede from the Institute for Policy Studies highlight an *Imagine 2030* report issued in 2016. They wrote, "21 percent of Bostonians spend 50 percent or more of their monthly income on housing. There are more than 40,000 applicants on waiting lists for public housing and Section 8 vouchers. The median household income in Boston is similar to the national median, but the median price of a home is 2.5 times higher."[5] They cited the high-end luxury real estate market as a culprit for the city's crisis.

I talked with Henry, a real estate agent who worked primarily with the second-home market on the North End waterfront, who helped elaborate how second homeowners contributed to Boston's affordability crunch. A lot of his buyers first considered New York as a second-home destination but quickly found the pace of the city too overwhelming, and expensive:

Two hundred miles away up north there's a place called Boston. They start coming in. They say, "Wow, no traffic. People are a little friendly. Restaurants are still good, but not as good as New York." I think the area is much better than New York, because New York, as you know, is quite expensive. . . . You're talking about if you want to live in that downtown and then you probably have to pay probably 150 percent more than Boston. People start thinking about maybe Boston is a good idea.

From Henry's perspective, Boston's relative affordability explained why wealthy people who were not from Boston readily paid the price for the luxury condominiums being built there. It was all relative. "When you have so many people coming to buy a house, they don't understand the market," Henry continued. "They purchase $1 million condos for them, they say that this is comfortable. . . . They think everything for them is reasonable." To second homeowners looking to purchase a luxury condo, Boston appeared to be a deal, particularly compared it its Northeast corridor neighbor, New York. The high-end clients Henry worked with willingly paid the price.

Yet it is not without consequences. Non-Boston residents who come into the city's real estate market with relatively more wealth than the average Bostonian inflate property values as they are willing and able to pay higher, often exorbitant, prices for condos. Since he capitalized on these high-end purchases, Henry did not have many complaints: "We're not complaining about that because more buyers is more sell, and more sell is more commission." Henry's market was primarily second-home buyers from the United States, Europe, and Asia. Yet other real estate agents I spoke with who dealt exclusively with U.S.-born buyers narrated these same processes, as Marcia did when we spoke:

Let's say they have a one-and-a-half to two-million-dollar home in the suburbs. . . . They'll come in the city and buy a two-bedroom home for a million dollars, and they want to keep the other home, because it's a totally different lifestyle. . . . I would say the typical people are in their fifties if they're coming back in the city. They've made a couple hundred thousand dollars a year their whole life, so they have a decent . . . I shouldn't say decent, excuse me. They have a couple million dollars of net worth. That's the person that wants to basically spend that kind of money, because you don't get that much in the city. They have this excess money, and they want to spend it on real estate in the city. . . . They like the idea of being in the city, but they don't want to be here maybe in the summer, or they don't want to be here in the winter if they have a second home in Florida. They're kind of buying a part-time lifestyle here.

The people Marcia worked with have high-paying jobs and a few million dollars in net worth, money they specifically made by not living in the city throughout their careers. This, she carefully noted, was money they accrued while living in the suburbs. The people she worked with were willing to pay the price for the amenities they wanted, and they often saw it as a deal compared to New York. If a second-home buyer was flexible about where they wanted to be located and wanted to be (relatively) mindful of price, Boston provided access to the wide array of amenities for almost half the price of New York. Luxury real estate in Boston was a bargain—comparatively.

When city councilors talked about the impact of high-end blight on Boston's affordability, this is the process to which they were referring. People with excess money, generated in places outside of Boston—whether in the suburbs, abroad, or across the country—have been willing to pay exorbitant prices for the location and amenities they value, themes expressed by the people with whom I talked for this book. Many did not want what they considered to be a deal on a home in a rapidly changing neighborhood where they might have found a return on their investment or proximity to so-called authentic people or places, as other scholars have found with some gentrifiers.[6] They wanted amenities. They wanted access to Boston's most prestigious areas. And they were willing to pay the price, artificially inflating the value of Boston real estate, only to leave it vacant most of the year.

Collective Efficacy

High-end blight is a problem not only of rising property values. Community leaders in neighborhoods across Boston expressed concern about how high-end blight undermines community life. At the end of a North End/Waterfront Neighborhood Council meeting, I found myself in casual conversation with four men who were seated at my table. One of the gentlemen asked why I was in attendance, as I clearly stood out as the youngest in the room by nearly twenty years. I detailed my project studying second homeowners in Boston. Another, a white man in his fifties and well dressed in beige slacks and a muted green button-down, was eager to mention the vacant units in the building across the street from him, citing the "dark windows" at night as the indicator. With indignation, the other men in the conversation then went on to name all the buildings in the area they noticed were dark at night, citing those located primarily on the waterfront in the North End and across the harbor in Charlestown, one of which they had heard houses an Apple executive. They echoed many of the problems that Terry and Margaret had originally highlighted in my observations of these meetings. They expressed that the luxury waterfront buildings had created a rapidly growing socio-economic and cultural divide in the neighborhood.

Margaret, a member of the North End/Waterfront Residents' Association, corroborated these concerns during an interview. She pointed to the luxury buildings on the waterfront that house affluent and transient residents as a problem for neighborhood cohesion. "The only people who can afford to live there [on the Waterfront]," she noted, "are so wealthy that they have multiple residences." She explained that the neighborhood association will often try to rally the people in the buildings on the Waterfront if there is a development issue that the neighborhood is concerned with. But, she explained, "with Waterfront people, very seldom will show up for anything like that. . . . They're not going to get involved. It's really almost not worth putting the effort in trying to get them involved." Henry, one of the luxury real estate agents I interviewed, lived in one of these homes on the Waterfront and echoed Margaret's observations:

> We have about 104 units altogether in that small community. The second home for all my neighbors is quite high. I'd have to say probably more than 50 percent. People just come in the summertime or people just come in at the wintertime. Most likely, sometimes you don't even see your neighbor because this is their second home. The more high-end, the more luxury building that you see, there's more people [who] are using it as a second home.

Henry suggested that many of the high-end Waterfront buildings are empty most of the year. As my conversation with Margaret unfolded, she continued to discuss the negative effects of empty high-end luxury buildings on neighborhood cohesion. I asked if there was a general perception among the residents' associations of the luxury buildings. She mused:

> For the most part, I would say that our association does not feel that that [luxury buildings on the Waterfront] is anything that fosters a stable community, or an involved community, or anything like that. They're just not involved. There, but they're not involved. They're basically passing through, and they want to be sure that they have a place to park, and that there's not too much garbage out front of the building. That's about as much as they care about.

During our conversation, Margaret was unable to name a single second homeowner she knew. She could not think of a time where she really had a conversation with anyone on the Waterfront. She found what I had found: they were just passing through. Boston was not their home, nor was it their community. Many even relished this sort of anonymity in the city.

Why would such absence be a problem for what Margaret called "a stable community"? The *New York Times* detailed a simple moment that captured the value in everyday presence for neighborhood life. Olympic Tower in Midtown Manhattan was composed of predominantly second homeowners. Years ago, there was a water leak in an apartment there that caused $500,000 in damage to the apartments below it. After the event, the *Times* wrote, "A building newsletter noted that the mess 'could have been completely avoided if a set of working keys for that apartment were maintained' at the concierge desk."[7] Knowing your neighbors is important in building the types of social connections necessary for what sociologists call *collective efficacy*. Collective efficacy generally refers to the process in which people trust and are willing to help their neighbors.[8] This leads to crime reduction, improved health, and social capital, among other things. But the people I met wanted no part of this element of community life.

In *The Death and Life of Great American Cities*, Jane Jacobs warned about the preponderance of high-rent tenants like the second homeowners I met. These tenants who concentrate in affluent neighborhoods, she argued, would undermine collective efficacy. The "high-rent tenants, most of whom are so transient we cannot keep track of their faces," she warned, "have not the remotest idea of who takes care of their street, or how."[9] High-rent tenants have amenities not available to more modest residences: doormen, a concierge, dog walkers, "delivery boys, and nurse maids."[10] These very amenities supplant what Jacobs considered to be the authentic, "built-in" eyes on the street, which are necessary for consistent, locally embedded social control and safety—a geographically bound, place-based community.

A few of the second homeowners I talked with rented out their home on Airbnb when they were not using it for themselves and preferred to outsource the eyes on the street. For instance, when looking for a second home, Dan had been adamant that it would be in a professionally managed building. He relied on the building's concierge because he was not always there to keep an eye on what was going on in his Airbnb rental unit. He elaborated:

> What happens is, the concierge, she's the eyes and ears in the building. They'll put a stop to anything that's obnoxious to other people. . . . The concierge is [also] good too. She'll just say in a certain way. . . . We had one guy, he was coming in every year for the month of October. After he

left last year, the concierge said: "Now is he going to be back next year?" I said, "I don't know, we'll see what happens next year." She's like, "Yeah, you might not think about renting to him." I don't get into it. I just say, "Oh, ok." . . . If it makes her uncomfortable, it makes me uncomfortable.

It's not just that Dan wanted to outsource his own local social control; he wanted a professional to do it. Dan did not know any other tenants in his building and did not rely on them when he wasn't around. In fact, he was just one of many transient residents in the building. He explained: "I joke about it all the time. Sundays. All Sunday in our building is rolling bags going out and rolling bags coming in." The content of owners association meetings, of which Dan has only attended one, falls squarely on this transience:

> It has a lot to do with the property management. There's always things going on in the building. There's always heating issues, cooling issues, elevator issues. Things just happen. People go away and they leave their tub dripping, then they come back two weeks later, and it's overflowed. Ruins the ceiling of somebody downstairs.

A concierge can do only so much when residents leave for weeks at a time and neighbors only know each other by the sounds of their suitcases. Only consistent presence can prevent a small drip from becoming an overflowing problem; developing local social ties and building collective efficacy can prevent damage to others.

Some Boston residents find the absence of building occupants troubling for collective decision-making efforts. In the summer of 2016, I walked into the French Cultural Center, a beautiful brownstone on a tree-lined street in Back Bay, one of Boston's most prestigious neighborhoods. I was there to attend Back Bay's neighborhood association meeting to observe the presence, or absence, of second homeowners in Boston's civic life, as well as to observe what, if any, concern local civic groups had about their in-migration. I walked in and sat down waiting for the meeting about the redevelopment of Back Bay Station to begin. A man in his late sixties wearing a pastel-colored polo tucked into his jeans sat next to me. He introduced himself as David.

We exchanged pleasantries, and I asked David if he lived in Back Bay. He said he did and asked why I was attending the meeting. I explained to him my project, that I was interested in understanding how second homeowners engage in the city and so I was observing meetings in neighborhoods where second homeowners tended to concentrate. Without further prompting, he said he was concerned about the international buyers who purchase property in Boston and leave it empty. By way of example, he told me about his own building of seventeen units. One of the units is owned—here he switched to a whisper—by a Chinese businessman whose son goes to an elite preparatory school in Andover, Massachusetts. With a sigh of frustration, he told me that 'they're never there,' and 'they're not involved at all.' He sits on the condo association board of his building and confided that their absence undermines their building's community efforts and the efforts of those who have a 'stake in the neighborhood.'

There is an undercurrent of trepidation about affluent, transient neighborhoods like this. In fact, Monica, a luxury real estate agent, tried to conceal from her non-second-home buyers the proportion of second homeowners in the luxury buildings she showed. "People actually, in general, prefer to hear that everybody in the building is living there full-time," she said, "but that's usually not the case." I got a glimpse into why this might be during my conversation with Linda, a board member of a South End civic association, whom I met at Flour Bakery, a bustling coffee shop on Washington Street in Boston's South End. Although I had exchanged numerous emails with Linda before our meeting, she asked me once again to clarify my project when we sat down. When I explained the details of my project further, Linda abruptly ended our interview, telling me definitively that there were 'no second homeowners in the South End.' It was a 'real neighborhood,' she insisted, unlike her hometown of Charleston, South Carolina, where a "great number of the mansions in the downtown area have been restored to a fare-thee-well but are empty most of the year. . . . The dark windows are a problem in neighborhood cohesiveness."

Linda thought we would be talking about second homeowners in Boston generally, not the South End specifically. And she seemed offended by the latter. She suggested I steer my search away from the South End and turn my attention downtown, where dark windows were, to her, much more visible across the new luxury high-rise units. I was at first perplexed by her defensive reaction. But I began to think about the interaction from Linda's point of view and what it meant to her when I said she lived in a neighborhood that houses second homeowners. There was *stigma* associated with such neighborhoods, a negative social label implying that the neighborhood was devoid of community.[11] High-end blight was understood as an affront to neighborhood community life.

The Specter of "Shady Foreign Buyers"

Although high-end blight is broadly understood as detrimental to community life in Boston, most of the people I met did not conceive of themselves as part of this problem, nor did most public discourse. Public conversations about the root of high-end blight in Boston focused on international wealth elites who buy real estate in the city as a safe-deposit box, leaving it empty most of the year. This discourse provided the resources for and *upheld* the moral preserve of the second homeowners I met, who distanced their everyday practices from the world's superrich to justify their in-migration.

The popular press about second homeowners in Boston, which echoed media outlets in other cities like New York and LA, tended to tie Boston's changing real estate landscape to acquisitions made by "shady foreign buyers" who leave their residences entirely vacant.[12] Journalists from the *Boston Globe* had focused on how luxury high-rises like Millennium Tower had become "a popular investment for international buyers looking for a place to store their cash" or as a "safe place to park their money."[13] In 2016, Tim Logan traced the financial motives of a local Concord resident, a Chinese immigrant, who purchased sixteen condos for a total of $15.6 million—paid in cash—on behalf of foreign investors from his home country. This investigative journalism highlighted the rise of foreign investment in Boston real estate, which had left entire floors of these new high-rise developments empty.[14] Indeed, Logan, a fastidious journalist at the *Globe*, had spent years tracing such sources of foreign investment in the city to reveal a web of money laundering in Boston real estate, the "specter of shady foreign buyers using US real estate to hide or launder illicit money."[15]

In 2018, Logan wrote an article for the *Boston Globe* admonishing the influx of foreign wealth that had come to dominate Boston's new luxury development projects. In the article, he referenced a report by Chuck Collins from the Institute for Policy Studies that traced the owners of twelve new luxury buildings in the city. The report, Logan wrote, "is the latest example of the growing concern among housing advocates that Boston's development boom is producing little that most locals can afford. In this case, study author Chuck Collins said, it appears that whole buildings are being constructed for global elites who are looking to park some cash." In response to such dubious transactions, Collins suggested that Boston employ an "empty-home tax" and a "surcharge on home sales above $2.5 million."[16] In Collins's words, "It's not a home. It's a wealth-storage unit." Collins's assessment of the luxury housing boom focused on the purchases made across nearly a dozen luxury buildings in Boston. He found that 64 percent of these units were not owner occupied, and a third of them were owned by a limited liability corporation. He targeted the international buyers using real estate to hide or launder money as the cause for concern. But there is more to know about the other two-thirds of these non-resident owners.

I never once saw specific critique on the pages of the *Boston Globe* about the types of second homeowners I interviewed for this book. In fact, nearly every article between 2015 and 2017 about "second homes" or "vacation homes" covered people buying second homes in rural, amenity-rich communities, not Boston. And this makes sense. Boston's total population hovers around 650,000 people.[17] Second homes make up less than 2 percent of the total housing stock. Of that 2 percent, there is likely great variety in types of ownership and no real way to discern between them, which is an issue for scholars and policymakers trying to determine exactly who owns real estate in Boston and why. Some are exclusively Airbnb owners, some are international wealth elites who use urban real estate as a safe-deposit box, some own a place to be near their children attending college, others are like the second homeowners I talked to for this book, and still others are a combination of these categories—the list could go on. But in Boston, upper-middle-class second homeowners, like those I met, are mostly ignored. When they *are* written about, they are generally subjects of uncritical puff pieces in the real estate or "Your Home" section of the entertainment-focused *Globe Magazine* that celebrates the style and decor of an enviable pied-à-terre. Second homes in such pieces are not framed as places to park illicit money but as "refuge[s] for suburban commuters . . . a welcoming resting place for a couple who live in Hingham and work in Cambridge."[18] Wealthy white suburbanites' motives are not questioned nor are their financial transactions subjected to background checks.

There are several reasons for this. Second homeowners like those I met are largely invisible in Boston. They are small in number, and their second homes make up only a small fraction of the local housing stock across the city. They also don't *want* to be known. They don't attend civic meanings, regularly socialize with neighbors, or attend most community events. The second homeowners I met furthermore resembled city leaders I met across Boston's affluent downtown neighborhoods—almost universally white, U.S.-born, highly educated, upper-middle-class people who often occupy the same spaces across the city.

However, although the people I met likely made up the smallest fraction of the non-permanent residents who occupy Boston's neighborhoods, they were participating in the very processes that many of the neighborhood leaders I talked with resented: the rise of Airbnb units, the dark windows and vacant units undermining collective community life, and the rise of high-end vacancy, increasing property values and making the city even more unaffordable to the rest. The people I met were connected to a larger history that makes neighborhoods in the central part of Boston a playground for elites. And attention to secondary homebuyers—of all types—should focus on not only their absence but also their presence. The stories of the people I met help show that some secondary homebuyers are not just leaving their homes dark and lifeless; there is a pattern to their emergence that tells a larger story about the city's growing affluence and exclusivity. In the end, the singular focus on international buyers—and their reported dubious purchases—fuels the moral preserve for the people I met. It provides them with distance from concerns over high-end blight and its effects on housing affordability and collective efficacy. It empowered their discourse of deservingness about the practices associated with their second homeownership in Boston, upholding their privilege.

Conclusion

In this book, I have demonstrated how buying a second home in the city and the country was a way for the people I met to balance their desire for a meaningful connection to urban and rural places with their desire to hold onto material interests in their hometowns. This strategic negotiation explained why they bought second homes in the city and the country, why they remained in their first homes in mostly suburban areas, and how this informed their community practices across these places. Understanding the motivations behind their actions has provided unique analytical leverage to explore how they are at once connected to multiple processes of place-based inequality within and between the city, the country, and the suburbs.

I want to end by discussing how studying this process, the place-identity projects of the people we followed in this book, contributes to a broader understanding of the social world. First, it gestures to the complex way that affluent people engage in community life in the twenty-first century. Second, it highlights the value of studying the relationship between place identity and social class to understand how communities are made and for whom. Third, it clarifies how a cultural approach to understanding affluent people's relationship to place can inform policies made about second-homeowner in-migration.

Understanding Affluent People in Communities

In 1929, urban and community sociologist Harvey Zorbaugh observed that the wealthy residents of Chicago's Gold Coast, the most affluent neighborhood in the city, divided their associations between their neighborhood and other, more "fashionable" locations during the summer and winter months. Their interests are "scattered," he argued, and their solidarity is that of "caste rather than contiguity." Zorbaugh concluded in no uncertain terms that they "can scarcely be called a community."[1] When people like those I met are subjects of inquiry in community studies like those on the Gold Coast, their affluence is often studied for the ways in which it is *spatialized*. That is, affluent people are studied within a delimited geography—a neighborhood, a gated community, a school district, a street, or even an entire town or county. But Zorbaugh points to a fundamental characteristic of affluent people who live within these geographies: their interests are *scattered*.

After spending over two years talking to second homeowners in Rangeley and Boston, I learned the value of analyzing affluent people beyond the confines of a singular municipality. Not only did I learn that the people I met maintained scattered community interests in the ways that Zorbaugh alluded to nearly a century prior, but I also learned that these interests were patterned and relational in ways that sustained their privileged relationship to place across the multiple communities where they lived and owned second homes.

This encouraged me to rethink my own orientation to the *community question* in sociology.[2] Although research has problematized geographic propinquity to study people's orientations to community, there remains an emphasis on understanding community engagement within a singular municipality or metropolitan region.[3] This is particularly true when sociologists study people who move from one community to another and the effect this has on local life. Sociologists study gentrifiers who have moved to urban, rural, and small city areas, who propel community change and churn.[4] They study billionaires and the middle and upper middle classes who have uprooted their lives to find the good life in natural-amenity-rich communities, sometimes imposing their notions of nature and rural life onto rural people and places.[5] They also study advantaged and affluent people who hoard access to resources in the suburbs in ways that reproduce residential segregation and limit opportunity for others.[6] Even when I set out to understand second homeowners, I had intended to analyze their practices in relation to their second-home host communities. But I learned that studying them in geographic isolation obscured the complexities of their community engagements. Their practices were connected to these multiple existing processes of place-based community inequality simultaneously and in ways that were relational. Understanding these practices was particularly important as the cities and communities they traversed were increasingly dependent on private practices and philanthropic support of people like them for local growth.[7]

After spending time considering their orientation to community life, I was able to understand how they were distinct from every other upper-middle-class person who moved to affluent suburban communities to hoard access to resources like schools, housing, and jobs, which has contributed significantly to educational, wealth, and health inequalities.[8] I was also able to understand how they were distinct from other groups of people who make locational decisions, often explicitly sacrificing access to job opportunities or high-quality schools, to move permanently to urban and rural communities as gentrifiers or amenity migrants to find a sense of place belonging, which has contributed to economic inequality, residential segregation, and community conflict.[9] The people I met did not want to—nor did they have to—choose between access to resources and a sense of place belonging. The second home allowed them to have *both*, making their geographic reach and connection to larger social problems multiple, simultaneous, and relational. A reliance on municipal boundaries to study affluent people's orientation to community life thus obscures the relational, place-based processes I learned about from talking to people who traverse these boundaries.

Understanding the Relationship between Social Class and Place Identity

When I began studying second homeowners, I knew I wanted to understand their relationship to place-based communities—to the people, to the culture, to the social life they fashioned in their second-home host communities. I did not expect the people I met to talk at length about their identities, this sense that they were rural and urban people who felt unmoored from the places where they would rather be. And I did not expect to learn as much as I did about the tensions between these desires and their other desires to hold onto material interests in their hometowns. These findings, however, pushed me to clarify how social class lies at the heart of the recursive relationship between place and identity, which motivated how they engaged with the communities where they lived and owned second homes.

Much has already been written about the relationship between place and identity. Sociologists have explored how places can influence identity, including how distinct cultures of places change how people view themselves, how regional identities combine with other identity categories like race and gender to produce a distinct local identity, and how rural, urban, and suburban places influence ideologies of the world.[10] Scholars have also explored how identities can influence places, including how people's actions are explained, in part, by how they understand themselves in relationship to the communities where they live.[11] I found that there were four ways in which social class influenced this dynamic relationship—how place influences how people think of themselves and how self-conceptions motivate people to influence the places where they live.

First, social class helped explain why the people I met developed *felt* place identities.[12] They remained in their hometowns for access to value-generating resources, even if they would rather have been somewhere else. This is because upper-middle-class people in part secure their socio-economic position through modest wealth, high-earning professions, and access to resources they have by virtue of where they live.[13] These findings capture the importance of understanding concepts like place identity as personally held, not necessarily bound to one's permanent geographic location, and analyzing the conditions, like social class, that explain how and why it is *felt*.[14]

Second, social class shaped how they acted on their felt identities. Anyone can have a felt place identity; it is not unique to the people I talked with. Yet, not everyone has an equal ability to buy a second home to fulfill this internal desire and to make places more like how they imagine them. Scholars have studied how people who move to new places can adopt a new identity or way of thinking about themselves.[15] So, too, have scholars captured that when people experience a rupture in place attachment, they are forced to craft a new narrative about who they are in relation to where they are.[16] But in this case, the people I met were not forced to adopt a new method of thinking about themselves in relation to where they were. Their social-class position enabled the people I met to *enact* their felt place identity, transforming it into a *project*. Future work can therefore analyze how, when, and why place identities are pursued through action.

Third, social-class position influenced the relative weight and style of their place-identity project. Much has been written about how the cultural orientations of diverse groups of people influence the trajectories of a given community—artists, doormen, gentrifiers, landlords, building inspectors, real estate appraisers and agents, and so on.[17] People like those I met not only had enough money to buy a second home elsewhere but also had a wealth of social, economic, cultural, and political capital that extended beyond the walls of their real estate investments. They could support parades, renovate homes, patronize local businesses, and attend community meetings—practices typically associated with middle-class community power.[18] But they also had a wealth of resources not available to the middle class. They had more material weight to philanthropically support institutions that they perceived to be stewards of the city and the country, defining what urban and rural life should be, even in their absence. In fact, it is precisely because they were not permanent residents, who can participate in local governance, that they had to rely on nonprofit institutions as their community representatives to maintain this sense of place.

This suggests the importance of studying the place projects of people who are not necessarily consistently present in everyday community life to understand how, why, and for whom places are constructed. Affluent college alumni or other community-focused donors, for instance, maintain visions for what their places of interest should look and feel like, and they can use their time and money to enact these visions. Communities are constructed by a wide range of actors who tie their identities to places but may not necessarily show up at municipal hearings, homeowners' association meetings, or even weekly farmer's markets. This is particularly important as larger social and economic forces empower social actors' everyday philanthropic and consumptive practices. Resources are not allocated evenly across municipalities. If and how a community grows (or does not) depend in large part on the ways in which people—however present or absent—invest their time and money.[19]

Finally, place identity also informed their social-class identity. It did so in ways that justified their privileged social location. Their relationships to the city and the country—and to culture and nature, respectively—provided a "moral preserve" in a "landscape of materialist desires."[20] It allowed them to view themselves as different from other types of elite second homeowners who engaged in what they perceived to be more morally dubious projects, like international wealth elites who bought property in cities all over the world or other second homeowners whose everyday practices they framed as more class conspicuous. They viewed their affiliations and engagements with select parts of the city and the country as morally deserving, compared to other elites' more ostentatious practices. Their place-identity projects provided a source of identity and lifestyle choices they found to be more authentic and legitimate, all of which justified buying a second home in someone else's community. While much attention has been paid to how elites use affiliation with nature and the country to solve their ethical class dilemmas, these findings encourage attention to the multiple places that privileged people use to uphold and justify their social-class position.

Understanding Culture to Inform Tax Policy

Using a cultural approach to study affluent people's relationship to the multiple communities where they live and own second homes has value beyond the academy. Understanding this relationship to place has implications for tax policy targeting second homeownership.

Some cities and states have begun to think about second homeowners as a social problem and are considering policies to curb their influence. Most public and political discourse centers on taxation of secondary residences, broadly defined. Cities across the globe are considering policies to deter the purchase of vacation or investment homes.[21] Paris has proposed increasing the property tax rate by five times for second-home properties to deter unused properties.[22] Boston's own city councilors have called for increased taxation for "property flippers" and "speculators" to help mitigate Boston's affordable-housing crisis. Because there is no clear way to demarcate the type of vacant property beyond the residential tax exemption, these policies would include the non-permanent residents I followed in this book.[23]

In Maine, where civic leaders have sounded the alarm about an emergent affordable-housing crisis, legislators have begun to consider taxing vacation homes that are vacant more than six months out of the year in an effort to fund an affordable-housing infrastructure through a real estate tax transfer (a program called HOME, "housing opportunities for Maine") for more economically disadvantaged communities.[24] A lot of the concern about this potential tax policy is that it will deter second homeownership entirely. The case of Rangeley shows how complicated it is to disincentivize second homeownership, as many rural communities are nearly exclusively reliant on the money brought in by the second-home tourism industry.

To be sure, whether admittedly or not, financialization has made possible the purchase of a second home for the people I interviewed. If buying a second home was a financially risky decision, it is unlikely many I talked with would have followed through with such a purchase even though they distanced themselves from financial incentives. But investment potential alone did not explain what motivated the second homeowners I spoke with, nor did it explain their local engagement. Rather than financial potential, they were invested in aligning themselves with the places that gave them the feeling of being an urban or rural person and they often paid a premium to find this sense of place. Their local engagements were not about maximizing the investment potential of their second home but maximizing the ways the second-home destinations complemented their city or country selves.

Joyce did not donate to the Museum of Fine Arts or work in the rose bed garden to close the rent gap and increase the value of her own second-home property. She did it because she viewed herself as an urban person, part of a high-cultural environment and lifestyle. Jeff did not buy an acre of property across the dirt road from his second home in Rangeley to protect his financial portfolio. He did it so he could preserve his quiet retreat set in nature while he kayaked in the lake, listened to the birds, and walked the dirt road with his dog. Many I met even told me that they did not care what might happen to the value of their properties because they wanted to pass it onto their children someday. They did not want to sell it off to fund their retirement because for many, it *was* their retirement.

In both cases, understanding the cultural motivations that underlie these second-home purchases reveals how inelastic the second-home market can be—these extra taxes might not have operated as a deterrent for the people I met. However, because of this, these policies could *work* to recoup lost capital. Many of the people I met in Rangeley and Boston explicitly noted that they did not care if they were taxed more or about the financial potential of their second home; they were willing to pay the price. Cristobal Young and colleagues write about this process with millionaires and billionaires. States and countries worry about taxing the rich. If they have time and money, won't they just move somewhere else? They debunk this claim by showing how wealth elites are more tied to place than most people think. They often remain in places where they are successful.[25] Understanding people's relationship to place, then, has implications for tax policy. The people I met underscore how important it is to capitalize on their presence. Many of the people I met expressed being largely disconnected from the aspects of the communities where they own second homes that were not associated with their sense of place, only paying their property tax bill and nearly singularly funding organizations they associated with their limited notions of *rural* or *urban*. But if they were willing to stay—and most were—taxing them more could help redistribute money to fund other local institutions which they eschew.

In the immediate future, communities can think about how they could levy extra taxes on second homeowners for public goods and services their municipalities need. They could earmark more funds for local services like education that some second homeowners, including those I talked with, evade—either strategically or de facto—through mobility.[26] Taxation for affordable housing is another possible avenue. In other localities like Aspen, Colorado, Jenny Stuber has shown how a real estate tax transfer earmarked for housing the local workforce has made a hyper-affluent resort town more affordable for those who live and work there.[27]

These kinds of policies matter materially and symbolically. At the material level, they work to redistribute resources to those who have been systematically denied them. Symbolically, such policies can make some second homeowners more attuned to their local influence and locational choices, of which they might otherwise be unaware. This may be particularly effective for people like those I talked to for this book, who did not see their everyday social practices as necessarily problematic as they compared themselves to second homeowners they perceived to be more egregious, like those who buy multimillion-dollar homes or hire "help." They mostly preferred to keep to themselves. Such an explicit taxation, then, might bring forth the implications of living somewhere part-time (e.g., educational or housing inequality), beyond the real estate transaction.

Of course, the only real way to limit the influence of the people we followed in this book is to fundamentally rethink the way resources are distributed across localities, particularly public goods like schools, health care, and internet access. Schools are disadvantaged in places like Rangeley and Boston because people like those I talked to are unwilling to live in these destinations full-time, withholding significant capital that might infuse the schools with more resources. The only reason their locational choices matter is because schools allocate resources based on the local tax base. If school funding were evenly allocated across districts, their second-home choices would be less consequential. The same goes for other public goods like hospitals and internet access. Reliance on market competition or private donors to fund medical centers or attract broadband coverage makes the distribution of resources across localities uneven. As Mary Pattillo argues in her analysis of public schooling, discussing more equitable division of resources "invokes concepts that have disappeared from and are even perhaps taboo. . . . Words like provision, state responsibility, and entitlement all require the state to meet people where they are as opposed to requiring citizens to seek out, navigate, and work for public benefits."[28] A broader, more equitable distribution of public goods and resources would have undermined the power of the suburbs as a site for opportunity hoarding for the people I talked with. It would also have lessened the influence of the everyday practices of the people I met that contributed to deepening inequality within urban and rural places. It would mean that people could not build their sense of place on others' disadvantage.

Here, There, Everywhere

During my conversation with Doris Flynn about her daily routine in her waterfront condo in Boston, she casually mentioned another aspect of her life: "On the other hand, on the other side of the world, we have a home in Scotland." The home in Scotland was distinct from their home in Boston. It was not a connection to their shared past as city people but a connection to her family heritage. For many of the people I met, the term "second home" was a misnomer.[29] It was a mere colloquialism used to describe one of possibly multiple residences that were not considered a primary home. I often did not have to directly broach the subject of whether they owned more than one residence; it was often casually mentioned in passing during our conversations. I learned about family homes in Cape Cod, Maine, Chicago, upstate New York, coastal Florida, and Washington, D.C., and the list goes on.

For most of the people I talked with who had more than one "second home" there was a recurring theme. These homes were typically family oriented—homes to share with relatives or homes to live closer to relatives or homes to re-create parts of their family's past. The relationship between place and identity is multifaceted. While this book detailed the specific place-identity projects of becoming a city person or a country person and the stakes of these everyday practices, notions of identity and family are also tied to place. This explains why Doris and Richard reconstructed their family's home in Scotland from rubble to match the indigenous environment—what it looked like decades ago when Richard's grandmother lived there. Many of the people I met moved away from their primary ties long ago to live in communities for access to jobs and schools, instead holding onto place-based family ties through mobility. These multiple homes allowed them to have, in Bruce and Joyce's words, "the best of all worlds."

This type of mobility was normal, expected, and an everyday part of life for the people I met. They were not geographically bound to just one area. They maintained municipally unbound, geographically dispersed community commitments, making selective claims in many places at once. And I learned that this privilege extends even beyond the boundaries of the communities I covered in this book.

Epilogue

In the winter of 2020, everything changed. In January 2020, the United States confirmed its first case of Covid-19 from a sample in Washington State.[1] In an unprecedented moment on March 11, the National Basketball Association canceled the remainder of its season due to a positive Covid-19 case. On March 15, New York City began shutting down public schools to prevent the accelerating spread of the disease. And in the weeks that followed, school systems, colleges, businesses, and nearly every facet of social life shut down for a near-nationwide quarantine in an effort to flatten the curve. An entirely new lexicon of everyday life appeared—*quarantine, social distancing, masks, hand sanitizer, essential workers, risk, death.* The pandemic upended life as we knew it. It also laid bare America's deep inequality.

New York City was among the first major metropolitan regions to be hit by an outbreak of Covid-19. The city quickly descended into lockdown, with only essential services open. The early wave ravaged the densely packed city, sending thousands of New Yorkers to increasingly strained emergency rooms. At the peak of the pandemic in April 2020, the city reported a seven-day average of 829 deaths a day with the elderly and front-line essential workers hit the hardest.[2] The early days of the pandemic were chaotic. Basic groceries and household supplies became difficult to procure, hospitals were at full capacity, and death spread throughout the city. What emerged was a stark divide between those who were able to rely on others for essential services to avoid disease risk and the essential workers who were exposed to risk daily. This divide fell across racial and class lines.

The pandemic altered the daily routine of many white-collar workers who were employed outside of essential services. These workers went remote. People found themselves learning, teaching, consulting, managing, and researching, all from their homes on their cell phones and laptops. An entire segment of the city's population was soon found scrambling to construct home offices within crammed apartment units to join Zoom meetings and take conference calls.

But not everyone had to stay to endure the risk of death and the unpleasant conditions of lockdown. The most privileged few were able to rely on others for essential services and temporarily move to evade the epicenter of the pandemic. New York City's wealthiest neighborhoods saw an almost 40 percent decrease in their population between March 1 and May 1, 2020, measured by cell-phone tracking data and analyses of garbage pickups.[3] Many of these out-migrants moved to their second homes on the shores of Long Island, the Hamptons, and New Jersey.[4]

Some of the earliest reports of this phenomenon came from waterfront communities in New Jersey, where New York dwellers fled to take up residence in their second homes.[5] Here, they could escape disease risk, procure groceries, consume greenspace, and enjoy more square footage for the duration of remote work and lockdown. But these second homeowners were not met with open arms. Municipalities urged second homeowners to stay home to avoid spreading disease into rural vacation communities that lacked the capacity to deal with overflowing emergency rooms.[6]

As more cities began closing schools and offices, remote rural vacation communities beyond the New York metropolitan region began to grapple with the unwelcome influx of out-of-towners looking to escape. Second homeowners were met with contempt from states, municipalities, and local residents, a relationship that was often already strained even before the pandemic.[7] The relationship between locals and second homeowners became so fraught during this period that one Maine resident who had to temporarily drive a rental car with Massachusetts plates went viral for the message she wrote on her back windshield: "If my husband would stop hitting deer, I'd stop driving rentals! I'm not a Masshole!"[8]

These tensions emerged from deep-seated resentment of second homeowners, a highly privileged sector of the American population. Like many natural disasters, the pandemic laid bare what those with power and privilege can avail themselves of to keep safe, often at the expense of others.[9] At the extreme end, early reports across the globe traced the out-migration of billionaires to their disaster bunkers, stocked with food, supplies, and even medical treatments, in remote parts of the world.[10] On the comparatively ordinary end of the elite spectrum, many second homeowners were part of a white-collar workforce that was able to avoid most risk exposure in everyday life by virtue of working at home and paying others to procure life's basic necessities, like groceries. Given these new structures of remote work, second homeowners were unbound from where they permanently reside, enabled to flee disease risk and to live more comfortably under the conditions of lockdown in the comfort of their own second homes. However, their escape came with health risks for local host communities, who feared disease spread and critically overextended intensive care units.[11]

Covid-19 and Second Homes in Rangeley

According to news media in the early days of the Covid-19 pandemic, most rural communities bristled at the thought of second homeowners "invading" their communities, particularly during what would usually be the off season—"mud season"—of March–June. Municipal officials across New York, New Jersey, Florida, Massachusetts, and even coastal Maine put out warnings to second homeowners to stay home. But not in Rangeley. In April 2020, a municipal leader wrote an open letter on a community forum to explain how the town would handle second homeowners:

> It cannot be said enough how proud we are of Rangeley residents. You are treating this pandemic with the seriousness it requires. Our request to all of our residents is that you understand we have seasonal residents (second homeowners) that have the right to be in their homes no matter where they are coming from. The police chief and I would further request that they self-quarantine for as long as necessary. The importance of this can never be understated. If these folks are in need of services, whether it's food, medical attention, whatever it might be, have them call and we will get them the help and/or services they need.

Rangeley municipal officials welcomed second homeowners with open arms. Such welcoming attitudes from local officials were unsurprising to me after studying Rangeley for over ten years. Local leaders framed second homeowner in-migration as a virtue, a local blessing. Their local place identity emerged in many ways from the looking-glass self, a perception of their town as a safe haven as imagined through the eyes of second homeowners. Among some of my first interviews in the field in 2013, I listened to locals claim Rangeley as a reprieve for shell-shocked New Yorkers after 9/11 or an oasis away from discrimination for many Jewish families throughout the early twentieth century. It only made sense that locals would understand Rangeley as a refuge when the world had its eyes on big cities as the epicenter of pandemic death and chaos.

And a refuge it became. Well into the summer of 2020 and the next year, the town witnessed a housing and population "boom" as people "sought a safe haven from the pandemic."[12] Median home prices and home sales soared as new buyers found a safe haven in this isolated rural community. The influx of new residents and second homeowners during a time of year when most businesses shut down until the summer season was a welcomed addition during a precarious economic moment. Some businesses flourished. Much of this, however, had come at a local cost. Housing prices continued to increase as most jobs in town remained low-wage, service-sector work with stagnant wages. As landlords capitalized on the growing second-home market, some renters were displaced.[13] And local services in such a small town struggled to supply resources for an increased population.

Perhaps the most significant change in the Rangeley region was in the school system. The Rangeley Lakes Regional School typically enrolls around 200 students. However in 2020, the school district enrolled almost 25 new students, which was a significant increase for such a small town.[14] Rangeley's school district held the option for in-person classes, unlike many school districts in other parts of New England that maintained entirely remote school years. This perhaps made Rangeley newly attractive to families who would normally, as I found, disparage its school system in comparison to their own.[15] When most school districts returned to in-person classes in 2021, it is perhaps unsurprising that Rangeley's school district enrollment began to drop again.[16] Liability to Rangeley continued, then, to be limited.

Covid-19 and Second Homes in Boston

Most reports out of Boston during the initial and subsequent waves of Covid-19 were not that second homeowners were flocking to the city. In the news media, cities were portrayed as ground zero for the pandemic. Pictures abound of overflowing hospital rooms, crowded sidewalks with masked passersby, and nearly deserted public transit as many worked from home. Most articles in the *Boston Globe* during this period focused on the intensive out-migration of people from Boston to new destinations like the suburbs or to second-home communities.[17]

In the fall of 2021, I talked with Leslie, a luxury real estate agent whom I had interviewed back in 2014. Before the pandemic, second homeowners made up about 20 percent of Leslie's sales. Most of these were white, highly educated empty nesters from the suburbs or exurbs looking for a full-service building in Back Bay or the Waterfront, proximate to the city's cultural amenities. According to Leslie, when the pandemic hit in early 2020, second homeowners "just stopped buying." He elaborated:

> Some of the buildings which second homeowners like are new, newer elevator buildings, and during Covid, especially early on . . . we weren't really clear how this was spread, and so people didn't want to be sharing common spaces with people. All the things that people came into the city for were shut down. The restaurants weren't open or they were very limited. The gyms weren't open. The theaters weren't open. You really couldn't go to the hospital unless you had something urgent to do. But it really just stopped.

He said it was like somebody "pressed pause on a video with the markets. It just stopped." But even with the out-migration from cities, Leslie noted that he never sold any second homeowners' units. It appears as if many held onto them despite the pandemic. And as of 2021, the second-home market appeared to be rebounding. For Leslie, it had bounced back to nearly 20 percent of his sales again. The only change in this market, he noted, was that people were no longer looking for luxury, full-service buildings. They wanted brownstones with more square footage and fewer shared public spaces like elevators and lobbies, new desired features that emerged from living with an airborne disease.

Other sources confirmed these trends. In the summer of 2021, the *Boston Globe* interviewed a series of Boston real estate brokers, developers, and executives, who had found only a blip in the luxury real estate market due to Covid. Many developments aimed at attracting second-home buyers had picked up selling at rates even higher than in 2019, before the pandemic began.[18] The decline of elite dwellers in the city, then, was not an enduring trend. It was a fleeting moment in recent urban history. As the world opened back up, as vaccinations increased, as people became more comfortable living with daily risk, elites reclaimed the city again as their own.

Second Homeowners during Covid-19

The second homeowners I talked to for this book were drawn to urban and rural places for the identity fulfillment they got from becoming a city or country person in second-home communities. They situated who they felt they were with where they felt they belonged through place-identity projects, involving the construction of their selves using place-specific attributes, meanings, and practices. The social changes brought on by Covid could have potentially changed a lot of what I found. It was possible that the new structure of remote work and school could have promoted more time spent in rural areas. It was also possible that Covid-related closures of museums, theaters, restaurants, symphonies, and virtually all public life might have undermined urban second homeowners' identity pursuits. But did it change anything? As of November 2021, only three of the second homeowners in Boston I had interviewed had sold their second home. The three who did also rented their homes to others via Airbnb, suggesting that possible financial constraints due to Covid-related revenue loss contributed to their unplanned departure. Two of the second homeowners I interviewed in Rangeley had sold their second homes. One sold the home because the spouse passed away and another sold their home during the summer of 2020 for reasons unknown.

Paul and Carol Baker have devoted even more time to Rangeley since the last time I spoke to them, spearheading local conservation efforts. Carol has since taken on a more formal and involved role at the RLHT, monitoring for invasive species across the region's lakes system. When I had talked with Paul and Carol back in 2013, Carol had been laying the groundwork for more local involvement, taking classes on invasive species endemic to the northern region. Such involvement investing in and protecting rurality was always part of her plan as she lived out her country self in Rangeley's lakes and forest.

Despite media portrayals of the great urban exodus, it seems that the pandemic did not entirely undermine Richard and Doris Flynn's relationship to Boston. In the summer of 2020 during the pandemic, Doris's typical haunts had all closed their doors to visitors. The MFA, the BSO, and the theater had all shut down for nearly six months. But during these closures, Doris helped bring new forms of high culture to the city, helping spearhead an open-air art exhibit in her neighborhood. As an elected member of her neighborhood organization dedicated to the promotion of public art, she worked with the city of Boston to secure grant money for this Covid-friendly cultural experience. As someone who had been thinking about these second homeowners for years, I was not at all surprised. For Richard and Doris, the city was never just about amenities. It was never just about attending places like the Museum of Fine Arts, specifically. It was about becoming the type of person who lives in an urban place and does urban—high-cultural—activities in whatever form is most readily available. And against even the greatest odds, Doris found new ways to satiate her city self.

Tables

TABLE 3. Change in "for Seasonal, Recreational, or Occasional Use" in American Global Cities, 2000–2019

	# second homes 2000	% of total housing stock 2000	# second homes 2019	% of total housing stock 2019
New York, NY (1)	28,157	0.9	75,935	2.1
Los Angeles, CA (7)	4,876	0.4	13,850	0.9
Chicago, IL (8)	4,549	0.4	12,007	1.0
Washington, DC (10)	2,207	0.8	3,428	1.1
San Francisco, CA (13)	3,762	1.1	8,316	2.1
Boston, MA (21)	1,568	0.6	4,626	1.6
Miami, FL (30)	2,901	1.9	12,074	5.8

Note: Numbers denote ranking from Kearney global city index. "The GCI assesses how globally engaged cities are across five dimensions: business activity, human capital, information exchange, cultural experience, and political engagement" (Kearney 2020). *Source*: 2000 Census data summary file 1 and 2019 American Community Survey 5-year estimates.

TABLE 4. Rangeley Second Homeowners' Permanent Home Residence: Top Seven States

State	Count (1,167)	% of total (2,342)
Maine	450	38.5
Massachusetts	272	23.3
New Hampshire	99	8.4
New York	47	4.0
Connecticut	46	3.9
New Jersey	41	3.5
Florida	34	2.9

Note: While I critique using this method for Boston, given that the majority of Rangeley's vacant housing stock is "for seasonal, recreational, or occasional use," and not other types of vacant properties (e.g., for rent, for sale, or other), property tax assessment data can more closely capture the permanent residences of second homeowners. It furthermore aligns with the census estimates on second homeownership in the town. *Source*: 2014 Rangeley Tax Assessment Data.

TABLE 5. Demographic Characteristics of Census Tracts with Highest Density of Second Homes in Three U.S. Cities, 2015–2019 ACS

	Neighborhood	Total housing stock	% second homes	Median home value	Median household income	% white alone
New York City, NY		3,546,601	2.1	$609,700	$63,998	42
-Tract 10200	Midtown	314	64	n/a	n/a	55
-Tract 11202	Midtown	561	46	$1,875,000	$141,563	82
-Tract 11203	Midtown	1,202	40	$973,700	$159,792	71
-Tract 10400	Midtown	993	38	$1,161,800	$125,882	63
-Tract 11401	Midtown	1,370	37	$2,000,001	$250,001	85
Los Angeles, CA		1,493,108	0.9	$642,400	$67,418	52
-Tract 267901	Century City	2,042	12	$1,146,700	$118,393	74
-Tract 189701	HLWD Hills	2,680	12	$1,115,700	$100,256	71
-Tract 274202	Venice Beach	2,786	11	$1,671,500	$128,766	76
-Tract 265602	Westwood	1,835	11	$1,149,100	$117,629	75
-Tract 262303	Brentwood	1,271	8	$2,000,001	$250,001	85
Chicago, IL		1,214,450	0.9	$272,700	$58,247	50
-Tract 81500	Near N. Side	4,231	22	$505,500	$107,847	66
-Tract 320400	Loop	1,029	21	$663,800	$168,958	61
-Tract 81402	Streeterville	4,317	11	$535,600	$119,387	63
-Tract 81201	Streeterville	3,839	11	$875,800	$94,288	77
-Tract 320100	New Eastside	9,808	10	$553,800	$109,167	68

Source: Steven Manson, Jonathan Schroeder, David Van Riper, Tracy Kugler, and Steven Ruggles, IPUMS National Historical Geographic Information System: Version 16.0 [data set] (Minneapolis: IPUMS, 2021).

TABLE 6. Boston Neighborhood Change from 1990 to 2019

	% white alone 1990	% white alone 2019	Median household income 1990	Median household income 2019	Median home value 1990	Median home value 2019	% 25+ BA or higher 1990	% 25+ BA or higher 2019
Boston	*62.8*	*44*	*$29,180*	*$71,259*	*$160,100*	*$532,700*	*29.9*	*49.7*
Back Bay	88.7	73.4	$38,981	$111,185	$471,884	$1,140,183	72.9	84.4
Downtown	61.7	55.6	$26,537	$88,750	$286,899	$902,900	43.3	63.0
Beacon Hill	85.6	83.7	$37,275	$110,841	$414,347	$983,233	67.7	91.0
North End	98	87.9	$29,371	$103,999	$337,590	$694,375	37.9	81.0

Source: Data for 1990–2010 come from Geolytics, "Neighborhood Change Database 1990–2010"; 2019 data come from Boston Planning and Development Agency 2019.

TABLE 7. Change in "for Seasonal, Recreational, or Occasional Use": Boston, 1990–2019

	1990 total housing stock	1990 % SRO	2019 total housing stock	2019 % SRO
Boston	*250,863*	*0.7*	*294,418*	*1.6*
Back Bay	8,365	1.9	11,971	10.4
Downtown	6,628	1.4	9,966	10.1
Beacon Hill	6,541	0.8	6,148	6.6
North End	4,771	0.6	5,829	6.1

Source: Data for 1990–2010 come from Geolytics, "Neighborhood Change Database 1990–2010"; 2019 data come from Boston Planning and Development Agency 2019.

Methods

Methodology: Rangeley

This project began with a two-week pilot study in the summer of 2013. It was difficult to find affordable short-term housing, and as a result I lived in an RV on a family friend's property for the duration of my stay. During this time, I interviewed three second homeowners and began to develop familiarity with the lay of the land by frequenting the local shops, restaurants, bars, and community events. In the winter of 2013, I rented a second-floor, one-bedroom apartment in a converted farmhouse near the center of the town on Main Street, and I lived in Rangeley until the end of the summer, August 2014.

The ethnographic portion of this project aimed to observe interactions among and between second homeowners and permanent residents, or lack thereof. To do this, I sampled a variety of civic, nonprofit, and political organizations in the town to measure the presence and/or absence of second homeowners in the formal, organized sphere of public life, as well as to gauge permanent residents' public perceptions and attitudes toward second homeowners. In total, I observed fifteen meetings. This included observing and meeting with members from the chamber of commerce (1), board of selectmen (4), annual town meeting (1), planning board (1), church events (2), Rangeley Region Guides and Sporting Association (1), library board (1), Rangeley Friends of the Arts (2), school board (1), and the Rangeley visioning (1).

As a way to observe other important facets of local life that extended beyond formal, organized civic and political meetings, this project furthermore relied on data collected through participant observation in coffee shops, bars, bakeries, restaurants, museums, bookstores, and community events—fairs, farmer's markets, parades, festivals, lectures, home tours, board of selectmen meet the candidates night, and so on—to measure the presence and/or absence of second homeowners in the public community realm.[1] I also analyzed an array of community data including newspaper

TABLE 8. Industry of Workers, Rangeley, 2000–2015

Industry of Workers	2000	2015
Civilian employed population sixteen years and over	498	528
Agriculture, forestry, fishing and hunting, and mining	7.6%	5.5%
Construction	12.7%	15.2%
Manufacturing	4.8%	2.7%
Wholesale trade	8%	0%
Retail trade	17.3%	18.8%
Transportation and warehousing, and utilities	2%	1.5%
Information	1.2%	2.3%
Finance and insurance, and real estate and leasing	7%	5.7%
Professional, scientific, and management, and administrative and waste management	8.4%	3.4%
Educational services, and health care and social assistance	13.1%	16.7%
Arts, entertainment, and recreation, and accommodation and food services	13.9%	15.7%
Other services, except public administration	5.8%	7.4%
Public administration	4.6%	5.3%

Source: 2000 data come from U.S. Census; 2015 data come from American Community Survey, selected economic characteristics, 5-year estimates 2011–15.

articles, historical texts, municipal records, property tax records, donation databases, and community forums.

Last, I drew upon in-depth and extended participant observation at two local commercial establishments: during the summer I worked alongside permanent residents at a restaurant that primarily served second homeowners and seasonal visitors, and during the winter I worked at the local mountain as a ski instructor where I worked alongside both second homeowners and permanent residents. There are three important limitations to these sources of data. First, because these interactions tended to take place within the occupational settings in the service industry, the interactions I observed were inherently embedded in a relationship of consumption and production, and my observations may thus be skewed toward these relationships. Second, because of the types of jobs I worked, I tended to interact with permanent residents who were on the front lines of the tourist industry in town. However, in both cases because the majority of employed residents in Rangeley work in these types of industries, it at the very least is representative of a significant portion of the local workforce (see table 8).

TABLE 9. Second-Homeowner Sample by Method of
Recruitment in Rangeley

	Total people	Total interviews
Rangeley Bistro	8	5
The Mountain	9	5
Real estate agents	5	3
Snowball through local residents and other second homeowners	15	9
Total	37	22

Third, and finally, I offer an important caveat to working at the local restaurant. On the whole, it was one of the more expensive restaurants in town. Therefore, it appealed to the second homeowners and tourists with more disposable income, and it tended to attract fewer families with young children. Thus, my observations at this restaurant may very well have been different if I worked at the local pizza place or coffee shop nearby. While these may be a limited source of data, they are representative of many of the instances in which some second homeowners and permanent residents interact—through the second homeowners' patronage of local business establishments.

Because the primary aim of this project was to uncover second homeowners' narratives and practices, I interviewed thirty-seven second homeowners across twenty-two interviews. Some interviews were conducted with husbands and wives and some with neighbors who wished to be interviewed together. Table 9 notes this distribution and the method of recruitment.

I solicited participants through multiple access points in town to diversify my sample. I solicited participants through the jobs I worked, through local meetings I attended, and through connections I made with permanent residents who introduced me to their second-homeowner acquaintances. These interviews, which lasted from one to three hours, were conducted at the places of the second homeowners' choosing, which allowed me to observe part of their daily routines and practices.[2] Although the second homeowners I met discussed not participating in much of Rangeley's public life and not maintaining many local social ties, I did meet some of them at commercial establishments in town (like the restaurant, the IGA, or the mountain) and I did meet some of them through other people. However, their engagement with these spheres was limited or bounded, and the people they connected me with were typically acquaintances—not close friends.

I occupied a unique position in the Rangeley community as both an insider and outsider. I am a "Mainer," but I am not from Rangeley nor am I (nor is anyone in my family) a second homeowner. I found it relatively easy to build rapport with permanent residents due to aspects of my personal history. I grew up in a small city in central Maine that was predominantly working and middle class, which I found gave me more local credence than if I had grown up in Portland or one of its many affluent suburbs—places that I heard some people refer to pejoratively as "northern Massachusetts." I also come from a family of farmers and steelworkers and have a working knowledge of all the primary outdoor recreation activities found in this area, which helped me navigate different local milieus—from skiers to snowmobilers and from historians to construction workers. Furthermore, due to the time I spent working at the restaurant and the ski mountain, I was able to meet and develop relationships with a variety of local folks that I sustained over the course of my fieldwork. However, everyone I encountered in town also knew that I was an outsider, a sociologist there to study second homeowners in their community. While I became a normal presence at work, at meetings throughout town, and in most commercial establishments, I knew I would never gain full access to permanent residents' world.

With second homeowners I was, in some ways, an insider; neither of us were from Rangeley. This seemed to encourage the second homeowners I met to talk openly with me about their feelings about the community—sometimes disparagingly so. However, because I was not a second homeowner and they knew I was a sociologist (originally from Maine) studying their relationship to the community, it is likely that they felt pressure to downplay their social position in this environment. My presence and questions possibly heightened their class consciousness, influencing the narrative they developed about their in-migration. I aimed to bridge these barriers and triangulate data through the multiple sources of data collection I detailed above.

Methodology: Boston

This research was conducted over the course of two years while I lived in Jamaica Plain in Boston. I began this project by observing community meetings to measure the presence or absence of second homeowners in civic life and to gauge the degree to which they are framed as a problem for civic leaders. I attended ten community meetings in neighborhoods where second homeowners most heavily concentrate in Boston: the North End/Waterfront, Back Bay, and Downtown. I chose these neighborhoods because of their high concentration of second homeowners, which enabled observation of the presence or absence of these residents in civic and political life. Meetings included residents' associations, neighborhood associations, and meetings hosted by the Boston Redevelopment Authority, which covered development projects taking place in these neighborhoods.[3] To provide contextual background for the perceptions of second homeowners and to gain an understanding of how they did or did not engage in civic and political life, this project furthermore relied on interviews with six community leaders, interviews with five real estate agents, and analyses of newspapers, community forums, and archival data. The interviews with community leaders and real estate agents were meant to mirror the type of data that I collected in Rangeley through observations of everyday life—observations that were only possible because of the small population of Rangeley and very high density of second homeowners in the region.

Real estate agents were contacted by email. I determined which real estate companies to contact by selecting companies that specialized in high-end real estate in the neighborhoods with the highest concentration of second homeowners. The real estate agents I spoke with broadly specialized in areas proximate to the center of the city: the North End, Seaport, Downtown, Back Bay, and Beacon Hill. I furthermore contacted neighborhood associations in areas where second homeowners concentrate and was able to connect with community leaders in Beacon Hill, Downtown, North End/Waterfront, South End, and Back Bay. I also interviewed an employee from the Boston Symphony Orchestra and corresponded with an employee from the Boston tax assessor's office.

To understand the narratives and practices of second homeowners in Boston, this case drew on twenty-four in-depth interviews with individual second homeowners. I did not interview husbands and wives together, except for respondents I call Bruce and Joyce, because I spoke with everyone except one over the phone. Gusterson argues for a different set of methods for "studying up" than social scientists typically utilize for participant observation. Gusterson advocates for "polymorphous engagement," whereby one "interacts with informants across a number of dispersed sites, not just in local communities, and sometimes in virtual form; and it means collecting data eclectically from a disparate array of sources in many different ways."[4] Indeed, there were peculiarities of the Boston case of second homeowners, which proved challenging for data collection yet ultimately fruitful to understand second homeowners' relationship to place. I thus collected data "eclectically from a disparate array of sources in many different ways."

Second homeowners are an elusive population, in part because of their transience—the very essence of second homeownership means that they live between two or more places—and in part because many choose not to participate in the formal, public sphere of their second-home communities.[5] To gain access to this elusive population I relied on a wide variety of sampling methods: neighborhood email lists and websites, Airbnb and VRBO (vacation rentals by owner), and Boston's tax assessment data.[6]

Because many neighborhood email lists are private to residents, I relied on informants to post calls for participants on my behalf. I sampled neighborhoods that had the highest concentration of second homes.[7] I furthermore turned to Airbnb and VRBO, where I contacted property owners who explicitly mentioned in their listing that they use their property occasionally as a vacation home for themselves.

Finally, I utilized Boston's tax assessment data to determine second homes/owners. I identified properties that met all three of the following criteria: single-family or condo homes, not owner occupied, and listed a zip code outside of Boston for the permanent mailing address. This strategy has been used before. However, it was difficult to parse intended use of each residential unit. The Boston City Assessing Office corroborated that while the city tracks non-residents through the residential exemption, it is nearly impossible to decipher the differences between those who own homes exclusively as rental properties (that are occupied by tenants full-time) and those who own them for vacation, leisure, or investment (e.g., units that are vacant and unrented).[8] I then randomly contacted residents by mail, in which I asked a series of demographic questions and whether they would like to participate in an in-depth interview.

All interviews with second homeowners were done over the phone, with the exception of one. The very difficulty of soliciting second homeowners for interviews, coupled with the challenge of setting up a time to meet in person—nearly all opted to talk over the phone—revealed the characteristics of these homeowners and some of the differences between them and those in the rural village. Second homeowners in Rangeley invited me over to their homes, and I often spent hours with them, chatting over coffee or sitting with them outside overlooking their home's scenic views. Second homeowners in Boston rarely knew when they would be in town or if they had the time to meet with me once they were. At least three of the second homeowners I interviewed over the phone did so while they were themselves in transit—driving in a car, grocery shopping, or walking to pick their children up at school. I also could not *see* second homeowners

TABLE 10. Second-Homeowner Sample
by Method of Recruitment in Boston

	Total
Neighborhood listserv	5
Mail-in survey	11
Airbnb/VRBO	6
Personal network	2
Total	24

in everyday life as I did in Rangeley, making ethnography of their everyday lives difficult to capture.

Altogether, this set of sampling methods provided me with a largely diverse group of second homeowners throughout many of the Boston neighborhoods. However, it is important to note that the findings in this project were wholly dependent on who responded to my inquiries. Many of the second homeowners I contacted declined to participate. Contacting second homeowners by mail yielded the most response. Table 10 reveals the breakdown of the sample by method of recruitment. No second homeowners were successfully recruited from real estate agents or from neighborhood community leaders.

My educational position at a well-known university in the Boston area helped me gain entrée with the second homeowners in Boston I met. However, aspects of my social position as a young graduate student without formal credentials made it difficult to cast a wide net of second homeowners to interview. It is likely that upper-middle-class second homeowners who are well-educated responded to my call for participants because they had an appreciation of graduate work. In fact, many of them discussed this, remembering what it was like to be in graduate school or telling me about family members who were earning graduate degrees—and they wanted to help me out. People who are even more transient are less likely to find the time or desire to talk about their relationship to Boston. Or, as one real estate agent told me about his most high-end clients: "They have high status; they don't want to be bothered." This may have influenced why I found so many people with a significant place identity tied to Boston.

However, like in the case of Rangeley, I was not a second homeowner. This outsider status may have limited how forthcoming people were about their everyday practices, as their social-class position was heightened during our conversations, particularly as I asked them questions about how and if they involve themselves in neighborhood and community life in Boston. It's possible that many wanted their everyday practices to appear normal and inconsequential to a researcher trying to understand second-homeowner in-migration into cities, downplaying their class status, influence on communities, and everyday practices. I addressed this issue by relying on "polymorphous data collection," detailed above, with and through neighborhood civic associations, real estate agents, nonprofit organizations, neighborhood observations, newspapers, and analyses of donor databases and property tax records to triangulate what they said and what they did.

Methods: Analysis

Collecting data across two cases produces a large data set. To analyze this large amount of data, I coded my interview, textual, and observational data using NVIVO software. I first broke the data up into large chunks of analyzable text that aligned with the thematic topics of interest I covered in my interview and observational guides, aligning with what Deterding and Waters have recently called "flexible coding" methods.[9] My interview guides broadly covered my informants' background, their relationship to their first home, why they chose a second home where they did, what they did when they were there, the types of organizations they were involved with or donated to, how and if they developed social ties, and what they thought of their second-home community.

I then engaged in focused coding, in which I inductively analyzed each section of texts to look for emerging themes and patterns across both cases. From these sections, I noticed the following themes that emerged specifically from the large chunks of interview text from the categories "background/ primary homes," "view of Rangeley/Boston," and "time spent in Rangeley/ Boston": identity dissatisfaction with their orientations to their first-home community, a desire for a sense of place in their second-home communities, and social practices that align with the meanings they attached to these place categories. After memoing and returning to extant literature from rural, urban, and cultural sociology, I was able to develop the concept, *place-identity project* to connect these findings.

My observational guides generally covered how local people reacted to second homeowners' presence or absence. During the focused coding of these large chunks of text, I was able to notice patterns in the discourses that were developed around both types of second homeownership across cases—high-end blight in Boston and resource dependency in Rangeley.

NOTES

Introduction

1. All names of people from interviews and observations herein are pseudonyms. To protect the confidentiality of these informants, some small details of their lives have also been changed. All place-names herein are real.

2. https://www.thefreedomtrail.org/.

3. In the past twenty years, rates of second homeownership have increased by 34 percent (statistics derived from Census 2000 and 2020 American Community Survey five-year estimates). I define second homeownership herein by drawing upon the work of sociologists, geographers, and tourism and mobility studies (Coppock 1977; Hall and Müller 2004; Stiman 2020a; Armstrong and Stedman 2013; Hall and Müller 2018; Müller and Hoogendoorn 2013). Hall and Müller loosely define second homes by acknowledging the variety of second-home types: "there is a great variety of terms that refer to second homes: recreational homes, vacation homes, summer homes, cottages, and weekend homes. . . . The term 'second home' is used as an umbrella for these different terms, which all refer to a certain idea of usage" (2004, 4). I adopt this similar approach, by acknowledging the heterogeneity of second-home types and usage, but I generally refer to second homes and second homeowners as those who own a housing unit for vacation or leisure use but whose permanent residence is elsewhere. This is also the language I used to solicit calls for participants. While "multiple homes" (Paris 2010) is often more appropriate to describe some of the affluent participants in this sample who own more than two properties, I defer to the colloquial term "second home." This is furthermore how the participants in this sample referred to their residences.

4. See Stiman 2020a for an elaboration.

5. According to the National Association of Realtors, vacation properties and investment properties located in urban areas or central cities account for nearly 20 percent of all secondary properties, which has increased over the past ten years (National Association of Realtors 2017). Fifteen percent of vacation properties and 23 percent of all investment properties are located in urban areas or central cities. This has increased since 2010, when 17 percent of all second-property purchases, including both vacation and investment purchases, were in urban areas or central cities. See Paul Bishop, Jessica Lautz, Arun Barman, and Danielle Hale, "National Association of Realtors Profile of Home Buyers and Sellers 2010," https://www.slideshare.net/wmleads/nar-2009-home-buyers-and-sellers.

6. Badger 2022.

7. National Association of Realtors 2021b.

8. Ballentine and Kantor 2021.

9. Khater, Kiefer, and Yanamandra 2021.

10. Demsas 2021.

11. National Association of Realtors 2017.

12. For examples of highly segregated second-home destinations, see Dolgon 2005; Fernandez, Hofman, and Aalbers 2016; Park and Pellow 2011; Winkler 2013.

13. García 2022.

14. Ibid., 34.

15. Scholars have found that some local populations view tourism as a means with which to prevent economic decline (Long, Perdue, and Allen 1990; Smith and Krannich 1998), while others find that the new dependence on tourism comes with a host of social and economic problems (Milman and Pizam 1988). As such, scholars have found there to be a threshold at which local populations are more accepting of tourism; as communities become more dependent on tourism and become tourist destinations, their tolerance for tourists and non-residents decreases (Long, Perdue, and Allen 1990). Other scholarship has turned to how local populations perceive second homeowners, one segment of the tourism economy. Some debate the extent to which second-home development is a "curse" or a "blessing" for rural locales whose economic base is now largely dependent on tourism and consumption (Coppock 1977; Hall and Müller 2004). Regardless of the economic benefits or disadvantages, the in-migration of second homeowners is found to at times conflict with longtime residents' community values, land-use practices, and resource management strategies (Clendenning, Field, and Kapp 2005; Gosnell and Abrams 2011; Jaakson 1986). Some research suggests that conflicts are perhaps even more heightened in rural locales with a higher density of second homeowners (Rye 2011), and other work finds that permanent residents are more likely to perceive culture clash between themselves and second homeowners in areas with a high concentration of seasonal homes (Armstrong and Stedman 2013). However, other research analyzes the local conditions of second-homeowner acceptance, finding that local populations' perceptions of second homeowners depend on the outcomes of second-home tourism and whether or not second homeowners make a social or economic contribution to the local community (Farstad 2011).

16. Miles 2020.

17. Treisman 2020.

18. Ortiz 2020.

19. Fernandez, Hofman, and Aalbers 2016.

20. Ibid.; Kadi, Hochstenbach, and Lennartz 2020; Ronald and Kadi 2017; Stiman 2019.

21. Roberts 2011.

22. Bolongaro 2021.

23. Lees 2003; Butler and Lees 2006.

24. I situate this book within the long-standing theoretical framework in urban and community sociology that seeks to analyze how the meanings people hold about a given locale have the power to influence its construction and use (Borer 2006; Brown-Saracino 2010, 2015; Douglas 2012; Firey 1945; Gieryn 2000; Hummon 1990; Hunter 1982; Kaufman and Kaliner 2011; Kusenbach 2008; Milligan 1998; Ocejo 2014, 2019; Suttles 1972).

25. For exemplary rural cases, see Armstrong and Stedman 2013; Farstad 2011; Hall and Müller 2004; Schewe et al. 2012; Stedman 2006; Winkler 2013. For exemplary urban cases, see Fernandez, Hofman, and Aalbers 2016; Kadi, Hochstenbach, and Lennartz 2020; van Loon and Aalbers 2017. For important exceptions that trace the mobility of the elite, see Hay 2013; Paris 2010.

26. I situate this in the robust literature that explains how social class influences migration patterns, including how social class mediates long-term residential decision making, the use of social networks, locational decisions after environmental disasters, and horizontal immobility (Harvey et al. 2020; Krysan and Crowder 2017; Lareau 2014; Lareau and Goyette 2014; Rhodes and Besbris 2022b, 2022a; Rosen 2017). Upper-middle-class suburbanites who own second homes in either the city or the country can tell us more about the geographic reach—the multiple and simultaneous locations—of some upper-middle-class people today. For an overview of the multiple places in which upper-middle-class people make claims over place, see Paulsen and Stuber 2022.

27. This is not to say that economic conditions are separate from this second-home housing purchase. Intergenerational housing wealth made possible by housing policies and practices has enabled generations of predominantly white middle- and upper-middle-class families to purchase primary, secondary, and multiple residences.

28. For notable examples, see Oldenburg 1999; Putnam 2001; Slater 1990.

29. On the framing of the suburbs as part of the American dream, see Jackson 1985.

30. Charles Tilly (1998) defines opportunity hoarding as a distinct method of social closure in which people within a bounded social network secure resources for themselves and those within their networks at the direct expense of others. More recently, Matthew Desmond (2023) has made the case that opportunity hoarding is yet another mechanism by which poverty has been maintained for centuries in America; they are two sides of the same coin.

31. Briggs, Popkin, and Goering 2010; Logan and Molotch 1987; Massey 1996; Massey and Denton 1993; Sampson 2012; Sharkey 2013; Wilson 2012.

32. Massey and Denton 1993.

33. On the effects of gentrification for longtime residents, see Brown-Saracino 2010; Hyra 2017; Levy and Cybriwksy 1980; Pattillo 2007; Golding 2016.

34. Girouard 2023.

35. Massey and Denton 1993.

36. Bartram 2022; Besbris 2020; Korver-Glenn 2021; Levine 2021; Rosen 2020.

37. Bayurgil 2021; Herbert 2021; Summers 2019; Tuttle 2022b.

38. Farrell 2020a; Pattillo-McCoy 2000; Tissot 2015; Brown-Saracino 2010; Girouard 2023.

39. Dolgon 2005; Farrell 2020a; Fernandez and Aalbers 2016; Fernandez, Hofman, and Aalbers 2016; Stuber 2021; Winkler 2013.

40. Aalbers 2019; Brown-Saracino 2010; Makris and Gatta 2020.

41. Farstad and Rye 2013.

42. This orientation to causality originates from early social theorists like Max Weber, who was committed to multicausality to explain social phenomena. For example, while Weber agreed that material conditions and technological advances were part of the rise of capitalism in the West, he argued that the cultural conditions that motivated people to seek profit and the accumulation of capital, the spirit of capitalism, were essential for it to take hold the way it did. I similarly acknowledge that large-scale material conditions are central to the story about the rise of upper-middle-class suburbanites buying second homes; however, I explore how the place-based cultural motivations encourage everyday upper-middle-class people to participate in this process, which helps connect what people do to these broader social forces (Weber 2013).

43. Brown-Saracino 2010; Hummon 1990. On culture's relationship to structure and agency, see Wray 2014. For examples of how research links the motivations of people to their actions, see Alkon and Traugot 2008; Borer 2006; Brown-Saracino 2010, 2015; Deener 2007; Firey 1945; Gieryn 2000; Grazian 2003; Greene 2014; Hunter 1975, 1982; Kaufman and Kaliner 2011; Milligan 1998. According to Brown-Saracino (2010), this cultural approach—understanding what people do and why—enables researchers to link the motivations of people to their actions, all of which provides a piece to the puzzle of how inequality is produced and reproduced.

44. Gieryn 2000, 471.

45. Brown-Saracino 2010; Douglas 2012; Ocejo 2019.

46. Sherman 2021; Bell 1994; Gosnell and Abrams 2011; Hoey 2014; Farrell 2020a.

47. Kaufman and Kaliner 2011.

48. Firey 1945.

49. Anguelovski 2015.

50. Phadke 2013.

51. For an overview of neoliberalism and place, see Brenner and Theodore 2005; Lees 2003.

52. On the consequences of growth as an ideology, see Logan and Molotch 1987.

53. For an analysis and history of uneven transportation access in Boston, see Levine 2021. On rural medical deserts, see Brown and Schafft 2011.

54. See Brown-Saracino 2010; Douglas 2012; Parker and Ternullo 2022. For an important exception, see Richard Ocejo's (2019) analysis of gentrifiers in the Hudson Valley who left New York City, in which this movement shapes how they understand themselves and their place within their new community.

55. Farrell 2020a; Stuber 2021; Gosnell and Abrams 2011; Sherman 2021.

56. Scholarship has captured a great deal about how second homeowners engage with community life within their rural second-home host communities—their sense of community, place attachment, local social ties, and/or local institutional involvement (Armstrong and Stedman 2013, 2019; Pitkänen, Adamiak, and Halseth 2014; Schewe et al. 2012; Stedman 2006). Much of this research used large-scale data sets to analyze these processes. The present book builds on this robust body of research by gathering interpretive data from second homeowners themselves across the multiple place categories where they reside to understand these very processes.

57. Bell 1994; Breen 1996; Brown-Saracino 2010; Cain 2020b; Dolgon 2005; Douglas 2012; Hull 2012; Ocejo 2011; Parker and Ternullo 2022; Pattillo 2007; Sherman 2021.

58. Hunter and Suttles 1972; Janowitz 1952; Kusenbach 2008; Wellman and Leighton 1979.

59. There is an array of cultural elements that sociologists study to understand this link: repertoires and rituals, cultural capital, frames, symbolic boundaries, social norms, discourse and narratives, and institutions (Wray 2014). This book focuses on second homeowners' *identity narrative construction*: how they understand themselves and their place in the world, and how this self-understanding *guides* their everyday actions.

60. Cuba and Hummon 1993a, 1993b.

61. Gieryn (2000) suggests that place "is a unique spot in the universe . . . [it has] physicality . . . [and it is invested] with meaning and value" (465).

62. Lawler (2014) suggests that identities can be understood as narratives that we build to tell a story about who we are to others.

63. Cuba and Hummon 1993a, 1993b.

64. Cuba and Hummon (1993a) ask how people identify with places of different scales—dwelling, community, region—to construct a theory of place identity although still rely on individuals' immediate geographic location to explain affiliation with place.

65. Ibid.

66. Although some scholarship has moved beyond these categorical ways of thinking about local places in a globalizing and urbanizing world, people still experience these place categories as real and meaningful. For an elaboration of this, see Bell 1992.

67. Goffman 1963, 105; see also Milligan 2003, 383.

68. Trujillo 2022.

69. By exploring how place identity is felt, social scientists can analyze place identity not as dependent on one's immediate geographic location but as an *independent* variable, patterning various possible orientations to social life, from voting behaviors to environmental action to philanthropic practices.

70. According to structural symbolic interactionism, identity theory is based on the "premise that society impacts self impacts social behavior" (Stryker 2008, 20). In this conceptualization, people have multiple identities situated within organized systems of "role relationships in which they participate" (ibid.). Using the second home as a place-identity project could thus be conceptualized as a method through which the people I met specify their self, what Sheldon Stryker (2008) refers to as identity salience.

71. Lawler 2014.

72. Ibid.

73. For other notable examples, see Pattillo's (2007) discussion of middle-class Black gentrifiers who view themselves as "middlemen" and Brown-Saracino's (2010) analysis of gentrifiers whose ideologies are characterized by social preservationism.

74. Ocejo 2014.

75. Bartram 2022.

76. I draw on notable research to elaborate the relationship between social class and how people both interpret places and make residential choices (Pattillo 2007; Paulsen and Stuber 2022; Rhodes and Besbris 2022a, 2022b; Stuber 2021).

77. Scholars have written about how ruptures in place attachment can cause people to develop new identities in relation to place and how moving to a new place can cause someone to develop a new sense of self (Brown-Saracino 2018; Milligan 2003; Ocejo 2011). Attention to social class can explain why some people do not always have to adopt new identities; they have the financial resources to imprint their own sense of self onto the places where they live.

78. On how proximity to nature is a site "moneyed people" find "secure" and "legitimate," see Bell 1994.

79. Sherman 2018, 411.

80. Bell 1994, 138.

81. Bell 1994; Farrell 2020a; Sherman 2021.

82. Sherman 2018, 412; Sherman 2019.

83. There is a wealth of research explaining such forces, building on research from W.E.B. Du Bois (1899) and Cedric Robinson (2005), which broadly examines how the social construction of race explains the valuation of places. For notable contemporary examples, see Dantzler, Korver-Glenn, and Howell 2022; Loughran 2017; Mayorga, Underhill, and Crosser 2022; Rucks-Ahidiana 2021; Seamster 2015; Tuttle 2022b.

84. Hornsby and Judd 2015; Priest 2009.

85. Much of the theorizing about amenity destinations emerges from one specific geographic context—the American West—to such a degree that scholars suggest that it is perhaps a "regional literature" (Gosnell and Abrams 2011, 305). This derives from an empirical warrant. The American West has witnessed rapid social and economic changes since the 1970s (Gosnell and Abrams 2011; Shumway and Davis 1996; Vias and Carruthers 2005), and thus scholars have attended to the consequences of such sudden changes for longtime populations. By attending to a town in New England, I build on other important work in this region where there is a "longstanding history of second homeownership and a tradition of seasonal visitation" (Armstrong and Stedman 2013, 320; Armstrong and Stedman 2019) to advance knowledge about the "linkages and continuities, as well as regional specificities" (Gosnell and Abrams 2011, 305), between and among geographies across the United States.

86. In Rangeley's tax assessment data from 2014, out of the 2,342 property assessments in the sample, 1,167 were "second homeowners," that is, people who own property in Rangeley, but Rangeley is not their primary residence. This closely aligns (almost 50 percent) with the census data, which cites 57 percent of the housing stock in Rangeley as labeled "for seasonal, recreational, or occasional use" (U.S. Census Bureau 2010). Given these data, I aggregated the total number of residents who come from each state. The largest percent of the total number of second homeowners come from Maine, 38 percent, which mirrors my own sample. Of the 450 second homeowners from Maine only 37, or 8 percent, come from the top five most populous cities in Maine: Portland (66,194), Lewiston (36,592), Bangor (33,039), South Portland (25,002), and Auburn (23,055) (U.S. Census Bureau 2010). Only 7.5 percent of the total second-homeowner population comes from New York or New Jersey (see table 4). While I critique this method of using property assessment data as a way of measuring second homeownership, given that the majority of Rangeley's vacant housing stock is "for seasonal, recreational, or occasional use," and

not other types of vacant properties (e.g., for rent, for sale, or other), it can more closely capture the permanent residences of second homeowners. It furthermore aligns with the census estimates on second homeownership in the town.

87. ACS 2019 5-year estimates.

88. On defining the upper middle class, see Gilbert 2011.

89. On multiple property ownership as an indicator of affluence, see Paris 2010.

90. For notable research that highlights this process, see Brown-Saracino 2010; Zukin and Kasinitz 1995.

91. See table 3.

92. See tables 5 and 6.

93. See table 7.

94. Collins and de Goede 2018.

95. The luxury real estate agents I spoke with corroborated that their typical second-home buyers were predominantly retirees from the suburbs or, in the case of one real estate agent, international buyers. Given my diverse sampling methods, the findings of this book are thus dependent on who responded to my call for participants. As discussed more in the methodological appendix, it is thus not surprising that people who expressed some sort of place identity were more likely than others, who perhaps were less connected to the city, to respond.

96. For an elaboration on how "methodological stumbles" in generating an interview sample can generate "substantive insights" about that very sample, see Brown-Saracino 2014.

97. ACS 2019 5-year estimates.

98. Farrell 2020b; Story and Saul 2015.

99. Drawing from their occupational status and educational attainment, the people I met broadly fell into this defined social-class category. I use Dennis Gilbert's (2011) model of American social-class structure to define the class boundaries of the people I interviewed for this book. Gilbert defines three distinct groups of social classes in America using a combination of occupation, education, and income. The "privileged classes" lie at the top of this schema. Gilbert divides this broad category into two distinct classes: the "capitalist class," who constitute the top 1 percent of households, and the "upper middle class," who constitute the top 14 percent of households. The comparative boundaries of this social-class category are with the capitalist class and the middle class. The capitalist class are typically investors, executives, and heirs, have undergraduate, graduate, and professional school degrees, usually from elite institutions, and make over $1 million in household income annually. The middle class, a group that Gilbert considers part of the "majority classes," tend to work as lower-level managers, semiprofessionals, non-retail sales workers, and craftsmen, have at least high school and some college education, and make $70,000 annually. It is important to acknowledge the contention among academics in America in defining these social-class categories. As Lauren Rivera (2016) argues, the label "upper-middle" often obscures the privileges of many of these people. The term associates them with a "middle" category, when in fact this group accounts for the top 15–20 percent. However, because "upper-middle" is a term that is used frequently in academic and popular discourse, it provides a heuristic for categorizing the types of people I talked to for this book who are not the middle class and are not in the top 1 percent. However, they are, by any measure, privileged.

100. Bachaud 2022. In 2019, 72 percent of those in the top fifth of the income distribution were white (Joo and Reeves 2017).

101. Khan 2012, 362.

102. Ibid.

103. Sherman 2019.

104. Second homeownership is often understood as an urban-to-rural phenomenon, in which urban residents seek out a reprieve in the rural countryside (for overviews, see Gosnell and Abrams 2011; Lichter and Brown 2011). Lichter and Brown summarize the changes rural areas

have experienced in an "urban society." Of note, they argue that rural destinations have become "landscapes of consumption" for urban residents. New "rural places of consumption provide spatial arenas for interaction between rural natives and urban visitors . . . many urban dwellers own second homes and pay local property taxes in rural areas rich in natural amenities" (2011, 575).

105. Determining the permanent location of second homeowners is methodologically challenging. Most publicly available data sets that are widely used by scholars who study housing, like the Home Mortgage Disclosure Act, which provides local-level data on mortgage acquisitions, only link the housing unit purchased to its location, not to the individual's permanent address. The same is true for data sets like the American Housing Survey. In Andrea Armstrong and Richard Stedman's (2019) analysis of permanent residency of second homeowners in the Northeast from a representative mail-in survey, they rely on Esri's urban/suburban/rural designation to define place category and found that suburban residents accounted for the majority, 42 percent of second homeowners. Urban residents accounted for 23 percent and rural residents for 33 percent.

106. Many permanent-resident place designations are based on the urban-rural gradient provided by the U.S. Census, which is generated from county-level characteristics. There is thus little distinction on the *types* of places where second homeowners come from *within* these larger county categories. For an exception and discussion of this process, see Armstrong and Stedman 2019.

107. There are no uniform measures for defining place categories outside the census designations "urban," "urbanized area," and "rural" (Forsyth 2012; Golding and Winkler 2020). The census offers a locational method for defining suburbs as places located within Metropolitan Statistical Areas that are not part of the core city; thirty-five of the households I spoke with aligned with this category of suburban (for a discussion of this measure, see Forsyth 2012). To define the place categories of second homeowners' primary residences, I rely on the Urbanization Perceptions Small Area Index (UPSAI), which emerged from the 2017 AHS Neighborhood Description Study. The U.S. Department of Housing and Urban Development (HUD) created an index from the answers to the neighborhood description question in HUD's 2017 American Housing Survey. The question "asked respondents whether they considered their neighborhood to be 'urban,' 'suburban,' or 'rural.'" Bucholtz, Molfino, and Kolko (2020) then created a database using machine learning to predict how people would interpret all tract-level regional and neighborhood measures. This method is advantageous because it captures how people interpret and experience these place categories that do not have a clear operationalization. The category "suburb" includes places that other measures or colloquial usages might also define as small towns, small cities, or even exurban communities. As Kenneth Jackson (1985) suggests, suburbia is a contested concept across disciplines, as "suburbia is both a planning type and a frame of mind based on imagery and symbolism" (4). Thus, the UPSAI enables interpretive definitions of these place categories as they are experienced at the tract level. These designations closely align with how my respondents themselves described these place categories.

108. Forsyth 2012.

109. The people who live in places designated in the table as "rural" are often classified as what Golding and Winkler (2020) refer to as "exurban." Golding and Winkler write that "while no concise definition exists, exurbs are typically understood to be rural spaces with low density housing on the far outskirts of cities, where labor market and services of the urban core are accessible via commute" (2020, 839). The people who live in places designated in the table as "urban" are primarily from what is considered to be a small city, with a population of less than 100,000 people (Ocejo, Kosta, and Mann 2020).

110. Teaford 2018.

111. Median household income is $15,000 higher; the towns are 83 percent white on average. Numbers were calculated from ACS 2019 1-year estimates, averaging their hometown's median household income vs. their state's median household income. Racial demographics, "white alone," were calculated from ACS 2019 5-year estimates.

112. Lareau 2014; Rury and Saatcioglu 2011. For a discussion of the contemporary dynamics of suburbia across the globe, see Maginn and Anacker 2022.

113. Girouard 2023; Massey and Denton 1993.

114. Rury and Saatcioglu 2011; Ryan 2010.

115. Lareau 2014.

Part I. The Suburbs and Everywhere in Between

1. Jon Teaford (2018) provides an overview of how metropolitan areas in the United States have been divided through *incorporation*. See also Wyndham-Douds (2023), who finds that incorporated suburbs are less racially diverse and whiter than nonincorporated suburbs and this exclusion is more pronounced in suburbs incorporated after the postwar period.

2. Teaford 2018.

3. This type of municipal incorporation is still used as a method to hoard educational resources in the United States. Since 2000, communities are splitting from their school districts to form incorporated townships and cities as a method to create their own school districts (EdBuild 2019). For a notable example, see St. George's Parish in Baton Rouge (Harris 2019).

4. Massey and Denton 1993.

5. For an exemplary case of this process, see Ryan 2010, which traces the historic and contemporary racial segregation of Richmond Public Schools and Henrico County Public Schools.

6. On nature as racialized as a white space, moving from the country to the city to the suburbs, see Loughran 2022.

7. For an overview of the history and development of the suburbs, see Jackson 1985.

8. For an overview of the academic and popular discourse about suburbs from "dreamscape" to "nightmare," see Maginn and Anacker 2022.

9. Zukin 1989.

10. David Ley (1994) makes the case that gentrification is predicated on the "new middle class," whose political and ideological orientations to the city/suburbs emerge in part from the civil rights movement.

11. Bonilla-Silva, Goar, and Embrick 2006.

12. On the demand-side conditions of gentrification, see Ley 1994.

13. Hines 2010a; Ocejo 2019.

14. Kolko 2017; Parker et al. 2018.

15. On the racial and economic heterogeneity of the suburbs, see Clerge 2019; Lacy 2007, 2016.

16. Logan 2014. According to this report, on average, white families across all economic groups live in neighborhoods that have lower rates of poverty than those of Black and Hispanic families. Lower-income whites still live in neighborhoods with lower poverty rates than those of affluent Black Hispanics. See also Massey and Tannen (2018), who find that the suburbs are still predominantly white.

17. On affluent people's migration to the country, see Hoey 2014; Salamon 2007; Sherman 2021. On affluent people's migration to the city, see Ley 1994; Zukin 1989.

18. For an elaboration of how the first-home locations of my interview participants counter dominant findings in second-home scholarship that emphasize primarily urban to rural migration, see Stiman 2020a.

1. Ennui

1. Slater 1990, 10.

2. Ibid., 14.

3. Putnam 2001; Slater 1990; Whyte 2013; Watt 2009.

4. Putnam 2001; Slater 1990.

5. Gans 1982a; Lacy 2007, 2016.

6. For an overview of the meanings attached to and amenities found in suburban areas, see Hummon 1990.

7. Ibid.; Brekhus 2003.

8. For a discussion of community, mobility, and belonging in "undistinctive [suburban] places," see Allen and Watt 2022. For a discussion of the cultural representation of liminality in American suburbs, see Luccarelli and Roe 2022.

9. Cuba and Hummon 1993a.

10. Simmel [1903] 2005.

11. Hummon 1990.

12. Ibid.; Williams 1975.

13. Williams 1975, 291. Williams argues that the changing modes of production explain the changing cultural images of the city and the country. With the rise of capitalism, for instance, "the city" was meant to represent "capitalism or bureaucracy or centralised power" and "the country" has meant "rural retreat" (290–91). Thus, to understand the meanings people attach to the city or the country, Williams posits that it is crucial to examine the changing modes of production and how these changes produce a different vocabulary of city and country life.

14. For exemplary discussions of the suburbs as ambiguously defined places, see Forsyth 2012; Golding and Winkler 2020; Jackson 1985; Lacy 2016.

15. David Hummon (1990) articulated distinct community ideologies of urbanites, suburbanites, and small-town residents, finding that those who live in these respective destinations adhere to a set of ideological frameworks associated with these distinct place characteristics. Community ideologies are "a system of belief that uses conceptions of community to describe, evaluate, and explain social reality, and that does so in such a manner as to motivate commitment to community." They enable residents to "define what types of places exist" and in doing so provide a "symbolic language" that helps residents clarify their home—whether small town, urban, or suburban—but also "provides a guide to the essential features of other types of places as well . . . the ideology provides the landscape with a simple, oppositional (polarized) structure" (38).

16. Corey Dolgon draws upon Raymond Williams to make this case for explaining the cultural images of the city (2005, 237).

17. On the multiple vocabularies of suburbia, see Brekhus 2003.

18. Only two of the second homeowners I interviewed had direct ties to Rangeley by living in Rangeley at one point in time or having family members who either lived in Rangeley or owned a second home there.

19. Most of the Boston second homeowners I interviewed had direct ties to the city. Nine had gone to college in Boston, seven had previously worked in Boston, three had children who were or had been in college in Boston, and one had family ties.

20. Krysan and Crowder (2017) have found that in making housing choices, people rely both on their own homogeneous social networks and on past experiences of where they once lived or worked, all of which reproduce residential segregation, intergenerationally. The people I met similarly relied on past experiences to make (second-home) housing choices. Armstrong and Stedman (2019) have found that this type of attachment to place matters greatly in explaining second homeowners' orientation to place.

21. For an overview of such forms of migration, see Benson and O'Reilly 2009; Cohen and Sirkeci 2011; FitzGerald and Arar 2018.

22. Milligan defines the process of nostalgia as something that "often emerges after displacement as individuals attempt to regain a sense of identity continuity through recognizing and redefining a shared past. Loss results in identity discontinuity, which nostalgia can repair by creating a shared generational identity to mend the lost one" (Milligan 2003, 381; see also Davis 1979).

23. Davis 1979, 18, as cited in Milligan 2003, 384.

2. A Land of Opportunity

1. U.S. News and World Report 2021.

2. On rural restructuring, see Lichter and Brown 2011.

3. Shelley Kimelberg (2014) has explicitly explored this process in Boston Public Schools (BPS) for middle-class families. At the time of her research, BPS was predominantly comprised of Black and Hispanic low-income students. She found that middle-class families are willing to take risks by sending their children to elementary schools in BPS. However, these families acknowledged that they would reevaluate their choices to send their children to Boston's public schools and move to the suburbs if their children's high schools did not match up with their understandings of a quality school—this, she suggested, was linked to their concerns over their children's future successes. She argued that they have the *privilege of risk.* Thus, where children will go to school is a defining feature of choosing where to live, and middle-class families have the ability to move for access to quality schools (see also Pattillo 2015).

4. U.S. News and World Report 2021. In fact, most of the second homeowners I talked with lived in top-ranked public-school districts, with 57 percent of households living in places with a Niche score of at least an "A–" and 80 percent of households living in places with at least a "B–." I utilized niche.com to decipher these rankings. It is important to note that these rankings are notoriously problematic, often reflecting socioeconomic and racial inequalities and not actual school quality. However, I use this here as a measure because these subjective understandings of school rankings are known to often influence white, affluent families' locational choices (for an explanation of how locational choices are influenced by school rankings, see Holme 2009).

5. For a brief overview of this history, see Allison 2004. For a contemporary example of this process, see Kimelberg 2014.

6. For an overview of this process, see Rury and Rife 2018; Rury and Saatcioglu 2011. Even today, sociologist Annette Lareau (2014) finds that white middle-class and upper-middle-class families rely on their own racially and economically homogeneous social networks to choose where to live and where their kids will go to school, readily reproducing the geographies of social inequality.

7. Loughead 2019.

8. On community "lost," see Simmel [1903] 2005; Tönnies 1887; Wirth 1938. On "community found," see Fischer 1982; Gans 1982b; Simmel [1903] 2005; Wirth 1938.

9. For a network analytic approach, see Wellman 1979; Wellman and Leighton 1979.

10. Corcoran 2008, 270.

11. Other scholars who study affluent suburban people have found similar processes. Watt (2009) builds on Savage's (2010) concept of "elective belonging," in which people prefer to live with people like themselves, to develop the concept of "selective belonging," or "the spatially uneven attachment rooted in residents' schizophrenic relationship to the suburban area" (Watt 2009, 2874). Such suburbanites selectively affiliate themselves with local institutions they associate with themselves and distance themselves from institutions associated with working-class residents. I build on this to show how affluent people's relationship to place is not only selective within the sphere of a singular community but also selective across communities.

12. U.S. News and World Report 2021.

13. Hoey 2014; Ocejo 2019; Sherman 2021.

14. On how the upper middle class secure their social position, see Sherman 2019.

15. Tilly 1998.

16. On rural "brain drain," see Carr and Kefalas 2009.

17. Reeves 2018.

18. Rury and Saatcioglu 2011.

19. See also Desmond 2023.

20. On the geographies of the superrich, see Fernandez, Hofman, and Aalbers 2016; Hay 2013.

21. Suburban neighborhoods today are more racially and economically heterogeneous than they were in decades prior. Some are more racially diverse, some concentrate poverty, and others are new immigrant destinations (Clerge 2019; Lacy 2016). However, evidence suggests that predominantly white suburban communities still concentrate affluence today (Airgood-Obrycki 2019; Owens 2012).

22. For a contemporary example of how suburban residents resist measures that would make their communities more inclusive, see Girouard 2023.

23. Middle-class and upper-middle-class people and families have the time and resources to make long-term housing choices that align with their residential preferences, unlike low-income families who are faced with constraints that limit choices and undermine desired preferences (Harvey et al. 2020; Rhodes and Besbris 2022b). The people I met thus had both the economic and social capital to make not just singular, long-term housing decisions but multiple housing decisions.

24. Richard Ocejo (2011) finds that early gentrifiers use *nostalgia narratives* to construct new local identities. Melinda Milligan (2003) finds that in the face of displacement, individuals call upon nostalgia to construct new identities, repairing identity continuity.

25. Scholars like Max Besbris (2020) and Debbie Becher (2014) specify the mutually constitutive relationship between use and exchange value in housing markets—that buyers cannot fully separate use value and exchange value when making a housing purchases. For the people I talked with, while financial conditions enabled second-home purchases, many explicitly distanced their second-home purchases from its exchange value. For instance, many claimed that they did not buy it as an investment or that their intent was not profit; their intent was rather to pass down the property in the family for future use (which of course is intimately tied to its exchange value for future generations). They thus *framed* the second home more in terms of its use value.

Part II. The Country

1. The Rangeley region is made up of the town of Rangeley and Oquossoc Village (which comprises a significant proportion of the region's population), Rangeley Plantation, Dallas Plantation, and Sandy River Plantation. Although they are technically different municipal entities, they all rely on the resources located in the town of Rangeley (e.g., most commercial establishments, the public library, and the grocery store). They also share a school district, the Rangeley Lakes Regional School District. Because of this, I generally refer to Rangeley as this larger region as this is also its colloquial use (see also https://www.rangeley-maine.com).

2. Following Colin Jerolmack (2021), I use single quotes to denote instances in which I reconstructed dialogue through my handwritten field notes. Double quotes are direct quotes from conversations that were recorded and transcribed verbatim.

3. While Brian Hoey suggests that second homeowners "explore potential selves and possibly even take on a situationally negotiated identity . . . understood by them as positively divergent from their typical selves," I found that for the second homeowners in my sample, this pursuit of a felt identity extended beyond rural spheres (2016, 71). I draw on Michael Bell's (1994) conceptualization of the "country person," a yardstick against which to measure a person's moral worth and claim to place in rural life in relation to others. The country self is part of second homeowners' identity narrative construction, a portion of one's identity that requires actualization and legitimization.

4. Bell 2007.

5. Ibid.

6. Raymond Williams (1975) argued that the country was historically framed as removed from human interests during a period of rapid urban industrialization. Others have built on this argument to explain how nature has been framed as a moral good and used as a mechanism to influence urbanization and place-making (Angelo 2021; Loughran 2022).

7. Loughran 2022.

8. Jackson 1985. Also of note, the Roosevelts frequented the Springwood Estate in Hyde Park, New York. The Vanderbilts kept a country estate on Long Island. The Rockefellers split time between the city and Kykuit in the Hudson Valley. The Boston Brahmins, a network of wealthy elites in Boston, maintained "country estates" in Brookline, Longwood, Chestnut Hill, and all along the North Shore to retreat from the city, consuming a bucolic rural lifestyle (Farrell 1993).

9. For instance, the Rockefellers maintained a summer estate on Mount Desert Island in Maine. The Carnegies set up a secondary residence in the Hamptons. The Vanderbilts constructed the Breakers in Newport, Rhode Island. And the Roosevelts frequented Campobello Island in New Brunswick.

10. Farrell 1993.

11. Taylor 2016.

12. Timothy 2004.

13. For an overview, see Gosnell and Abrams 2011.

14. Armstrong and Stedman 2013. Today, second homeownership has expanded yet again into the Mountain West, where previously remote communities now grapple with the influx of newcomers, including the middle and upper middle class and also the world's superrich (Farrell 2020a; Gosnell and Abrams 2011; Shumway and Davis 1996).

15. Stiman 2020b.

16. Harrill 2004; Long, Perdue, and Allen 1990; Smith and Krannich 1998; Stiman 2020b.

17. Clendenning, Field, and Kapp 2005; Milman and Pizam 1988; Winkler, Deller, and Marcouiller 2015.

3. The Way Life Should Be

1. Bell 1994.

2. Nature has long been used by white middle- and upper-middle-class people as a cultural resource for social distinction (Loughran 2017). Historically, nature has been racialized as a white space, defined for white interests and activities. And proximity to this sphere generates cultural capital for people who can claim knowledge about outdoor activities, like hiking, skiing, and canoeing, and an appreciation for the forests, lakes, and hillsides where these activities take place (Finney 2014).

3. Bell 1994, 86.

4. Ibid., 119.

5. Ibid., 138.

6. For an elaboration of how billionaires engage in these same practices, see also Farrell 2020a.

7. Sherman 2021, 12.

8. In *The Presentation of Self in Everyday Life*, sociologist Erving Goffman wrote about the performative aspects of social-class identity to maintain front, which sometimes entail downplaying social-class sign equipment. He writes, "Commonly we find that upward mobility involves the presentation of proper performances and that efforts to move upward and efforts to keep from moving downward are expressed in terms of sacrifices made for the maintenance of front . . . perhaps the most important piece of sign-equipment associated with social class consists of the status symbols through which material wealth is expressed. . . . However, many classes of persons have many different reasons for exercising systematic modesty and for underplaying any expressions of wealth, capacity, spiritual strength, or self-respect" (1975, 36–38).

9. Palmer 2004; Priest 2009; Moody 2023.

10. For an elaboration of Rangeley camps, see Priest 2009.

11. Khan 2012.

12. Sherman 2018.

13. Ibid., 412.

4. My Vacationland

1. See Scofield 2008. "Doctor's Island" was how I heard the island referred to during my time in Rangeley. As of 2017, the owner of the island has tried to change the name to Maneskootuk Island (Hanstein 2017).

2. See https://rlht.org/whipwillow-easement/.

3. These data come from an administrator of the Rangeley Lakes Heritage Trust at the time of my fieldwork.

4. See RLHT.org. Most recent information accessed spring 2021.

5. On newcomers using philanthropy to engage with community life and to justify their in-migration, see also Sherman 2021.

6. On nonprofit community-based organizations becoming non-elected neighborhood representatives, see Levine 2016.

7. Zukin 1995.

8. Town of Rangeley 2012, 2.

9. For an overview of the history of comprehensive plans in Maine, see Cucuzza, Stoll, and Leslie 2020.

10. Town of Rangeley 2012, 5.

11. The town has seen an increase in service-sector, tourism-based jobs to the area, in which the majority of the permanent population is employed; restaurant, retail, and recreation make up the largest portion of employed residents (Maine Department of Labor: Center for Workforce Research & Information 2014).

12. Town of Rangeley 2012, 74.

13. Ibid., 74–75.

14. Ibid., 4.

15. Ibid.

16. In 2014, around the time when I was in the field, Rangeley's median household income was $51,250 and 6.7 percent of individuals were below poverty. This is in comparison to Franklin County, which had a median household income of $41,446 and a poverty rate of 15.3 percent (2010–14 ACS 5-year estimates).

17. Reeder and Brown 2012; Sherman 2018.

18. Winkler 2013; Park and Pellow 2011; Farrell 2020a.

19. Town of Rangeley 2012, 44.

20. According to the Maine Housing Authority's Housing Affordability Index, the median home price in 2017 in Rangeley was $220,000, while the home price that the median income can afford was $194,420. Franklin County's median home price was $128,000, while the median income can afford a home for $153,062. In Rangeley in 2017, 54 percent of households could not afford a median home (Maine State Housing Authority 2017).

21. Town of Rangeley 2012.

22. Freeman and Schuetz 2017; Hyra 2017.

23. Since the time of the research, I have observed community leaders discuss various ways to provide affordable workforce housing for the community, such as utilizing Tax Increment Financing (TIF) as a tool to attract developers to the area (The Irregular 2020). Philanthropy, however,

has proven to be the most effective tool. For example, in 2021, philanthropists donated a large sum of money to support workforce housing at the local ski resort (Skelton 2021a).

24. For an elaboration of these tensions, see Mueller 2021.

25. Stern, Adams, and Elsasser 2009.

26. Ibid.

27. Skelton 2021b.

28. Brown and Schafft 2011.

29. Ibid.

30. U.S. Department of Health and Human Services 2022.

31. Lear 2021.

32. Winkler, Deller, and Marcouiller 2015.

33. This is not to say that all second homeowners in Rangeley or other rural regions exclusively direct their time and efforts toward conservation at the expense of other community institutions. There are many everyday people and philanthropists who aim to uplift other community institutions. However, this present book calls attention to the collective impact of relying on private actors to support public resources and community growth.

5. Open for Business

1. Smith 1980, 192.

2. The 2020 census counted 1,222.

3. Town of Rangeley 2012.

4. For an overview of residents' perceptions of tourism development, see Harrill 2004.

5. Baker 2022; Chu-O'Neil 2019.

6. Lamont 2009; Willis 1965.

7. Lamont 2009, 19.

8. Sherman 2009.

9. In Rangeley, second homeowners are often discussed in tandem with tourism; second homeownership is discursively framed as the heart of the local tourism economy, although second homeowners are never framed as "tourists."

10. In theory, it is a form of direct democracy that enables citizens to have a voice in local municipal affairs. In practice, however, town meetings are not always representative of the community at large, often favoring certain actors and voices over others (Mansbridge 1983). Its value to me as a researcher was that the town meeting could lay bare dominant public community discourse about second homeowners and their in-migration.

11. Understanding local reactions to exogenous forces helps articulate a place's unique character (Paulsen 2004).

12. Cooley 1902.

13. See Ellis 1982; Palmer 2004; Priest 2009. It is important to note that the emergence of tourism came at the expense of Maine's Abenaki people; they were "severely constrained by state and private encroachment, destruction of their fishing resources, and criminalization of their hunting and trapping activities" (Hornsby and Judd 2015, 36). As such, place histories are often partial and problematic, as they romanticize one segment of the local population while overlooking marginalized, locally embedded populations. In doing so, place histories cement the legacy and legitimacy of one group over another (Breen 1996; Brown-Saracino 2007, 2010; Dolgon 2005).

14. Priest 2009.

15. Ibid., 1.

16. New York Angler 1876. On Rangeley's history as a hunting and sporting destination, see Ellis 1982; Palmer 2004; Priest 2009.

17. Ellis 1982.

18. Gosnell and Abrams 2011; Vias and Carruthers 2005.

19. Palmer 2004; Priest 2009.

20. Sherman 2018, 2021.

21. McCormick 2017.

22. For notable examples, see Sherman 2018, 2021; Winkler 2013; Gosnell and Abrams 2011.

23. See also Sherman 2018, 2021.

Part III. The City

1. White and Rancatore 2017.

2. At the time of the research, the Boston Planning and Development Agency was called the Boston Redevelopment Authority.

3. Wirth 1938; Ocejo, Kosta, and Mann 2020.

4. Gans 2009.

5. Hoyt 2003.

6. Suttles 1972.

7. DiMaggio 1982.

8. Loughran 2022.

9. Firey 1945; Suttles 1972; Zorbaugh 1929.

10. For a comprehensive overview of this history, see Massey and Denton 1993.

11. For a comprehensive overview of this economic history, see Wilson 1997.

12. Loughran 2017.

13. Greenberg 2008; Loughran 2022; Zukin 1995.

14. Greenberg 2008; Zukin 1995.

15. Zukin 1995.

16. For notable examples, see Brown-Saracino 2010, 2013; Hyra 2014; Ley 1994; Smith 1979; Zukin 1989.

17. Glass 1964; Ley 1994; Zukin 1989.

18. Zukin 1995.

19. Ibid.; Clark 2004. See also Loughran 2017.

20. Chevalier, Corbillé, and Lallement 2012.

6. City Mouse

1. See Jacobs 2002, 15–17.

2. Some in the sample cited attendance at neighborhood events. However, the events they attended were typically culturally, not civically, oriented (e.g., neighborhood wine tastings and cocktail hours).

3. Hosman 2018b, 2018a.

4. For an overview of Jamaica Plain and a discussion of its gentrification, see Cain 2020a, 2020b.

5. For an overview of Roxbury and a discussion of gentrification, see Cain 2020a, 2020b.

6. Brown-Saracino 2010; Deener 2012; Douglas 2012; Hosman 2018b; Tissot 2015.

7. Back Bay was originally the bay of the Charles River, but by the 1880s a series of landfill projects transformed this area from a tidal basin to a highly sought-after neighborhood with brownstones built along French-inspired, tree-lined boulevards (Hughes 1988). The city offered land parcels to institutions at discounted rates to encourage cultural development of the area. Soon, the neighborhood was home to the Boston Society for Natural History, MIT, and still-standing

famous institutions like Trinity Church. Back Bay became home to Boston's "social and intellectual elite" (Hughes 1988).

8. Firey 1945.

9. Aalbers 2019.

10. On super-gentrification in New York, see Lees 2003.

11. Butler and Lees 2006; Lees 2003; Stuber 2021.

12. This singular vision of Boston life mirrors Chevalier, Corbillé, and Lallement's (2012) finding that foreign pied-à-terre owners in Paris seek out a particular kind of Paris, one rooted in its historic sites and archetypical locales—what is perceived to be an authentic, real Paris and "Parisianity."

13. Bell 1994.

14. On lifestyles as a form of social closure, see Bourdieu 1984.

15. Sherman 2018.

16. Bell 1994.

17. On class blindness as a method to justify and ignore privileges, see Sherman 2021.

18. Bell 1994.

19. Loughran 2022; Williams 1975.

20. Bell 1994, 119.

21. Sherman 2019.

22. As of 2021, roughly two-thirds of all Black Bostonians live in Dorchester, Roxbury, and Mattapan (Ofulue 2021).

23. Zawadi Rucks-Ahidiana (2021) explicitly makes this connection between gentrification and racial capitalism.

24. See Stiman 2019.

25. Allison 2004.

26. Boston Redevelopment Authority 1988.

27. In the 1980s, the Boston Redevelopment Authority provided evidence for early to mid-stages of gentrification taking place in the central-city neighborhoods: "newcomers to downtown, West End, Waterfront and Bay Village . . . tend to be middle-aged and younger adults who are well educated, employed in professional and managerial positions, and have relatively high income . . . and are predominantly white" (1988, 3). Along with the Back Bay and Beacon Hill districts, the central district maintained the highest median household income and lowest percentage of people in poverty in 1985. Furthermore, the central district witnessed a rise in housing units being converted from apartments to condominiums. The central district enjoyed the greatest share of investments among the planning districts, with $3.7 billion in development between 1975 and 1989, over 40 percent of the entire city's development investments (Boston Redevelopment Authority 1988, 25).

28. The South End is a highly affluent but also diverse neighborhood. However, gentrifiers and wealthy residents of the area are known to control the type of diversity they value in the neighborhood (Tissot 2014). And as Rucks-Ahidiana (2021) argues, gentrifiers who purportedly value diversity tend to value non-Black diversity or non-contentious Black culture.

29. Mayorga, Underhill, and Crosser 2022. Urban sociologists refer to this general process as *racial capitalism*, in which racism and capitalism are intimately linked and all processes of urban, suburban, and rural growth and change are "rooted in constructions of race, racialization, and differentiation" (Dantzler, Korver-Glenn, and Howell 2022, 168).

30. Levine 2021; Small 2009.

31. On central-city investments, see Boston Redevelopment Authority 1988, 25. City leaders heeded the concerns from civic associations in Beacon Hill. A sampling of issues in civic organizations in historically Black neighborhoods in Boston like Roxbury, Dorchester, and Mattapan highlights these processes in which Black and brown neighborhoods fight for resource access. In Mattapan, civic leaders and residents discuss how to develop and maintain access to

affordable housing in the neighborhood without it leading to displacement, how to provide quality vocational schooling to neighborhood students, and how to promote more equitable transit access (Skelly 2021). In Dorchester's Codman Square, residents discuss how to address mental health and community violence, how to expand transit access, and how to provide careers to the neighborhood's youth (Codman Square Neighborhood Council 2010). Roxbury has a long history of community activism in the face of state-sponsored and private neglect, encouraging "development without displacement" through their neighborhood initiatives like community land trusts to promote public housing and public youth services.

32. On racialization and affluent in-migrants' residential choices, see Rucks-Ahidiana 2021.

33. Aalbers 2019; Lees 2003; Ocejo 2019.

7. A Brahmin Ethos

1. See the U.S. National Park Service: https://www.nps.gov/places/boston-public-garden.htm.

2. See https://friendsofthepublicgarden.org/about/who-we-are/.

3. Fenway Alliance 2022.

4. This type of cultural consumption is distinct from the cultural consumption practices of many gentrifiers analyzed in extant research, who seek perceived authenticity through old-timers' institutions and neighborhoods, older industrial spaces, bohemia, artist enclaves (Brown-Saracino 2010; Deener 2007; Lloyd 2010; Zukin 1989), and non-white neighborhoods (Hyra 2017; Pattillo 2007). Many of the second homeowners I interviewed avoided these very spaces of consumption for the pursuit of high-cultural amenities.

5. The rose beds are an important historic cultural destination in Boston, which relies on volunteers from the Friends of the Public Garden to work in conjunction with the city's department of Parks and Recreation to maintain the gardens (Friends of the Public Garden 2021).

6. In preliminary analyses, I uncovered different orientations to city life governed by different motivations for buying a second home, in which some people I talked with were primarily culturally oriented, and a very small contingent was economically oriented. However, I explain these differences as *temporal*, which can tell us more about how place-identity projects are tied to notions of the city and types of homeownership—as in the case of Stan, whose practices align with different stages of Boston's development. His second home in Boston was originally purchased as a primary home. When he first bought this house he engaged with the city through classic place-entrepreneurial practices such as renovating his home and attending civic meetings. But when he followed a job outside of Boston, he decided to *keep* his primary home as a secondary home. His engagement then changed when he moved out of the city and as the city entered new stages of gentrification (on waves of gentrification, see Aalbers 2019); his work to transform his neighborhood into his vision was "complete" and his primary home became his secondary home. He and others I met who purchased during this time period still sometimes engaged in civic activities, but most I talked with began seeing the city as a cultural endeavor as their understandings of what the city was changed and, in the case of Stan, as the type of homeownership changed. Most in this small group purchased their home for utilitarian reasons, like being close to work. However, when they decided to keep it as a home for their leisure use in retirement, their orientation to it changed. It is important to note that most didn't want to live in the city permanently for similar reasons: Boston public schools. The majority of the second homeowners I spoke with, however, purchased a second home after 2000 and explicitly intended to use it as a method to be proximate to high culture. I thus suggest that type of ownership and the stages of gentrification of the city can matter for how people engage in communities. For an overview of how time living in a neighborhood matters for community engagement, see McCabe 2016.

7. They also donated to various religious institutions that they occasionally frequented while in town, animal shelters, and medical research institutions, such as Dana Farber and Boston

Children's Hospital. Yet their primary and overlapping donations were directed toward institutions of high culture.

8. For an overview of the social bases of philanthropy, see Barman 2017.

9. WBUR 2021.

10. DiMaggio 1982.

11. Farrell 1993, 31.

12. DiMaggio 1982, 48.

13. Such institutions were also built on the basis of social exclusion, as they simultaneously championed the Immigration Restriction League in 1894 and the New England Watch and Ward Society from 1878 to the 1920s (New England Historical Society 2016).

14. Molotch, Freudenburg, and Paulsen 2000.

15. Gieryn 2000, 468.

16. Selling arts and culture in Boston also relies on promoting the little-c cultural milieu, the everyday cultures of people across Boston's mosaic of neighborhoods. This is why as visitors step off the plane at Logan airport they see an assortment of advertisements for Boston's distinct neighborhoods. For instance, an advertisement for East Boston reads, "Visit Eastie! Come discover one of America's most authentic neighborhoods," with images from around the neighborhood, including a view of Boston's harbor and pizza from the iconic Santarpio's restaurant.

17. Lopez 2019.

18. ArtsBoston 2019.

19. The comparison cities include Baltimore, Chicago, Cleveland, Minneapolis, New York, Philadelphia, and San Francisco (Koo and Curtis 2015).

20. Koo and Curtis 2015.

21. ArtsBoston 2022; Koo and Curtis 2015.

22. Koo and Curtis 2015, 20.

23. ArtsBoston 2022.

24. I draw from Jeremy Levine (2016), who suggests that community-based organizations are non-elected neighborhood representatives for community governance. In this case, public-private partnerships like the Fenway Alliance become stewards of community interests.

25. Fenway Alliance 2022.

26. Ibid.

27. City of Boston 2017.

28. Fenway Alliance 2022.

29. Zukin 1995.

30. For an overview of the development of urban parks in the twentieth and twenty-first centuries, see Loughran 2022.

31. Zukin 1995.

32. On public-private partnerships in a postindustrial city, see Greenberg 2008.

33. MFA Boston 2015.

34. For notable examples of how a neighborhood's brand and identity can contribute to its upscaling, see Deener 2007; Lloyd 2010; Parker 2018; Ocejo 2014.

35. As of 2020, Fenway was one of the most rapidly gentrifying neighborhoods in Boston (Pan 2020).

36. On how neoliberalism has changed urban growth, see Logan and Molotch 1987; Greenberg 2008; Brenner and Theodore 2005. On the rise of public-private partnerships in community governance, see Levine 2021, 2016.

37. Logan and Molotch 1987; Levine 2021; Pacewicz 2016.

38. Other scholars have furthered this argument to suggest that the racialization of space is central to explaining which neighborhoods receive attention and which do not. For a notable explanation of this process, see Rucks-Ahidiana 2021.

39. Calculated using Boston's property tax assessment data for 2022, tallying all MFA property owned in the Avenue of the Arts, 15.2 acres.

40. Each year, the city requests a real dollar value from tax-exempt cultural, educational, and medical institutions across Boston, against which these institutions can contribute to the city through offering a range of "community benefits" or direct cash donations. In 2020, the city of Boston designated a total PILOT value for the Boston Symphony Orchestra as almost $30 million, requesting only $121,443 in return. The organization provided half of that requested in "community benefits" and the other half as a cash contribution. The PILOT value of the Museum of Fine Arts is calculated at nearly $300 million, for which the city requested a little over $2 million in return. The MFA contributed just over $1 million in "community benefits," including free programming and admissions for certain people, educational opportunities for teens, and various beautification projects, and provided $61,393 as a cash contribution. This met only 53 percent of the city's requested amount (City of Boston 2020; MFA Boston 2020).

41. Critics have called into question the "community benefits" dimension of the PILOT program. There is now political momentum to require cash payments. See McDonald 2021.

42. City of Boston 2022b.

43. City of Boston 2019.

8. High-End Blight

1. Herbert 2021; Rosen 2020.

2. O'Malley and Campbell 2018.

3. According to the City of Boston, "65% of Bostonians are renters and more than half of them spend more than 30% of their monthly income on rent, leaving them struggling to save and vulnerable to housing instability" (City of Boston 2022a). See also Bluestone et al. (2015), who explain how the surge in luxury development projects close to downtown, rapidly increasing condo prices, and a citywide affordable-housing crisis are pushing out low- and middle-income Boston residents.

4. Treffeisen 2018. On Boston's luxury housing boom, see Collins and de Goede 2018.

5. Collins and de Goede 2018, 7.

6. Brown-Saracino 2010; Douglas 2012; Ley 1994; Ocejo 2019; Pattillo 2007.

7. Roberts 2011.

8. Sampson 2012.

9. Jacobs 1961, 39.

10. Ibid., 40.

11. Goffman 1963.

12. Logan 2018.

13. Ross 2014; Fernandes 2015.

14. Logan 2016.

15. Logan 2018.

16. Ibid.

17. According to the 2021 U.S. Census, Boston's population was 654,776.

18. Katz 2019.

Conclusion

1. Zorbaugh 1929, 68.

2. For an overview of the community question, see Wellman 1979; Brown-Saracino 2011.

3. For an important exception to analyzing people within the delimited sphere of their communities, see Ocejo 2019.

4. Brown-Saracino 2010; Ocejo 2019; Douglas 2012; Tissot 2014.

5. Farrell 2020a; Hines 2010b; Gosnell and Abrams 2011; Sherman 2021; Winkler 2013.

6. Rury and Saatcioglu 2011; Rury and Rife 2018; Girouard 2023.

7. For an overview of growth, see Logan and Molotch 1987.

8. On opportunity hoarding in the suburbs, see Girouard 2023; Rury and Saatcioglu 2011.

9. On groups who make explicit locational sacrifices for a sense of place belonging, see Harrison 2017; Hoey 2014; Ocejo 2019.

10. Brown-Saracino 2018; Hummon 1990; Kazyak 2012; Robinson 2014.

11. Brown-Saracino 2010; Ocejo 2019, 2011; Douglas 2012.

12. For other important research in this area that captures how people use places other than their hometowns to give their identities meaning, see Lauder 2022.

13. Lareau 2014.

14. For an overview of how scholars often use "place of residence" as a variable that intersects with other identities such as political identity, gender, race, and age, see Armstrong and Stedman 2019. As a result, understanding place identity as a variable that is independent of one's primary home can help explain, for instance, why scholars have found on survey data that place attachment often matters more than second homeowners' permanent geographic location in explaining patterns of rural local environmental concern (Armstrong and Stedman 2019).

15. On how city-specific sexual identity cultures shape sexual identity, see Brown-Saracino 2018.

16. On how ruptures in place attachment force people to craft new narratives, see Milligan 1998; Ocejo 2011.

17. Jason Kaufman and Matthew Kaliner (2011) argue that places transform and become distinct through an "increasingly common contemporary process: the migration of people to and from places for cultural, as opposed to (or as well as merely) economic reasons." They suggest that this is "both a cause and an effect of endogenous socio-economic, socio-cultural, and sociopolitical transformations" (150). For an overview of the debate about how places are accomplished, see also Molotch, Freudenburg, and Paulsen 2000. On the diverse groups of people who influence the trajectories of place, see Bartram 2022; Bayurgil 2021; Besbris 2020; Brown-Saracino 2010; Deener 2012; Herbert 2021; Korver-Glenn 2021; Rosen 2020; Zukin 2010.

18. Brown-Saracino 2010; Douglas 2012; Lees 2003; Ocejo 2014, 2019; Pattillo 2007.

19. Logan and Molotch 1987.

20. Bell 1994, 138.

21. Barcelona, for example, began more heavily regulating multiple property owners on Airbnb (Burgen 2017).

22. Burgen 2017; O'Sullivan 2016.

23. Adamg 2018. A hearing on vacancy held by Boston city councilors Ed Flynn, Lydia Edwards, Matt O'Malley, and Andrea Campbell in 2019 called for changes to the tax structures that allow landlords to monopolize a high number of properties and foreign real estate investors to purchase luxury units only to leave them vacant.

24. Billings 2021.

25. Young et al. 2016.

26. Molly Vollman Makris and Mary Gatta (2020) have documented the problem of second homeowners' orientation to the educational system in Asbury Park, New Jersey, where those who are not permanent residents are less inclined to care about underfunded educational systems. This has real implications for people who live there who rely on the infusion of tax dollars and social capital from middle-class and upper-middle-class people to support public schools.

27. Stuber 2021.

28. Pattillo 2015, 63.

29. Many geographers and scholars of housing studies highlight this distinction. "Second home" is used colloquially but often does not capture the material reality of *multiple* homeownership for many elites. See, for example, Kadi, Hochstenbach, and Lennartz 2020; McIntyre, Williams, and McHugh 2006.

Epilogue

1. CDC 2022.
2. New York Times 2020.
3. Quealy 2020; Sandoval 2020.
4. Bellafante 2020.
5. Nir and Tully 2020.
6. Ibid.; Miles 2020.
7. Editorial Board 2020.
8. Joey 2020.
9. Quealy 2020.
10. Neate 2020.
11. Nir and Tully 2020.
12. Valigra 2020.
13. Bever 2020.
14. Valigra 2020.
15. Ibid.
16. Maine Department of Education 2021.
17. Kaufman 2021; Sperance 2021.
18. Logan 2021; Gardizy 2021.

Appendix B. Methods

1. On observing other facets of local life beyond meetings, see Brown-Saracino and Stiman 2017.
2. Kusenbach 2003.
3. At the time of my research, the Boston Planning and Development Agency (BPDA) was called the Boston Redevelopment Authority (BRA).
4. Gusterson 1997, 116.
5. Brown-Saracino and Stiman 2017.
6. I furthermore attempted to solicit participants through neighborhood and civic associations and luxury real estate agents; however, no second homeowners responded to my requests through this method. Through real estate agents, I actively tried to pursue interviewing international buyers; however, no real estate agents were able to connect me with buyers. Only one out of the five real estate agents I spoke with dealt with international buyers. The other four noted their primary second-homeowner demographic is U.S.-based retirees.
7. Successfully posted: South End, Back Bay, Beacon Hill, Downtown, Jamaica Plain, and the North End/Waterfront.
8. DeLaney and Pizzuti 2005.
9. Deterding and Waters 2021.

REFERENCES

Aalbers, Manuel B. 2019. "Introduction to the Forum: From Third to Fifth-Wave Gentrification." *Tijdschrift Voor Economische En Sociale Geografie* 110 (1): 1–11.

Adamg. 2018. "Boston Councilor Would Tax Property Flippers and Other Housing Speculators." Universal Hub. 2018. https://www.universalhub.com/2018/boston-councilor-would-tax -property-flippers-and.

Airgood-Obrycki, Whitney. 2019. "Suburban Status and Neighbourhood Change." *Urban Studies* 56 (14): 2935–52.

Alkon, Alison Hope, and Michael Traugot. 2008. "Place Matters, But How? Rural Identity, Environmental Decision Making, and the Social Construction of Place." *City & Community* 7 (2): 97–112.

Allen, David, and Paul Watt. 2022. "Place Attachment in Non-Place Spaces? Community, Belonging and Mobilities in 'Post-Suburban' South East England." In *Suburbia in the 21st Century: From Dreamscape to Nightmare?*, ed. Paul J. Maginn and Katrin B. Anacker. New York: Routledge.

Allison, Robert J. 2004. *A Short History of Boston*. Beverly, MA: Commonwealth Editions.

Angelo, Hillary. 2021. *How Green Became Good: Urbanized Nature and the Making of Cities and Citizens*. Chicago: University of Chicago Press.

Anguelovski, Isabelle. 2015. "Healthy Food Stores, Greenlining and Food Gentrification: Contesting New Forms of Privilege, Displacement and Locally Unwanted Land Uses in Racially Mixed Neighborhoods." *International Journal of Urban and Regional Research* 39 (6): 1209–30.

Armstrong, Andrea, and Richard C. Stedman. 2013. "Culture Clash and Second Home Ownership in the US Northern Forest." *Rural Sociology* 78 (3): 318–45.

———. 2019. "Understanding Local Environmental Concern: The Importance of Place." *Rural Sociology* 84 (1): 93–122.

ArtsBoston. 2019. "The Arts Factor Report." Boston: ArtsBoston. http://artsboston.org/wp -content/uploads/2019/06/ArtsBoston_ArtsFactorBook19_Digital.pdf.

———. 2022. "ArtsBoston Audience Lab—Creating Diversity with Data." ArtsBoston: Audience Lab. 2022. https://www.artsboston.org/audience-lab/.

Bachaud, Nicole. 2022. "How Mortgage Applications for Vacation Homes Spiked Early in the Pandemic." *Zillow Research* (blog), March 15. https://www.zillow.com/research/vacation -homes-mortgage-applications-30827/.

Badger, Emily. 2022. "The Housing Shortage Isn't Just a Coastal Crisis Anymore." *New York Times: The Upshot*, July 14.

Baker, Billy. 2022. "With Its Ski Resort Open Again, Everyone Is Rooting for Rangeley, Maine." *Boston Globe*, January 8, https://www.bostonglobe.com/2022/01/08/metro/with-its-ski -resort-open-again-everyone-is-rooting-rangeley/.

Ballentine, Claire, and Alice Kantor. 2021. "Why Buying a Second or Even Third Home Is Becoming More Popular than Ever." Bloomberg.com. https://www.bloomberg.com/news/features /2021-10-15/why-buying-a-second-home-is-real-estate-s-newest-trend.

Barman, Emily. 2017. "The Social Bases of Philanthropy." *Annual Review of Sociology* 43 (January): 1–20.

Bartram, Robin. 2022. *Stacked Decks: Building Inspectors and the Reproduction of Urban Inequality.* Chicago: University of Chicago Press.

Bayurgil, Ladin. 2021. "Fired and Evicted: Istanbul Doorkeepers' Strategies of Navigating Employment and Housing Precarity." *Social Problems* 69 (4): 1092–1108.

Becher, Debbie. 2014. *Private Property and Public Power: Eminent Domain in Philadelphia.* Oxford: Oxford University Press.

Bell, Michael. 1992. "The Fruit of Difference: The Rural-Urban Continuum as a System of Identity." *Rural Sociology* 57 (1): 65–82.

———. 1994. *Childerley: Nature and Morality in a Country Village.* Chicago: University of Chicago Press.

———. 2007. "The Two-Ness of Rural Life and the Ends of Rural Scholarship." *Journal of Rural Studies* 23 (4): 402–15.

Bellafante, Ginia. 2020. "The Rich Have a Coronavirus Cure: Escape from New York." *New York Times*, March 14. https://www.nytimes.com/2020/03/14/nyregion/Coronavirus-nyc-rich-wealthy-residents.html.

Benson, Michaela, and Karen O'Reilly. 2009. "Migration and the Search for a Better Way of Life: A Critical Exploration of Lifestyle Migration." *Sociological Review* 57 (4): 608–25.

Besbris, Max. 2020. *Upsold: Real Estate Agents, Prices, and Neighborhood Inequality.* Chicago: University of Chicago Press.

Bever, Fred. 2020. "Western Maine Is Having a Moment—More People Are Heading to Franklin County and Staying There." Maine Public. https://www.mainepublic.org/business-and-economy/2020-09-24/western-maine-is-having-a-moment-more-people-are-heading-to-franklin-county-and-staying-there.

Billings, Randy. 2021. "Bill Would Impose New Fees on Vacation Homes, Short-Term Rentals." *Press Herald* (blog), April 12. https://www.pressherald.com/2021/04/12/bill-would-impose-new-fees-on-vacation-homes-short-term-rentals/.

Bluestone, Barry, James Huessy, Eleanor White, Charles Eisenberg, and Tim Davis. 2015. "Greater Boston Housing Report Card 2015." Northeastern University: Kitty and Michael Dukakis Center for Urban and Regional Policy.

Bolongaro, Kait. 2021. "Justin Trudeau Vows Two-Year Ban on Foreign Home Buyers in Canada Election." Bloomberg.com. https://www.bloomberg.com/news/articles/2021-08-24/trudeau-vows-two-year-ban-on-foreign-home-buyers-if-re-elected.

Bonilla-Silva, Eduardo, Carla Goar, and David G. Embrick. 2006. "When Whites Flock Together: The Social Psychology of White Habitus." *Critical Sociology* 32 (2–3): 229–53.

Borer, Michael. 2006. "The Location of Culture: The Urban Culturalist Perspective." *City & Community* 5 (2): 173–97.

Boston Planning and Development Agency. 2019. "Boston Neighborhood Demographics, 2015–2019." https://data.boston.gov/dataset/neighborhood-demographics/resource/d8c23c6a-b868-4ba4-8a3b-b9615a21be07.

Boston Redevelopment Authority. 1988. *Central Neighborhood Profile, 1988.* http://archive.org/details/centralneighborh00bost.

Bourdieu, Pierre. 1984. *Distinction: A Social Critique of the Judgement of Taste.* Cambridge, MA: Harvard University Press.

Breen, T. H. 1996. *Imagining the Past: East Hampton Histories.* Athens: University of Georgia Press.

Brekhus, Wayne. 2003. *Peacocks, Chameleons, Centaurs: Gay Suburbia and the Grammar of Social Identity.* Chicago: University of Chicago Press.

Brenner, Neil, and Nik Theodore. 2005. "Neoliberalism and the Urban Condition." *City* 9 (1): 101–7.

Briggs, Xavier de Souza, Susan J. Popkin, and John Goering. 2010. *Moving to Opportunity: The Story of an American Experiment to Fight Ghetto Poverty.* Oxford: Oxford University Press.

Brown, David L., and Kai A. Schafft. 2011. *Rural People and Communities in the 21st Century: Resilience and Transformation.* Cambridge, MA: Polity.

Brown-Saracino, Japonica. 2007. "Virtuous Marginality: Social Preservationists and the Selection of the Old-Timer." *Theory and Society* 36 (5): 437–68.

———. 2010. *A Neighborhood That Never Changes: Gentrification, Social Preservation, and the Search for Authenticity.* Chicago: University of Chicago Press.

———. 2011. "From the Lesbian Ghetto to Ambient Community: The Perceived Costs and Benefits of Integration for Community." *Social Problems* 58 (3): 361–88.

———. 2013. *The Gentrification Debates: A Reader.* New York: Routledge.

———. 2014. "From Methodological Stumbles to Substantive Insights: Gaining Ethnographic Access in Queer Communities." *Qualitative Sociology* 1 (37): 43–68.

———. 2015. "How Places Shape Identity: The Origins of Distinctive LBQ Identities in Four Small U.S. Cities." *American Journal of Sociology* 121 (1): 1–63.

———. 2018. *How Places Make Us: Novel LBQ Identities in Four Small Cities.* Chicago: University of Chicago Press.

Brown-Saracino, Japonica, and Meaghan Stiman. 2017. "How to Avoid Getting Stuck in Meetings." In *Meeting Ethnography: Meetings as Key Technologies of Contemporary Governance, Development, and Resistance,* ed. Jen Sandler and Renita Thedvall, 88–105. New York: Taylor & Francis.

Bucholtz, Shawn, Emily Molfino, and Jed Kolko. 2020. "The Urbanization Perceptions Small Area Index: An Application of Machine Learning and Small Area Estimation to Household Survey Data." Department of Housing and Urban Development. https://www.huduser.gov/portal/AHS-neighborhood-description-study-2017.html#small-area-tab.

Burgen, Stephen. 2017. "Barcelona Cracks down on Airbnb Rentals with Illegal Apartment Squads." *The Guardian,* June 2, sec. Cities. http://www.theguardian.com/technology/2017/jun/02/airbnb-faces-crackdown-on-illegal-apartment-rentals-in-barcelona.

Butler, Tim, and Loretta Lees. 2006. "Super-Gentrification in Barnsbury, London: Globalization and Gentrifying Global Elites at the Neighbourhood Level." *Transactions of the Institute of British Geographers* 31 (4): 467–87.

Cain, Taylor. 2020a. "A Place for 'Families like Us': Reproducing Gentrification and Gentrifiers in Two Boston Neighborhoods." PhD thesis, Boston University.

———. 2020b. "Keeping the Family Home: Reproducing Gentrifiers in Two Boston Neighborhoods." *Journal of Urban Affairs* 42 (8): 1222–41.

Carr, Patrick J., and Maria J. Kefalas. 2009. *Hollowing Out the Middle: The Rural Brain Drain and What It Means for America.* Boston: Beacon Press.

Centers for Disease Control and Prevention (CDC). 2022. "CDC Museum COVID-19 Timeline." January 5. https://www.cdc.gov/museum/timeline/covid19.html.

Chevalier, Sophie, Sophie Corbillé, and Emmanuelle Lallement. 2012. "Le Paris des résidences secondaires: Entre ville réelle et ville rêvée." *Ethnologie Française* 42 (3): 441–49.

Chu-O'Neil, Stephanie. 2019. "Berry Family, Arctaris Impact Fund Reach Agreement for Sale of Saddleback." *Lewiston Sun Journal,* November 15. https://www.sunjournal.com/2019/11/15/berry-family-arctaris-impact-fund-reach-agreement-for-sale-of-saddleback/.

City of Boston. 2017. "Fenway Cultural District." Boston.gov. November 30. https://www.boston.gov/departments/arts-and-culture/fenway-cultural-district.

———. 2019. "FY20 Operating Budget | Boston.Gov." February 28. https://www.boston.gov/departments/budget/fy20-operating-budget.

———. 2020. "Fiscal Year 2020 Pilot Contributions." Boston. https://www.boston.gov/sites/default/files/file/2020/11/PILOT%20figures%20FY20%20Nov%203%202020%20rev1%20-%20Final.pdf.

———. 2022a. "Members of Rent Stabilization Advisory Committee Announced." Boston.gov. https://www.boston.gov/news/members-rent-stabilization-advisory-committee-announced.

———. 2022b. Payment in Lieu of Tax (PILOT) Program. https://www.boston.gov/finance /payment-lieu-tax-pilot-program.

Clark, Terry N. 2004. *The City as an Entertainment Machine*. Oxford: Elsevier.

Clendenning, Greg, Donald R. Field, and Kirsten J. Kapp. 2005. "A Comparison of Seasonal Homeowners and Permanent Residents on Their Attitudes toward Wildlife Management on Public Lands." *Human Dimensions of Wildlife* 10 (1): 3–17.

Clerge, Orly. 2019. *The New Noir: Race, Identity, and Diaspora in Black Suburbia*. Berkeley: University of California Press.

Codman Square Neighborhood Council. 2010. "A Community Call to Action/Presentation on the Health of the Community." *Codman Square Neighborhood Council* (blog), March 16. https://codmansquarecouncil.org/codman-square-health-council/a-community-call-to-action -presentation-on-the-health-of-the-community/.

Cohen, Jeffrey, and Ibrahim Sirkeci. 2011. *Cultures of Migration: The Global Nature of Contemporary Mobility*. Austin: University of Texas Press.

Collins, Chuck, and Emma de Goede. 2018. "Towering Excess: The Perils of the Luxury Real Estate Boom for Bostonians." Program on Inequality and the Common Good. Institute for Policy Studies. https://ips-dc.org/wp-content/uploads/2018/09/ToweringExcessReport -Sept10.pdf.

Colocousis, Chris. 2012. "'It Was Tourism Repellent, That's What We Were Spraying': Natural Amenities, Environmental Stigma, and Redevelopment in a Postindustrial Mill Town." *Sociological Forum* 27 (3): 756–76.

Cooley, Charles. 1902. "The Looking Glass Self." In *Social Theory: The Multicultural, Global, and Classic Readings*, 6th ed., 146–47. New York: Routledge, 2019.

Coppock, John. 1977. *Second Homes: Curse or Blessing?* Oxford: Pergamon.

Corcoran, Mary. 2008. "Communities of Limited Liability." In *Belongings: Shaping Identity in Modern Ireland*, 259–73. Dublin: Institute of Public Administration.

Cuba, Lee, and David M. Hummon. 1993a. "A Place to Call Home: Identification with Dwelling, Community, and Region." *Sociological Quarterly* 34 (1): 111–31.

———. 1993b. "Constructing a Sense of Home: Place Affiliation and Migration across the Life Cycle." *Sociological Forum* 8:547–72.

Cucuzza, Marina, Joshua S. Stoll, and Heather M. Leslie. 2020. "Comprehensive Plans as Tools for Enhancing Coastal Community Resilience." *Journal of Environmental Planning & Management* 63 (11): 2022–41.

Dantzler, Prentiss, Elizabeth Korver-Glenn, and Junia Howell. 2022. "What Does Racial Capitalism Have to Do with Cities and Communities?" *City & Community* 21 (3): 163–72.

Davis, Fred. 1979. *Yearning for Yesterday: A Sociology of Nostalgia*. New York: Free Press.

Deener, Andrew. 2007. "Commerce as the Structure and Symbol of Neighborhood Life: Reshaping the Meaning of Community in Venice, California." *City & Community* 6 (4): 291–314.

———. 2012. *Venice: A Contested Bohemia in Los Angeles*. Chicago: University of Chicago Press.

DeLaney, Robert Michael, and Linda K. Pizzuti. 2005. "Who Is Buying Urban Condominiums?: A Tale of Four Cities." Massachusetts Institute of Technology. https://dspace.mit.edu/handle /1721.1/33200.

Demsas, Jerusalem. 2021. "Covid-19 Caused a Recession. So Why Did the Housing Market Boom?" *Vox*. https://www.vox.com/22264268/covid-19-housing-insecurity-housing-prices-mortgage -rates-pandemic-zoning-supply-demand.

Desmond, Matthew. 2023. *Poverty, by America*. New York: Penguin Random House.

Deterding, Nicole M., and Mary C. Waters. 2021. "Flexible Coding of In-Depth Interviews: A Twenty-First-Century Approach." *Sociological Methods & Research* 50 (2): 708–39.

DiMaggio, Paul. 1982. "Cultural Entrepreneurship in Nineteenth-Century Boston: The Creation of an Organizational Base for High Culture in America." *Media, Culture & Society* 4 (1): 33–50.

Dolgon, Corey. 2005. *The End of the Hamptons: Scenes from the Class Struggle in America's Paradise.* New York: New York University Press.

Douglas, Gordon C. C. 2012. "The Edge of the Island: Cultural Ideology and Neighbourhood Identity at the Gentrification Frontier." *Urban Studies* 49 (16): 3579–94.

Du Bois, William Edward Burghardt. 1899. *The Philadelphia Negro: A Social Study.* Philadelphia: University of Pennsylvania Press.

EdBuild. 2019. "Fractured: The Accelerating Breakdown of America's School Districts." http://edbuild.org/content/fractured.

Editorial Board. 2020. "Our View: Don't Try to Escape COVID by Coming to Rural Maine." *Press Herald* (blog), March 31. https://www.pressherald.com/2020/03/31/our-view-dont-try-to-escape-covid-in-rural-maine/.

Ellis, Edward. 1982. *A Chronological History of the Rangeley Lakes Region.* Farmington, ME: Heritage Printing Company.

Farrell, Betty. 1993. *Elite Families: Class and Power in Nineteenth-Century Boston.* New York: State University of New York Press.

Farrell, Justin. 2020a. *Billionaire Wilderness: The Ultra-Wealthy and the Remaking of the American West.* Princeton: Princeton University Press.

———. 2020b. "Where the Very Rich Fly to Hide." *New York Times,* April 15, sec. Opinion. https://www.nytimes.com/2020/04/15/opinion/jackson-hole-coronavirus.html.

Farstad, Maja. 2011. "Rural Residents' Opinions about Second Home Owners' Pursuit of Own Interests in the Host Community." *Norsk Geografisk Tidsskrift/Norwegian Journal of Geography* 65 (3): 165–74.

Farstad, Maja, and Johan Fredrik Rye. 2013. "Second Home Owners, Locals and Their Perspectives on Rural Development." *Journal of Rural Studies* 30 (April): 41–51.

Fenway Alliance. 2022. "History & Mission." http://www.fenwayculture.org/fcd-history-and-mission.

Fernandes, Deirdre. 2015. "Boston Condo Market Prices Set Record in 2014." *Boston Globe,* January 15. https://www.bostonglobe.com/business/2015/01/15/boston-condo-market-prices-set-record/mD8TQ0Pbu2hskUTfmDTPJN/story.html.

Fernandez, Rodrigo, and Manuel B. Aalbers. 2016. "Financialization and Housing: Between Globalization and Varieties of Capitalism." *Competition & Change* 20 (2): 71–88.

Fernandez, Rodrigo, Annelore Hofman, and Manuel B. Aalbers. 2016. "London and New York as a Safe Deposit Box for the Transnational Wealth Elite." *Environment and Planning A: Economy and Space* 48 (12): 2443–61.

Finney, Carolyn. 2014. *Black Faces, White Spaces: Reimagining the Relationship of African Americans to the Great Outdoors.* Chapel Hill: University of North Carolina Press.

Firey, Walter. 1945. "Sentiment and Symbolism as Ecological Variables." *American Sociological Review* 10 (2): 140–48.

Fischer, Claude S. 1982. *To Dwell among Friends: Personal Networks in Town and City.* Chicago: University of Chicago Press.

FitzGerald, David Scott, and Rawan Arar. 2018. "The Sociology of Refugee Migration." *Annual Review of Sociology* 44 (1): 387–406.

Forsyth, Ann. 2012. "Defining Suburbs." *Journal of Planning Literature* 27 (3): 270–81.

Freeman, Lance, and Jenny Schuetz. 2017. "Producing Affordable Housing in Rising Markets: What Works?" *Cityscape* 19 (1): 217 36.

Friends of the Public Garden. 2021. "Rose Brigade." *Friends of the Public Garden* (blog). https://friendsofthepublicgarden.org/about/volunteer/rose-brigade/.

Gans, Herbert J. 1982a. *The Levittowners: Ways of Life and Politics in a New Suburban Community.* New York: Columbia University Press.

———. 1982b. *The Urban Villagers: Group and Class in the Life of Italian-Americans*. New York: Free Press.

———. 2009. "Some Problems of and Futures for Urban Sociology: Toward a Sociology of Settlements." *City & Community* 8 (3): 211–19.

García, Daniel. 2022. "Second-Home Buying and the Housing Boom and Bust." *Real Estate Economics* 50 (1): 33–58.

Gardizy, Anissa. 2021. "Is There Demand for High-End, Urban Living Post-COVID? Boston Condo Developers Say Not Much Has Changed." *Boston Globe*, July 25. https://www.bostonglobe .com/2021/07/25/business/is-there-demand-high-end-urban-living-post-covid-boston -condo-developers-say-not-much-has-changed/.

Gieryn, Thomas F. 2000. "A Space for Place in Sociology." *Annual Review of Sociology* 26 (1): 463–96.

Gilbert, Dennis. 2011. *The American Class Structure in an Age of Growing Inequality*. Thousand Oaks, CA: Pine Forge Press.

Girouard, Jennifer. 2023. "Getting Suburbs to Do Their Fair Share: Housing Exclusion and Local Response to State Interventions." *RSF: The Russell Sage Foundation Journal of the Social Sciences* 9 (1): 126–44.

Glass, Ruth. 1964. "Aspects of Change." In *The Gentrification Debates: A Reader*, ed. Japonica Brown-Saracino, 19–30. London: Routledge.

Goffman, Erving. 1963. *Stigma: Notes on the Management of Spoiled Identity*. New York: Simon and Schuster.

———. 1975. *The Presentation of Self in Everyday Life*. New York: Penguin Books.

Golding, Shaun A. 2016. "Gentrification and Segregated Wealth in Rural America: Home Value Sorting in Destination Counties." *Population Research and Policy Review* 35 (1): 127–46.

Golding, Shaun A., and Richelle L. Winkler. 2020. "Tracking Urbanization and Exurbs: Migration across the Rural-Urban Continuum, 1990–2016." *Population Research and Policy Review* 39 (5): 835–59.

Gosnell, Hannah, and Jesse Abrams. 2011. "Amenity Migration: Diverse Conceptualizations of Drivers, Socioeconomic Dimensions, and Emerging Challenges." *GeoJournal* 76 (4): 303–22.

Grazian, David. 2003. *Blue Chicago: The Search for Authenticity in Urban Blues Clubs*. Chicago: University of Chicago Press.

Greenberg, Miriam. 2008. *Branding New York: How a City in Crisis Was Sold to the World*. New York: Taylor & Francis.

Greene, Theodore. 2014. "Gay Neighborhoods and the Rights of the Vicarious Citizen." *City & Community* 13 (2): 99–118.

Gusterson, Hugh. 1997. "Studying Up Revisited." *PoLAR: Political and Legal Anthropology Review* 20 (1): 114–19.

Hall, Colin Michael, and Dieter K. Müller. 2004. *Tourism, Mobility, and Second Homes: Between Elite Landscape and Common Ground*. Clevedon: Channel View Publications.

Hall, Michael, and Dieter Müller. 2018. "Governing and Planning for Second Homes." In *The Routledge Handbook of Second Home Tourism and Mobilities*. New York: Routledge.

Hanstein, Ben. 2017. "Name Change Proposed for Rangeley Lake Island." *Daily Bulldog* (blog), October 17. https://dailybulldog.com/features/name-change-proposed-for-rangeley-lake-island/.

Harrill, Rich. 2004. "Residents' Attitudes toward Tourism Development: A Literature Review with Implications for Tourism Planning." *Journal of Planning Literature* 18 (3): 251–66.

Harris, Adam. 2019. "The New Secession." *The Atlantic*. https://www.theatlantic.com/education /archive/2019/05/resegregation-baton-rouge-public-schools/589381/.

Harrison, Jill Ann. 2017. "Rust Belt Boomerang: The Pull of Place in Moving Back to a Legacy City." *City & Community* 16 (3): 263–83.

Harvey, Hope, Kelley Fong, Kathryn Edin, and Stefanie DeLuca. 2020. "Forever Homes and Temporary Stops: Housing Search Logics and Residential Selection." *Social Forces* 98 (4): 1498–1523.

Hay, Iain. 2013. *Geographies of the Super-Rich.* Cheltenham: Edward Elgar Publishing.

Herbert, Claire W. 2021. *A Detroit Story: Urban Decline and the Rise of Property Informality.* Berkeley: University of California Press.

Hines, J. Dwight 2010a. "In Pursuit of Experience: The Postindustrial Gentrification of the Rural American West." *Ethnography* 11 (2): 285–308.

———. 2010b. "Rural Gentrification as Permanent Tourism: The Creation of the 'New' West Archipelago as Postindustrial Cultural Space." *Environment and Planning D: Society and Space* 28 (3): 509–25.

Hoey, Brian. 2014. *Opting for Elsewhere: Lifestyle Migration in the American Middle Class.* Nashville: Vanderbilt University Press.

———. 2016. "Negotiating Work and Family: Lifestyle Migration, Potential Selves and the Role of Second Homes as Potential Spaces." *Leisure Studies* 35 (1): 64–77.

Holme, Jennifer Jellison. 2009. "Buying Homes, Buying Schools: School Choice and the Social Construction of School Quality." *Harvard Educational Review* 72 (2): 177–206.

Hornsby, Stephen J., and Richard W. Judd, eds. 2015. *Historical Atlas of Maine.* Orono: University of Maine Press.

Hosman, Sarah Siltanen. 2018a. "Allston Christmas: How Local Rituals Reproduce Neighbourhood Temporality and Deter Gentrification." *Urbanities: Journal of Urban Ethnography* 8 (2): 69–78.

———. 2018b. "From 'Street Car Suburb' to 'Student Ghetto': Allston and Urban Change." PhD thesis, Boston University.

Hoyt, Austin. 2003. *Chicago: City of the Century.* PBS American Experience. https://www.pbs.org/wgbh/americanexperience/films/chicago/.

Hughes, Carolyn. 1988. "Back Bay/Bay State Road: Exploring Boston's Neighborhoods." Boston: Boston Landmarks Commission.

Hull, Cindy L. 2012. *Chippewa Lake: A Community in Search of an Identity.* East Lansing: Michigan State University Press.

Hummon, David M. 1990. *Commonplaces: Community Ideology and Identity in American Culture.* Albany: State University of New York Press.

Hunter, Albert. 1975. "The Loss of Community: An Empirical Test through Replication." *American Sociological Review* 40 (5): 537–52.

———. 1982. *Symbolic Communities: The Persistence and Change of Chicago's Local Communities.* Chicago: University of Chicago Press.

Hunter, Albert D., and Gerald Suttles. 1972. "The Expanding Community of Limited-Liability." Ed. Albert Hunter. *The Social Construction of Communities.* Chicago: University of Chicago Press.

Hyra, Derek. 2014. "The Back-to-the-City Movement: Neighbourhood Redevelopment and Processes of Political and Cultural Displacement." *Urban Studies*, 1753–73.

———. 2017. *Race, Class, and Politics in the Cappuccino City.* Chicago: University of Chicago Press.

The Irregular. 2020. "Economic Opportunities for Rangeley & Oquossoc." November 11. https://www.theirregular.com/articles/economic-opportunities-for-rangeley-oquossoc/.

Jaakson, Reiner. 1986. "Second-Home Domestic Tourism." *Annals of Tourism Research* 13 (3): 367–91.

Jackson, Kenneth T. 1985. *Crabgrass Frontier: The Suburbanization of the United States.* Oxford: Oxford University Press.

Jacobs, Jane. 1961. *The Death and Life of Great American Cities.* New York: Vintage.

Jacobs, Joseph, ed. 2002. *The Fables of Aesop.* Illustrated ed. Mineola, NY: Dover Publications.

Janowitz, Morris. 1952. *The Community Press in an Urban Setting.* New York: Free Press.

Jerolmack, Colin. 2021. *Up to Heaven and Down to Hell: Fracking, Freedom, and Community in an American Town*. Princeton: Princeton University Press.

Joey. 2020. "A Maine Woman Declares It's Her Husband's Fault She's Driving with Massachusetts Plates." WCYY. https://wcyy.com/a-maine-woman-declares-its-her-husbands-fault-shes-driving-with-massachusetts-plates/.

Joo, Nathan, and Richard V. Reeves. 2017. "White, Still: The American Upper Middle Class." *Brookings* (blog), October 4. https://www.brookings.edu/blog/social-mobility-memos/2017/10/04/white-still-the-american-upper-middle-class/.

Kadi, Justin, Cody Hochstenbach, and Christian Lennartz. 2020. "Multiple Property Ownership in Times of Late Homeownership: A New Conceptual Vocabulary." *International Journal of Housing Policy* 20 (1): 6–24.

Katz, Marni Elyse. 2019. "This Bright South End Pied-à-Terre Is a City Refuge for Suburban Commuters." *Boston Globe*, February 7. https://www.bostonglobe.com/magazine/2019/02/07/this-bright-south-end-pied-terre-city-refuge-for-suburban-commuters/tlDihCznVIaIJkfxj8MlNN/story.html.

Kaufman, Amanda. 2021. "'It's Mind-Boggling': On Cape Cod, Soaring Home Prices Create an Unprecedented Seller's Market." *Boston Globe*, May 20. https://www.bostonglobe.com/2021/05/20/metro/its-mindboggling-cape-cod-home-prices-are-soaring-creating-an-unprecedented-sellers-market/.

Kaufman, Jason, and Matthew E. Kaliner. 2011. "The Re-Accomplishment of Place in Twentieth Century Vermont and New Hampshire: History Repeats Itself, until It Doesn't." *Theory and Society* 40 (2): 119–54.

Kazyak, Emily. 2012. "Midwest or Lesbian? Gender, Rurality, and Sexuality." *Gender & Society* 26 (6): 825–48.

Kearney. 2020. "2020 Global Cities Index." https://www.kearney.com/global-cities/2020.

Khan, Shamus. 2012. "The Sociology of Elites." *Annual Review of Sociology* 38 (1): 361–77.

Khater, Sam, Len Kiefer, and Venkataramana Yanamandra. 2021. "Housing Supply: A Growing Deficit." Research Note. Freddie Mac. https://www.freddiemac.com/research/insight/20210507-housing-supply.

Kimelberg, Shelley McDonough. 2014. "Middle-Class Parents, Risk, and Urban Public Schools." In *Choosing Homes, Choosing Schools*, 207–36. New York: Russell Sage Foundation.

Kolko, Jed. 2017. "Americans' Shift to the Suburbs Sped Up Last Year." *FiveThirtyEight* (blog), March 23. https://fivethirtyeight.com/features/americans-shift-to-the-suburbs-sped-up-last-year/.

Koo, Juliana, and Elizabeth Cabral Curtis. 2015. "How Boston and Other American Cities Support and Sustain the Arts: Funding for Cultural Nonprofits in Boston and 10 Other Metropolitan Centers." Understanding Boston. The Boston Foundation. https://www.tbf.org/-/media/tbforg/files/reports/arts-report_jan-7-2016.pdf?la=en.

Korver-Glenn, Elizabeth. 2021. *Race Brokers: Housing Markets and Segregation in 21st Century Urban America*. Oxford: Oxford University Press.

Krysan, Maria, and Kyle Crowder. 2017. *Cycle of Segregation: Social Processes and Residential Stratification*. New York: Russell Sage Foundation.

Kusenbach, Margarethe. 2003. "Street Phenomenology: The Go-Along as Ethnographic Research Tool." *Ethnography* 4 (3): 455–85.

———. 2008. "A Hierarchy of Urban Communities: Observations on the Nested Character of Place." *City & Community* 7 (3): 225–49.

Lacy, Karyn. 2007. *Blue-Chip Black: Race, Class, and Status in the New Black Middle Class*. Berkeley: University of California Press.

———. 2016. "The New Sociology of Suburbs: A Research Agenda for Analysis of Emerging Trends." *Annual Review of Sociology* 42 (1): 369–84.

Lamont, Michèle. 2009. *The Dignity of Working Men: Morality and the Boundaries of Race, Class, and Immigration*. Cambridge, MA: Harvard University Press.

Lareau, Annette. 2014. "Schools, Housing, and the Reproduction of Social Inequality." In *Choosing Homes, Choosing Schools*, 169–206. New York: Russell Sage Foundation.

Lareau, Annette, and Kimberly Goyette. 2014. *Choosing Homes, Choosing Schools*. New York: Russell Sage Foundation.

Lauder, Landon H. 2022. "Cruising Boston and Providence: The Roles of Place and Desire for Reflexive Queer Research(Ers)." *Ethnography* 24 (2): 280–300.

Lawler, Steph. 2014. *Identity: Sociological Perspectives*. New York: John Wiley & Sons.

Lear, Alex. 2021. "Doctors: Telemedicine Can Be a 'Game Changer' . . . If You Have Good Internet." *Lewiston Sun Journal* (blog), March 14. https://www.sunjournal.com/2021/03/14/doctors-telemedicine-can-be-a-game-changer-if-you-have-good-internet/.

Lees, Loretta. 2003. "Super-Gentrification: The Case of Brooklyn Heights, New York City." *Urban Studies* 40 (12): 2487–2509.

Levine, Jeremy R. 2016. "The Privatization of Political Representation: Community-Based Organizations as Nonelected Neighborhood Representatives." *American Sociological Review* 81 (6): 1251–75.

———. 2021. *Constructing Community: Urban Governance, Development, and Inequality in Boston*. Princeton: Princeton University Press.

Levy, Paul R., and R. A. Cybriwksy. 1980. *The Hidden Dimensions of Culture and Class: Philadelphia*. New York: Routledge.

Ley, David. 1994. "Gentrification and the Politics of the New Middle Class." *Environment and Planning D: Society and Space* 12 (1): 53–74.

Lichter, Daniel T., and David L. Brown. 2011. "Rural America in an Urban Society: Changing Spatial and Social Boundaries." *Annual Review of Sociology* 37 (1): 565–92.

Lloyd, Richard. 2010. *Neo-Bohemia: Art and Commerce in the Postindustrial City*. New York: Routledge.

Logan, John R., and Harvey L. Molotch. 1987. *Urban Fortunes: The Political Economy of Place*. Berkeley: University of California Press.

Logan, John. 2014. "Separate and Unequal in Suburbia." Census Brief prepared for Project US2010. http://www.s4.brown.edu/us2010.

Logan, Tim. 2016. "With Millennium Tower, Boston Reaches New Heights as Foreign Money Magnet." *Boston Globe*, August 29. https://www.bostonglobe.com/business/2016/08/29/with-millennium-tower-boston-reaches-new-heights-foreign-money-magnet/keC5sjXE546tpvGmGsTVlM/story.html.

———. 2018. "Boston's New Luxury Towers Appear to House Few Local Residents." *Boston Globe*, September 10. https://www.bostonglobe.com/business/2018/09/10/boston-new-luxury-towers-appear-house-few-bostonians/BkBkDOtdY2LwXpg2OhEWoJ/story.html.

———. 2021. "Greater Boston's Housing Market Still Soaring, Putting Ownership Further out of Reach for Many." *Boston Globe*, May 19. https://www.bostonglobe.com/2021/05/19/business/greater-bostons-housing-market-still-soaring-putting-ownership-further-out-reach-many/.

Long, Patrick T., Richard R. Perdue, and Lawrence Allen. 1990. "Rural Resident Tourism Perceptions and Attitudes by Community Level of Tourism." *Journal of Travel Research* 28 (3): 3–9.

Loon, Jannes van, and Manuel B. Aalbers. 2017. "How Real Estate Became 'Just Another Asset Class': The Financialization of the Investment Strategies of Dutch Institutional Investors." *European Planning Studies* 25 (2): 221–40.

Lopez, Cynthia. 2019. "Boston's Arts Sector Attracts More Visitors than Sports Games, Report Says." WBUR. https://www.wbur.org/news/2019/06/04/arts-boston-economic-impact.

Loughead, Katherine. 2019. "2019 State Individual Income Tax Rates and Brackets." *Tax Foundation* (blog), March 20. https://taxfoundation.org/state-individual-income-tax-rates-brackets-2019/.

Loughran, Kevin. 2017. "Race and the Construction of City and Nature." *Environment and Planning A: Economy and Space* 49 (9): 1948–67.

———. 2022. *Parks for Profit: Selling Nature in the City.* New York: Columbia University Press.

Luccarelli, Mark, and Per Gunnar Roe. 2022. "Liminal Space, Film Noir, and the Production of the (American) Suburb." In *Suburbia in the 21st Century: From Dreamscape to Nightmare?* ed. Paul J. Maginn and Katrin B. Anacker. New York: Routledge.

Maginn, Paul J., and Katrin B. Anacker. 2022. *Suburbia in the 21st Century: From Dreamscape to Nightmare?* New York: Routledge.

Maine Department of Education. 2021. "Public Funded Attending Counts by School and Location." Maine: Maine Department of Education. https://www.maine.gov/doe/data-reporting/reporting/warehouse/enrollment.

Maine Department of Labor: Center for Workforce Research & Information. 2014. "Annual Private Industry Employment and Wages, Rangeley, ME." 2014. https://www.maine.gov/labor/cwri/qcew1.html.

Maine State Housing Authority. 2017. "2017 Housing Facts and Affordability Index for Franklin County." https://www.mainehousing.org/docs/default-source/policy-research/housing-facts/2017/franklincounty2017.pdf?sfvrsn=f7f9a015_4.

Makris, Molly Vollman, and Mary Gatta. 2020. *Gentrification Down the Shore.* New Brunswick, NJ: Rutgers University Press.

Mansbridge, Jane J. 1983. *Beyond Adversary Democracy.* Chicago: University of Chicago Press.

Massey, Douglas S. 1996. "The Age of Extremes: Concentrated Affluence and Poverty in the Twenty-First Century." *Demography* 33 (4): 395–412.

Massey, Douglas S., and Nancy A. Denton. 1993. *American Apartheid: Segregation and the Making of the Underclass.* Cambridge, MA: Harvard University Press.

Massey, Douglas S., and Jonathan Tannen. 2018. "Suburbanization and Segregation in the United States: 1970–2010." *Ethnic and Racial Studies* 41 (9): 1594–1611.

Mayorga, Sarah, Megan Underhill, and Lauren Crosser. 2022. "'I Hate That Food Lion': Grocery Shopping, Racial Capitalism, and Everyday Disinvestment." *City & Community* 21 (3): 238–55.

McCabe, Brian J. 2016. *No Place Like Home: Wealth, Community, and the Politics of Homeownership.* Oxford: Oxford University Press.

McCormick, Kate. 2017. "Rangeley Planning Board Approves Controversial Concrete Plant." *Kennebec Journal and Morning Sentinel* (blog), April 13. https://www.centralmaine.com/2017/04/13/rangeley-planning-board-approves-controversial-concrete-plant/.

McDonald, Danny. 2021. "City of Boston to Launch a Task Force Review of PILOT Program." *Boston Globe,* June 14. https://www.bostonglobe.com/2021/06/14/metro/city-boston-launch-task-force-review-pilot-program/.

McIntyre, Norman, Daniel Williams, and Kevin McHugh. 2006. *Multiple Dwelling and Tourism: Negotiating Place, Home and Identity.* Cambridge, MA: CABI.

Menear, Dee. 2013. "Rangeley Researching Pharmacy." *The Irregular,* September 11. https://www.theirregular.com/articles/rangeley-researching-pharmacy/.

MFA Boston. 2020. "Museum of Fine Arts Boston: Report of PILOT Program Contributions." https://www.boston.gov/sites/default/files/file/2020/08/Museum%20of%20Fine%20Arts%20FY20%20Community%20Benefit%20%20Report%20%28Letter%29.pdf.

Miles, Kathryn. 2020. "A Tiny Island Tries to Shut Out the Virus." *Politico,* March 28. https://www.politico.com/news/magazine/2020/03/28/a-tiny-island-tries-to-shut-out-the-virus-152382.

Milligan, Melinda J. 1998. "Interactional Past and Potential: The Social Construction of Place Attachment." *Symbolic Interaction* 21 (1): 1–33.

———. 2003. "Displacement and Identity Discontinuity: The Role of Nostalgia in Establishing New Identity Categories." *Symbolic Interaction* 26 (3): 381–403.

Milman, Ady, and Abraham Pizam. 1988. "Social Impacts of Tourism on Central Florida." *Annals of Tourism Research* 15 (2): 191–204.

Molotch, Harvey, William Freudenburg, and Krista E. Paulsen. 2000. "History Repeats Itself, but How? City Character, Urban Tradition, and the Accomplishment of Place." *American Sociological Review* 65 (6): 791–823.

Moody, Roger Allen. 2023. *Historic Sporting Camps of Moosehead Lake, Maine.* Unity, ME: North Country Press.

Mueller, J. Tom. 2021. "Defining Dependence: The Natural Resource Community Typology." *Rural Sociology* 86 (2): 260–300.

Müller, Dieter K., and Gijsbert Hoogendoorn. 2013. "Second Homes: Curse or Blessing? A Review 36 Years Later." *Scandinavian Journal of Hospitality and Tourism* 13 (4): 353–69.

National Association of Realtors 2017. "2017 NAR Investment & Vacation Home Buyer's Survey." Report in author's possession.

———. 2021a. "2021 Vacation Home Counties Report." Report in author's possession.

———. 2021b. "Vacation Home Sales Skyrocket as a Result of Pandemic." https://www.nar.realtor /newsroom/vacation-home-sales-skyrocket-as-a-result-of-pandemic.

Neate, Rupert. 2020. "Super-Rich Jet off to Disaster Bunkers amid Coronavirus Outbreak." *The Guardian*, March 11, sec. World news. https://www.theguardian.com/world/2020/mar/11 /disease-dodging-worried-wealthy-jet-off-to-disaster-bunkers.

New England Historical Society. 2016. "A Brief History of the Boston Brahmin." http://www .newenglandhistoricalsociety.com/brief-history-boston-brahmin/.

New York Angler. 1876. "Angling in the Mountains: Contrasts in the Sporting Regions of Maine and New York." *New York Times*.

New York Times. 2020. "New York Coronavirus Map and Case Count." *New York Times*, April 1, sec. U.S. https://www.nytimes.com/interactive/2021/us/new-york-covid-cases.html.

Nir, Sarah Maslin, and Tracey Tully. 2020. "Did New Yorkers Who Fled to Second Homes Bring the Virus?" *New York Times*, April 10. https://www.nytimes.com/2020/04/10/nyregion /coronavirus-new-yorkers-leave.html.

Ocejo, Richard. 2011. "The Early Gentrifier: Weaving a Nostalgia Narrative on the Lower East Side." *City & Community* 10 (3): 285–310.

———. 2014. *Upscaling Downtown: From Bowery Saloons to Cocktail Bars in New York City.* Princeton: Princeton University Press.

———. 2019. "From Apple to Orange: Narratives of Small City Migration and Settlement among the Urban Middle Class." *Sociological Perspectives* 62 (3): 402–25.

Ocejo, Richard E., Ervin B. Kosta, and Alexis Mann. 2020. "Centering Small Cities for Urban Sociology in the 21st Century." *City & Community* 19 (1): 3–15.

Ofulue, Camille. 2021. "Redlining in Boston: How the Architects of the Past Have Shaped Boston's Future." *Boston Political Review*, November 4. https://www.bostonpoliticalreview.org/post /redlining-in-boston-how-the-architects-of-the-past-have-shaped-boston-s-future.

Oldenburg, Ray. 1999. *The Great Good Place: Cafés, Coffee Shops, Bookstores, Bars, Hair Salons, and Other Hangouts at the Heart of a Community.* Boston: Da Capo Press.

O'Malley, Matt, and Andrea Campbell. 2018. "An Order for a Hearing Regarding Vacant Properties in the City of Boston." https://www.boston.gov/sites/default/files/file/document_files/2019 /09/0583_docket_vacant_properties.pdf.

Ortiz, Aimee. 2020. "'Group of Local Vigilantes' Try to Forcibly Quarantine Out-of-Towners, Officials Say." *New York Times*, March 30. https://www.nytimes.com/2020/03/29/us/maine -coronavirus-quarantine-tree.html.

O'Sullivan, Feargus. 2016. "If You Own a Vacation Home in Paris, Consider Yourself Warned." CityLab. http://www.citylab.com/housing/2016/06/paris-wants-to-raise-second-homes -taxes-five-times/487124/.

Owens, Ann. 2012. "Neighborhoods on the Rise: A Typology of Neighborhoods Experiencing Socioeconomic Ascent." *City & Community* 11 (4): 345–69.

Pacewicz, Josh. 2016. *Partisans and Partners: The Politics of the Post-Keynesian Society.* Chicago: University of Chicago Press.

Palmer, Donald. 2004. *Rangeley Lakes Region.* Portsmouth: Arcadia Publishing.

Pan, Deanna. 2020. "Boston Is the Third Most 'Intensely Gentrified' City in the United States, Study Says." *Boston Globe,* July 10. https://www.bostonglobe.com/2020/07/10/metro/boston-is-third-most-intensely-gentrified-city-united-states-study-says/.

Paris, Chris. 2010. *Affluence, Mobility and Second Home Ownership.* New York: Routledge.

Park, Lisa Sun-Hee, and David Naguib Pellow. 2011. *The Slums of Aspen: Immigrants vs. the Environment in America's Eden.* New York: New York University Press.

Park, Minkyung, Monika Derrien, Emilian Geczi, and Patricia A. Stokowski. 2019. "Grappling with Growth: Perceptions of Development and Preservation in Faster- and Slower-Growing Amenity Communities." *Society & Natural Resources* 32 (1): 73–92.

Parker, Jeffrey Nathaniel. 2018. "Negotiating the Space between Avant-Garde and 'Hip Enough': Businesses and Commercial Gentrification in Wicker Park." *City & Community* 17 (2): 438–60.

Parker, Jeffrey Nathaniel, and Stephanie Ternullo. 2022. "Gentrifiers Evading Stigma: Social Integrationists in the Neighborhood of the Future." *Social Problems.* https://doi.org/10.1093/socpro/spac026.

Parker, Kim, Juliana Menasce Horowitz, Anna Brown, Richard Fry, D'Vera Cohn, and Ruth Igielnik. 2018. "Demographic and Economic Trends in Urban, Suburban and Rural Communities." Pew Research Center. https://www.pewresearch.org/social-trends/2018/05/22/demographic-and-economic-trends-in-urban-suburban-and-rural-communities/.

Pattillo, Mary. 2007. *Black on the Block: The Politics of Race and Class in the City.* Chicago: University of Chicago Press.

———. 2015. "Everyday Politics of School Choice in the Black Community." *Du Bois Review: Social Science Research on Race* 12 (1): 41–71.

Pattillo-McCoy, Mary. 2000. *Black Picket Fences: Privilege and Peril among the Black Middle Class.* Chicago: University of Chicago Press.

Paulsen, Krista E. 2004. "Making Character Concrete: Empirical Strategies for Studying Place Distinction." *City & Community* 3 (3): 243–62.

Paulsen, Krista E., and Jenny Stuber. 2022. "On Place and Privilege: Varieties of Affluence in Cities and Neighborhoods." *Sociology Compass* 16 (6).

Phadke, Roopali. 2013. "Public Deliberation and the Geographies of Wind Justice." *Science as Culture* 22 (2): 247–55.

Pitkänen, Kati, Czesław Adamiak, and Greg Halseth. 2014. "Leisure Activities and Rural Community Change: Valuation and Use of Rural Space among Permanent Residents and Second Home Owners." *Sociologia Ruralis* 54 (2): 143–66.

Priest, Gary. 2009. *The Gilded Age of Rangeley, Maine.* Gary Priest Publishing.

Putnam, R. D. 2001. *Bowling Alone: The Collapse and Revival of American Community.* New York: Simon and Schuster.

Quealy, Kevin. 2020. "The Richest Neighborhoods Emptied Out Most as Coronavirus Hit New York City." *New York Times,* May 15, sec. The Upshot. https://www.nytimes.com/interactive/2020/05/15/upshot/who-left-new-york-coronavirus.html.

Ragatz, Richard Lee. 1977. "Vacation Homes in Rural Areas: Towards a Model for Predicting Their Distribution and Occupancy Patterns." In *Second Homes: Curse or Blessing,* ed. John Terence Coppock, 181–94. Oxford: Pergamon Press.

Reeder, Richard J., and Dennis M. Brown. 2012. "Recreation, Tourism, and Rural Well-Being." In *Tourism and Hospitality.* Palm Bay: Apple Academic Press.

Reeves, Richard V. 2018. *Dream Hoarders: How the American Upper Middle Class Is Leaving Everyone Else in the Dust, Why That Is a Problem, and What to Do about It*. Washington, DC: Brookings Institution Press.

Rhodes, Anna, and Max Besbris. 2022a. *Soaking the Middle Class: Suburban Inequality and Recovery from Disaster*. New York: Russell Sage Foundation.

———. 2022b. "Best Laid Plans: How the Middle Class Make Residential Decisions Post-Disaster." *Social Problems* 69 (4): 1137–53.

Rivera, Lauren A. 2016. *Pedigree: How Elite Students Get Elite Jobs*. Princeton: Princeton University Press.

Roberts, Sam. 2011. "Homes Dark and Lifeless, Kept by Out-of-Towners." *New York Times*, July 7, sec. New York. https://www.nytimes.com/2011/07/07/nyregion/more-apartments-are-empty-yet-rented-or-owned-census-finds.html.

Robinson, Cedric J. 2005. *Black Marxism: The Making of the Black Radical Tradition*. Chapel Hill: University of North Carolina Press.

Robinson, Zandria F. 2014. *This Ain't Chicago: Race, Class, and Regional Identity in the Post-Soul South*. Chapel Hill: University of North Carolina Press Books.

Ronald, Richard, and Justin Kadi. 2017. "The Revival of Private Landlords in Britain's Post-Homeownership Society." *New Political Economy* 23 (6): 786–803.

Rosen, Eva. 2017. "Horizontal Immobility: How Narratives of Neighborhood Violence Shape Housing Decisions." *American Sociological Review* 82 (2): 270–96.

———. 2020. *The Voucher Promise: "Section 8" and the Fate of an American Neighborhood*. Princeton: Princeton University Press.

Ross, Casey. 2014. "At $37.5m, Millennium Tower Condo Tops Most Everything." *Boston Globe*, October 23. http://www.bostonglobe.com/metro/2014/10/22/millenniumtower/rOlAlAcEiwMcHF9ThIkdQP/amp.html.

Rucks-Ahidiana, Zawadi. 2021. "Theorizing Gentrification as a Process of Racial Capitalism." *City & Community* 21 (3): 173–92.

Rury, John L., and Aaron Tyler Rife. 2018. "Race, Schools and Opportunity Hoarding: Evidence from a Post-War American Metropolis." *History of Education* 47 (1): 87–107.

Rury, John L., and Argun Saatcioglu. 2011. "Suburban Advantage: Opportunity Hoarding and Secondary Attainment in the Postwar Metropolitan North." *American Journal of Education* 117 (3): 307–42.

Ryan, James E. 2010. *Five Miles Away, A World Apart: One City, Two Schools, and the Story of Educational Opportunity in Modern America*. Oxford: Oxford University Press.

Rye, Johan Fredrik. 2011. "Conflicts and Contestations: Rural Populations' Perspectives on the Second Homes Phenomenon." *Journal of Rural Studies* 27 (3): 263–74.

Salamon, Sonya. 2007. *Newcomers to Old Towns: Suburbanization of the Heartland*. Chicago: University of Chicago Press.

Sampson, Robert J. 2012. *Great American City: Chicago and the Enduring Neighborhood Effect*. Chicago: University of Chicago Press.

Sandoval, Gabriel. 2020. "Garbage Pickups Tell a Tale of Two Cities, with Part of Manhattan Shrinking." *The City*, April 12. https://www.thecity.nyc/government/2020/4/12/21247125/garbage-pickups-tell-a-tale-of-two-cities-with-part-of-manhattan-shrinking.

Savage, Mike. 2010. "The Politics of Elective Belonging." *Housing, Theory and Society* 27 (2): 115–61.

Schewe, Rebecca L., Donald R. Field, Deborah J. Frosch, Gregory Clendenning, and Dana Jensen. 2012. *Condos in the Woods: The Growth of Seasonal and Retirement Homes in Northern Wisconsin*. Madison: University of Wisconsin Pres.

Scofield, Carolyn G. 2008. *The Island Maneskootuk: A Family Saga on Maine's Rangeley Lake*. Victoria, BC: Trafford.

Seamster, Louise. 2015. "The White City: Race and Urban Politics." *Sociology Compass* 9 (12): 1049–65.

Sharkey, Patrick. 2013. *Stuck in Place: Urban Neighborhoods and the End of Progress toward Racial Equality*. Chicago: University of Chicago Press.

Sherman, Jennifer. 2009. *Those Who Work, Those Who Don't: Poverty, Morality, and Family in Rural America*. Minneapolis: University of Minnesota Press.

———. 2018. "'Not Allowed to Inherit My Kingdom': Amenity Development and Social Inequality in the Rural West." *Rural Sociology* 83 (1): 174–207.

———. 2021. *Dividing Paradise: Rural Inequality and the Diminishing American Dream*. Berkeley: University of California Press.

Sherman, Rachel. 2018. "'A Very Expensive Ordinary Life': Consumption, Symbolic Boundaries and Moral Legitimacy among New York Elites." *Socio-Economic Review* 16 (2): 411–33.

———. 2019. *Uneasy Street: The Anxieties of Affluence*. Princeton: Princeton University Press.

Shumway, J. Matthew, and James A. Davis. 1996. "Nonmetropolitan Population Change in the Mountain West: 1970–1995." *Rural Sociology* 61: 513–29.

Simmel, Georg. [1903] 2005. "The Metropolis and Mental Life." In *The Urban Sociology Reader*, ed. Jan Lin and Christopher Mele, 23–31. New York: Routledge.

Skelly, Matthew. 2021. "Greater Mattapan Neighborhood Council Monthly Meeting." https://g-mnc.org/wp-content/uploads/2021/09/2021-05-03-GMNC-Monthly-Meeting.pdf.

Skelton, Kathryn. 2021a. "Couple Donate $1.5 Million for Workforce Housing at Saddleback; Officials Hope to See Saddleback House Break Ground in the Spring and Work toward an Opening Next Winter." *Portland Press Herald*, December 1, C3.

———. 2021b. "Franklin County's High-Speed Internet Question—Will Residents Pay to Bring Service to Town?" *Lewiston Sun Journal* (blog), March 21. https://www.sunjournal.com/2021/03/21/franklin-countys-high-speed-internet-question-will-residents-pay-to-bring-service-to-town/.

Slater, Philip E. 1990. *The Pursuit of Loneliness: American Culture at the Breaking Point*. Boston: Beacon Press.

Small, Mario Luis. 2009. *Villa Victoria: The Transformation of Social Capital in a Boston Barrio*. Chicago: University of Chicago Press.

Smith, Edmund. 1980. "How to Go Native in Maine." In *Over to Home and From Away*, ed. Jim Brunelle, 191–214. Portland, ME: G. Gannett Publishing Company.

Smith, Michael D., and Richard S. Krannich. 1998. "Tourism Dependence and Resident Attitudes." *Annals of Tourism Research* 25 (4): 783–802.

Smith, Neil. 1979. "Toward a Theory of Gentrification: A Back to the City Movement by Capital, Not People." *Journal of the American Planning Association* 45 (4): 538–48.

Sperance, Cameron. 2021. "New England Vacation Homes Are the Ultra-Seller's Market." Boston.Com Real Estate. http://realestate.boston.com/buying/2021/05/12/it-is-staggering-what-some-people-are-paying/.

Stedman, Richard C. 2006. "Understanding Place Attachment among Second Home Owners." *American Behavioral Scientist* 50 (2): 187–205.

Stern, Michael J., Alison E. Adams, and Shaun Elsasser. 2009. "Digital Inequality and Place: The Effects of Technological Diffusion on Internet Proficiency and Usage across Rural, Suburban, and Urban Counties." *Sociological Inquiry* 79 (4): 391–417.

Stiman, Meaghan. 2019. "Speculators and Specters: Diverse Forms of Second Homeowner Engagement in Boston, Massachusetts." *Journal of Urban Affairs* 41 (5): 700–720.

———. 2020a. "Second Homes in the City and the Country: A Reappraisal of Vacation Homes in the Twenty-First Century." *International Journal of Housing Policy* 20 (1): 53–74.

———. 2020b. "Discourses of Resource Dependency: Second Homeowners as 'Lifeblood' in Vacationland." *Rural Sociology* 85 (2): 468–94.

Story, Louise, and Stephanie Saul. 2015. "Stream of Foreign Wealth Flows to Elite New York Real Estate." *New York Times*, February 7. http://www.nytimes.com/2015/02/08/nyregion/stream -of-foreign-wealth-flows-to-time-warner-condos.html.

Stryker, Sheldon. 2008. "From Mead to a Structural Symbolic Interactionism and Beyond." *Annual Review of Sociology* 34 (1): 15–31.

Stuber, Jenny. 2021. *Aspen and the American Dream: How One Town Manages Inequality in the Era of Supergentrification*. Berkeley: University of California Press.

Summers, Brandi Thompson. 2019. *Black in Place: The Spatial Aesthetics of Race in a Post-Chocolate City*. Chapel Hill: University of North Carolina Press.

Suttles, Gerald D. 1972. *The Social Construction of Communities*. Chicago: University of Chicago Press.

Taylor, Dorceta E. 2016. *The Rise of the American Conservation Movement: Power, Privilege, and Environmental Protection*. Durham: Duke University Press.

Teaford, Jon C. 2018. "Dividing the Metropolis: The Political History of Suburban Incorporation in the United States." In *The Routledge Companion to the Suburbs*. New York: Routledge.

Tilly, Charles. 1998. *Durable Inequality*. Berkeley: University of California Press.

Timothy, Dallen. 2004. "Recreational Summer Homes in the United States: Development Issues and Contemporary Patterns." In *Tourism, Mobility, and Second Homes*, ed. Michael Hall and Dieter K. Müller, 133–48. Clevedon: Channel View Publications.

Tissot, Sylvie. 2014. "Loving Diversity/Controlling Diversity: Exploring the Ambivalent Mobilization of Upper-Middle-Class Gentrifiers, South End, Boston." *International Journal of Urban and Regional Research* 38 (4): 1181–94.

———. 2015. *Good Neighbors: Gentrifying Diversity in Boston's South End*. London: Verso Books.

Tönnies, Ferdinand. 1887. "Community and Society." In *The Urban Sociology Reader*, ed. Jan Lin and Christopher Mele. Vol. 13. London: Routledge.

Town of Rangeley. 2012. "Rangeley Comprehensive Plan." https://townofrangeley.com/263 /Comprehensive-Plan.

Treffeisen, Beth. 2018. "Malley Looks at Fees to Tackle Vacant Storefronts and Apartments." *Beacon Hill Times*, April 21. https://beaconhilltimes.com/2018/04/21/malley-looks-at-fees -to-tackle-vacant-storefronts-and-apartments/.

Treisman, Rachel. 2020. "Northeast: Coronavirus-Related Restrictions by State." NPR, December 1, sec. Shots—Health News. https://www.npr.org/2020/05/01/847331283/northeast -coronavirus-related-restrictions-by-state.

Trujillo, Kristin Lunz. 2022. "Feeling Out of Place: Who Are the Non-Rural Rural Identifiers, and Are They Unique Politically?" *APSA Preprints*, September.

Tuttle, Steven. 2022a. "Towards a Theory of the Racialization of Space." *American Behavioral Scientist* 66 (11): 1526–38.

———. 2022b. "Place Attachment and Alienation from Place: Cultural Displacement in Gentrifying Ethnic Enclaves." *Critical Sociology* 48 (3): 517–31.

U.S. Census Bureau. 2000. "Profile of General Population and Housing Characteristics." https:// factfinder.census.gov/faces/tableservices/jsf/pages/productview.xhtml?src=CF.

———. 2010. "Profile of General Population and Housing Characteristics." https://factfinder .census.gov/faces/tableservices/jsf/pages/productview.xhtml?src=CF.

———. 2016–20. "American Community Survey 5-Year Estimates. Selected Economic Characteristics 5-Year Estimates." https://factfinder.census.gov/faces/tableservices/jsf/pages /productview.xhtml?src=CF.

———. 2010–14. "American Community Survey 5-Year Estimates. Selected Economic Characteristics 5-Year Estimates." https://factfinder.census.gov/faces/tableservices/jsf/pages /productview.xhtml?src=CF.

U.S. Department of Health and Human Services. 2022. "Health Communication and Health Information Technology Workgroup." Healthy People 2030. https://health.gov/healthypeople/about/workgroups/health-communication-and-health-information-technology-workgroup.

U.S. News and World Report. 2021. "These Are the Best High Schools in Maine." https://www.usnews.com/education/best-high-schools/maine/rankings.

Valigra, Lori. 2020. "Western Maine Town Sees Coronavirus Boom as People Seek Safe Haven from Pandemic." *Bangor Daily News*, October 26. http://bangordailynews.com/2020/10/26/business/western-maine-town-sees-coronavirus-boom-as-people-seek-safe-haven-from-pandemic/.

Vias, Alexander C., and John I. Carruthers. 2005. "Regional Development and Land Use Change in the Rocky Mountain West, 1982–1997." *Growth and Change* 36 (2): 244–72.

Watt, Paul. 2009. "Living in an Oasis: Middle-Class Disaffiliation and Selective Belonging in an English Suburb." *Environment and Planning A: Economy and Space* 41 (12): 2799–3044.

WBUR. 2021. "Boston Brahmins | American Experience | PBS." https://www.pbs.org/wgbh/americanexperience/features/murder-boston-brahmins/.

Weber, Max. 2013. *The Protestant Ethic and the Spirit of Capitalism*. Ed. Max Weber. Trans. Stephen Kalberg. New York: Routledge.

Wellman, Barry. 1979. "The Community Question: The Intimate Networks of East Yorkers." *American Journal of Sociology* 84 (5): 1201–31.

Wellman, Barry, and B. Leighton. 1979. "Networks, Neighborhoods, and Communities: Approaches to the Study of the Community Question." *Urban Affairs Review* 14 (3): 363–90.

White, Merry, and Gus Rancatore. 2017. "How the North End Became Boston's Little Italy." *Boston Globe*, January 24. https://www.bostonglobe.com/magazine/2017/01/23/how-north-end-became-boston-little-italy/WcU3qSWkGiXuxkvHC3Ou6K/story.html.

Whyte, William H. 2013. *The Organization Man*. Philadelphia: University of Pennsylvania Press.

Williams, Raymond. 1975. *The Country and the City*. Oxford: Oxford University Press.

Willis, Paul. 1965. *Learning to Labor: How Working-Class Kids Get Working-Class Jobs*. New York: Columbia University Press.

Wilson, William Julius. 1997. *When Work Disappears: The World of the New Urban Poor*. New York: Vintage.

———. 2012. *The Truly Disadvantaged: The Inner City, the Underclass, and Public Policy*. 2nd ed. Chicago: University of Chicago Press.

Winkler, Richelle. 2013. "Living on Lakes: Segregated Communities and Inequality in a Natural Amenity Destination." *Sociological Quarterly* 54 (1): 105–29.

Winkler, Richelle, Steven Deller, and Dave Marcouiller. 2015. "Recreational Housing and Community Development: A Triple Bottom Line Approach." *Growth and Change* 46 (3): 481–500.

Wirth, Louis. 1938. "Urbanism as a Way of Life." *American Journal of Sociology*, 1–24.

Wray, Matt. 2014. *Cultural Sociology: An Introductory Reader*. New York: W. W. Norton.

Wyndham-Douds, Kiara. 2023. "Suburbs, Inc.: Exploring Municipal Incorporation as a Mechanism of Racial and Economic Exclusion in Suburban Communities." *RSF: The Russell Sage Foundation Journal of the Social Sciences* 9 (2): 226–48.

Young, Cristobal, Charles Varner, Ithai Z. Lurie, and Richard Prisinzano. 2016. "Millionaire Migration and Taxation of the Elite: Evidence from Administrative Data." *American Sociological Review* 81 (3): 421–46.

Zorbaugh, Harvey W. 1929. *The Gold Coast and the Slum: A Sociological Study of Chicago's Near North Side*. Chicago: University of Chicago Press.

Zukin, Sharon. 1989. *Loft Living: Culture and Capital in Urban Change*. New Brunswick, NJ: Rutgers University Press.

———. 1995. *The Cultures of Cities*. New York: Wiley-Blackwell.

———. 2010. *Naked City: The Death and Life of Authentic Urban Places*. Oxford: Oxford University Press.

Zukin, Sharon, and Philip Kasinitz. 1995. "A Museum in the Berkshires." In *The Cultures of Cities*, 79–108. New York: Wiley-Blackwell.

INDEX

affluence, 11, 16; in Boston, 4, 22, 144; in cit-ies, 6; geography and, 24; in hometowns, 43; impact in rural communities, 96–97; place-identity projects and, 145–47; in primary homes, 43–44; spatialization of, 106, 146; suburban, 28; suburbaniza-tion and, 30, 58; understanding affluent people in communities, 145–47

Airbnb owners, 22, 83, 102, 135, 139, 143–45, 172–73

alienation, 38, 97

amenity migration, 14–15, 50, 147, 179n85; dependence upon, 96–97; by middle class, 58; nature as amenity, 64; by upper middle class, 58. *See also* gentrification

Aspen, Colorado, 151–52

Bartram, Robin, 18

Becher, Debbie, 185n25

Bell, Michael, 19, 65; "country person" coined by, 185n3; "moral preserve" coined by, 66; on nature, 66; "pastoral-ism" coined by, 63–64

Besbris, Max, 185n25

Boston, Massachusetts: affluence in, 4, 22, 144; Boston Public Gardens, 122, 125; Boston Redevelopment Authority, 103, 171, 190n27; city life in, 191n6; Covid-19 and, 157–58; demographic characteris-tics, 24; elite in, 12, 106, 113, 127, 142–44, 158; Freedom Trail, 4–5, 125–26; from aways in, 115–16; high cultural institu-tions in, 122–30; high culture in, 109–17, 128; housing changes (1990–2019), 165; landmarks in, 4–5, 129–30; Lewis Wharf Hotel construction project, 102–5; Museum of Fine Arts, 3–5; Nazzaro Com-munity Center, 101, 102; neighborhood changes (1990–2019), 164; neighborhood meetings, 102–3; neighborhoods, 111–12, 117–21, 122–23, 140–41; North End,

101–3, 135–36; philanthropic participa-tion in, 48–49, 126–27; place identity in, 38, 107, 117, 121–22, 173; place-identity project in, 110, 120, 123; place making/place-making projects in, 107, 123, 127–28, 130–33; privilege in, 144, 146; public culture, 130–34; real estate in, 135–38, 193n3; schools in, 45–46, 184n3; second home in, 4, 42, 109–13, 116, 119–21, 124, 126, 135, 137–40; second homeowners in, 102, 104–5, 109–14, 122–26, 139–41; second homeownership case study, 20–26; sec-ond homeownership case-study analysis, 174; second homeownership case-study methods, 170–74; segregation in, 111–12, 117–18; sense of place in, 119, 123; social ties and, 124; super-gentrification/upscaling in, 117; superrich in, 114; taxation in, 132–33, 150; upper middle class in, 23, 113–14, 143; vacation homes in, 143; walk-ability in, 37; waves of gentrification in, 120, 126, 190n27, 191n6; white flight and, 46. *See also* high end blight

Boston Globe, 142–43, 157–58

Boston Symphony Orchestra (BSO), 122, 125–30, 159; value of, 193n40

Bourdieu, Pierre, 127

Brahmins, 186n8; Brahmin ethos, 128; as social class, 127; and social exclusion, 192n13

Brown-Saracino, Japonica, 14; on linking motivations to action, 177n43; on meth-odology, 180n95, 195n1; on places shaping identity, 194n15; and social preservation-ism, 179n73

BSO. *See* Boston Symphony Orchestra

camp, second homeownership as, 68–69

Campbell, Andrea, 134

capitalism, 57, 116, 177n42, 183n13; racial capitalism, 117, 190n23, 190n29

second homeownership: advantages of, 9; Boston case study, 20–26; Boston case-study analysis, 174; Boston case-study methods, 170–74; as camp, 68–69; in cities, 22; cities emptied by, 8; deservingness of, 59, 65, 66, 69, 117, 144; elites and, 6, 57; growth of, 6–7, 175n3; in Mountain West, 186n14; Rangeley case study, 20–26; Rangeley case-study analysis, 174; Rangeley case-study methods, 167–70; real estate and, 84, 180n95; segregation and, 7; as social problem, 6–9, 20; as status symbol, 57–58; upper-middle-class, in case study, 24–27. *See also specific topics*
selective belonging, 184n11
sense of place, 5–6; in Boston, 119, 123; in city life, 105; in hometowns, 11; public goods and, 152; second home for, 50, 52, 112; spatial inequality and, 12; by upper middle class, 52; value of, 117
Sherman, Jennifer, 19, 67, 90; on class blindness, 67, 116, 190n17; on social divides, 97
Sherman, Rachel, 19, 25, 69
Simmel, Georg, 35
site of legitimation, 19, 114, 117
Slater, Philip, 35–36
small-town life, 4
Smith, Edmund, 87
social capital, 185n23
social class: American social-class model, 180n99; Brahmins as, 127; class blindness, 67, 116; class status, 68–69; defining, in Rangeley, 65–69; divisions, with permanent residents, 95–96; divisions, with second homeowners, 95–96; elite justifying, 19; felt identity and, 148; justifying, 115; migration patterns and, 176n26; moral preserve for, 149; place identity and, 145, 147–49; second home and, 148. *See also* classlessness; elite; middle class; superrich; upper middle class; working class
social resources, 69
socio-spatial environment, 34, 121
spatial inequality: cultural processes for explaining, 12–16; neighborhood valuation and, 117–21; place and, 13; second homeowners shaping, 14; sense of place and, 12
structural symbolic interactionism, 178n70
Stuber, Jenny, 151–52, 176n26
subcultures, 48
suburbanites, 176n26; associations and distancing of, 184n11; ideology of, 183n15;

migratory patterns of, 46; upper-middle-class, 19, 28, 177n42; wealthy, white, 43
suburbanization, affluence and, 30, 58
suburban people, 38
suburbs, 10, 185n21; as amalgamation of urban and rural, 34; criticism of, 33; cultural and natural resources in, 31; history of incorporation, 30; as inward looking, 36; limited liability and, 48–50; middle class in, 31–32, 58; out-migration from, 32; privilege in, 48, 50; racism in, 31–32; schools in, 30–31, 46–47; segregation in, 31–32; self-governance of, 30; separation from place, 33; upper middle class in, 31–32
super-gentrification/upscaling, 110; in Boston, 117; cycle of displacement and, 114; Lees coining, 113; in neighborhoods, 18, 120; reasons for, 121; stages of, 22
superrich: in Boston, 114; in cities, 8; Farrell on, 116–17; in Mountain West, 186n14; as ostentatious, 19, 116
symbolic middle, aspiring to, 69

taxation, 30; in Boston, 132–33, 150; culture informing tax, 150–52; HOME program, 150; in Massachusetts, 47; MFA and, 133; PILOT program, 133; in Rangeley, 54–55, 92, 151; second home and, 151; for second homeowners, 151–52; for vacation homes, 150
Teaford, Jon, 182n1
Tilly, Charles, 50, 177n30
tourism: as blessing or curse, 59; dependence on, 82, 88–89, 94–95, 97, 150, 176n15; as economic strategy, 57–59, 82; marginalized peoples and, 188n13; in Rangeley, 75, 82–83, 88, 95, 188n9; second home and, 150, 176n15
town meetings, 188n10; Boston neighborhood meetings, 102–3; community meetings, 18; municipal meetings, 21, 55, 79; in Rangeley, 55, 79, 92, 98–99
transportation, 15
travel, 6, 111
Trudeau, Justin, 8

upper middle class: aspiring to symbolic middle, 69; in Boston, 23, 113–14, 143; characteristics of, 25; in cities, 107; cities revalued by, 107; consumption and, 117–19, 131; as elite subset, 25; gentrification and, 50; life-style choices, 19;

A NOTE ON THE TYPE

This book has been composed in Adobe Text and Gotham.
Adobe Text, designed by Robert Slimbach for Adobe,
bridges the gap between fifteenth- and sixteenth-century
calligraphic and eighteenth-century Modern styles.
Gotham, inspired by New York street signs, was designed
by Tobias Frere-Jones for Hoefler & Co.